FAITH POPCORN is an acknowledged top forecaster of consumer trends, and a key adviser to many Fortune 500 companies. She is the founder of Faith Popcorn's BrainReserve, a New York-based marketing consultancy whose clients include Bell Atlantic, BMW, Cigna, GE Capital, Hasbro, IBM, Lipton, McDonald's, Nabisco, and Procter & Gamble. She is also the author of the *The Popcorn Report* and co-author of *Clicking*. An internationally known speaker on consumer trends, Popcorn lives in New York City and Wainscott, NY, with her daughter, g.g.

LYS MARIGOLD was BrainReserve's Creative Director for twelve years and is the mother of five-year-old Skye Qi. She co-created *The Popcorn Report* and co-authored *Clicking*. When she's not winging the globe from Petra to Beirut to Istanbul to Shanghai, fulfilling her passion for archaeology and travel, she resides in East Hampton, NY, and occasionally New York City.

D1325056

Also by Faith Popcorn and Lys Marigold

The Popcorn Report
Clicking

EVEolution

The Eight Truths of Marketing to Women

Faith Popcorn and Lys Marigold

HarperCollinsBusiness
An Imprint of HarperCollins*Publishers*

HarperCollinsBusiness
an imprint of HarperCollins*Publishers*
77–85 Fulham Palace Road,
Hammersmith, London W6 8JB

www.**fire**and**water**.com/business

Special overseas edition 2000
This paperback edition 2001
1 3 5 7 9 8 6 4 2

First published in the USA by
Hyperion 2000

The authors gratefully acknowledge permission to use excerpts from the following:
Awakening Intuition by Dr. Mona Lisa Schultz, © 1998.
Used by permission of Three Rivers Press,
an imprint of Crown Publishers, a division of Random House, Inc.
Beauty Fades, Dumb is Forever by Judge Judy Sheindlin, © 1999.
Used by permission of Cliff Street Books, an imprint of HarperCollins Publishers Inc.
Cherishing Our Daughters by Dr. Evelyn Bassoff, © 1999.
Used by permission from Plume Publishing, an imprint of Penguin Putnam Inc.
Fire and Ice: The Charles Revson Story by Andrew Tobias, © 1976,
by permission of Sterling Lord Literistic Inc.
The First Sex: The Natural Talents of Women and How They are Changing the World
by Helen Fisher, © 1999. Used by permission of Random House, Inc.
In a Different Voice by Carol Gilligan, © 1993. Used by permission of Harvard Univeristy Press
It's a Jungle Out There, Jane by Dr. Joy Browne, © 1999.
Used by permission of Crown Publishers, a division of Random House, Inc.
Meditations for New Mothers © 1992 by Beth Wilson Saavedra.
Used by permission of Workman Publishing, Co., Inc., New York. All rights reserved.
Raising a Daughter by Jeanne Elium and Don Elium (contributor), © 1995.
Used by permission of Celestial Arts Publishing, a division of Ten Speed Press.
Reviving Ophelia: Saving the Selves of Adolescent Girls by Mary Bray Pipher, © 1995.
Used by permission from Ballantine Books, a division of Random House, Inc.
What Do Women Want? by Louise Eichenbaum and Susie Orbach, © 1999.
Used by permission from Berkley Publishing Group, a division of Penguin Putnam, Inc.
The Whole Woman by Germaine Greer, © 1999.
Used by permission of Alfred A. Knopf, a division of Random House, Inc.
Woman: An Intimate Geography by Nathalie Angier, © 1999. Used by permission of Houghton Mifflin.
Women's Bodies, Women's Wisdom by Dr. Christine Northrup, © 1998.
Used by permission of Bantam Doubleday Dell Publisher, a division of Random House, Inc.

The Authors assert the moral right to
be identified as the authors of this work

A catalogue record for this book
is available from the British Library

ISBN 0 00 710715 3
Set in Fairfield

Printed and bound in Great Britain by
Clays Ltd, St Ives plc

To Georgica Swan Pond Rose Petal Qi Xin Popcorn,
my little g.g.
With the hope that she will grow up in a more
EVEolutionary world.

. . . Faith Popcorn

To Skye Qi Marigold, my baby bat.
A compassionate dreamsinger and radiant adventurer—
she has taught me, brought me, profound love.

. . . Lys Marigold

Acknowledgments

A trillion, billion thanks to my revolutionary, EVEolutionary, and courageous team:

To Lys Marigold, my creative partner. For her genius as a pen-woman and brilliant communicator. A cultural savant, she inspires, she sees, she astounds me. An unerring barometer of what's smart, interesting, important, and futuristic; her instinct and intellect never, ever fail. But mostly for her loving loyalty. She EVEolved this work to where it needed to be with her whole heart and energy.

To Milly Massey, a consummate talent. An astounding think-upper and write-downer. For the exquisite clarity of her mind and soul. She is a treasure.

To Mary Kay Adams Moment, the compass that keeps me on-course as I navigate my life. For her patience, precision, integrity, intelligence, commitment. Her wise, calm hand, head, and heart have touched each page of this book. She worked beyond human endurance and then some more. She is everything good.

To Adam Hanft, for his breathtaking brilliance. He knows more about women than any man I've ever known.

To Mechele Flaum, my sister, my friend. For her passion and persistence. Without her relentless logic, her people poise, and her strategic insight, this book would not be.

To Julie Newton-Cucchi for her fabulous mind and ability to capture the EVEolutionary theorem and turn it into Consumer-Speak.

To Kate Newlin, my business partner. For being the ideal stand-by-me stand-in while I was working on this book. She is a strategist extraordinaire. A marketing mastermind who makes the BrainReserve Tank teem with ideas.

And to the rest of the terrific BrainReserve Team:

To Kathleen McLaughlin Cantwell, my assistant, who cheerfully makes the impossible possible every day—she IS the "Anticipation" Truth. To Michele Rodriguez-Cruz, Controller, whose many talents keep us on-track, on-time, and on-budget, and also to her super-smart associate, Kim Brown. To Tiffany Vasilchik, Senior Consultant, who without fail envisions, creates, and delivers. To Johanna Busch, our Director of Creative Design, who is a prodigy of presentation, and to Robin McIver, our Creative Director, who amazes me with her visual and verbal acuity. To Rachel Masters, Director of TalentBank, and lightning-quick study, who knows what's out there and brings it in here. She and Lauren Rothman checked, and finally conquered, massive amounts of input. To Billie Brouse, Managing Director, for her ability to get things (any thing) done in lightning time and who has imaginatively administered many of our assignments. To Eileen Daily, Seminar Director, who is a flawless combination of beauty, brains, and efficiency. To Alissa Stakgold, Consultant, whose dedication and discipline are indispensable. To Nadine Mahadeo Quinlan, BrainReserve Associate (and new mother to Samantha), without whom I cannot imagine my business, my home, or my life. And to Julie Bailey, who has lifted BrainReserve to a place I'd only dreamed of. To Sissey Miyake, for being there, there, there. Together they all create the essential BrainReserve, a consultancy for future thinking.

To Dawn Reilly, Sonia Trulli-Zaki, and Hong Bing Yao, g.g.'s loving and loved nannies, who gave me the gift of (almost) a guilt-free presence while working on this book. And to Nancy Chui Wong, Julia Matingyad, and Yang Sang Chin, who keep the spirit of the BrainReserve home warm and clean.

To my early EVEolutionaries, I'm eternally grateful—Ali Demos, Jen Levine, Laura Pedersen, Leslie Marshall, and Gene Stone—for their thinking and direction. To Helen Rees, Donna Sammons Carpenter, and Maurice Coyle of Wordworks, for their thoughtfulness and diligence.

Many thanks to all my publishing mentors, Amanda Urban, my agent and source for wisdom and clarity; and to everyone at Hyperion, especially Bob Miller, Senior Vice President and Managing Director, who kept the faith and was a creative inspiration through late, later, and latest. To Martha Levin, Editorial Director and Publisher, for her insight and foresight. To Maureen O'Brien, Senior Editor, who got it all started; Leslie Wells, our get-it-done (fast and perfectly) Executive Editor; Phil Rose, Art Director, and Lisa Stokes, Design Manager, for their patience and design acumen. To Ellen Archer, Vice President and Associate Publisher, and Jennifer Landers, Publicity Director, for producing the EVEolutionary buzz.

To Bob Edmonds, esteemed counsel, who kept our track clear and safe. To Gerry Schwartz and Mary Luria for their legal knowledge and encouragement in all things publishing. To Heidi Krupp, our savvy, smart PR-plus. To Dr. Jane Ellen Aronson for her constancy and support. To Jan Miller, who more than willingly shared her expertise. Finally, to Dr. Ethel Person, who sheds light when it sometimes appears that there is none.

And to all our clients and business associates who advised and counseled, I want to say "thank you." There have been thousands of women and men who helped me crystallize my thinking, and who added their own brilliance; they helped "Co-Parent" this book. These are but a few:

Valerie Ackerman, President, WNBA
Dr. Patricia Yarberry Allen, OBGYN
Sylvia Anapol, President, Max Racks
Natalie Angier, Author
Herbert M. Baum, President/COO, Hasbro, Inc.
Lynn J. Beasley, Executive Vice President, Marketing,
    R.J. Reynolds Tobacco Company
Norris Bernstein, Certified Management Consultant
Nancy Bauer, Deputy General Manager, Fleishman Hillard
Charlene Begley, Vice President Corporate Audit,
    General Electric Company
Gail Blanke, Founder, Life Designs
Michael Bloomberg, Founder/CEO, Bloomberg News
Claire Babrowski, Executive Vice President,
    Worldwide Restaurant Systems, McDonald's Corporation
Rick Burton, Professor, University of Oregon
Candice Carpenter, Co-Chairman of the Board, CEO, iVillage
Wayne S. Charness, Senior Vice President Corporate
    Communications, Hasbro, Inc.
Doug Conant, President, Nabisco Foods Company
Chip Conley, CEO, Joie de Vivre Hospitality
Lynn Crump-Caine, Senior Vice President Operations,
    McDonald's Corporation
Judsen Culbreth, Vice President, Scholastic Inc.
Jerry Della Femina, Chairman/CEO Della Femina/Jeary and Partners
Tim DeMello, Chairman/CEO, Streamline.com
Jami Dover, Vice President, Director Worldwide Marketing,
    Intel Corporation
Maria Eitel, Vice President, Corporate and Social Responsibility,
    Nike, Inc.
Phylis Esposito, Senior Partner, Manager, Mathias & Co.
Gail Evans, Executive Vice President, CNN
David Fink, Esq.
Helen E. Fisher, Anthropologist, Author
Sander A. Flaum, Chairman/CEO, Robert A. Becker, Inc.

Susan Fournier, Professor, Harvard School of Business
Michael D. Fraizer, President and CEO, GE Financial Assurance
Mary Furlong, CEO, Third Age Media, Inc.
Carol Gilligan, Professor, Harvard University
Joshua B. Gitlin, Brand Director, Opportunity Creating Investments,
　The Whirlpool Corporation
Ross Goldstein, Psychologist
Marc Graham, President, Jiffy Lube International
Sharon Hartley, Group Executive, Integrated Marketing Services,
　Hasbro, Inc.
Alan Hassenfeld, Chairman/CEO, Hasbro, Inc.
Dr. Pat Heim, President, The Heim Group
Joel Henkin, Senior Vice President, Bruskin Goldring Research
Geraldine Laybourne, Chairman/CEO, Oxygen Media
Rick Lenny, President, Nabisco Biscuit Company
Rick N. Kaplan, President, CNN USA
Monique Vasilchik Kelson, Esq., Tularik, Inc.
Jim Kilts, Chairman/CEO, Nabisco, Inc.
Celinda Lake, Lake, Snell and Perry
Carl Levine, Carl Levine Consulting and Licensing
Margo Lowry, Vice President, New Business Development,
　Campbell Soup Company
Lori Moskowitz Lepler, Founder, The Intuition Group
Gene McCaffrey, CEO, Valuevision
Julie McCarthy, Vice President of New Market Development,
　GE Financial Assurance
Stefanie Meyers, Computer Works, East Hampton, NY
Milton Moscowitz, Author
Melissa Moss, President, Woman's Consumer Network
Fran Myers, VP Marketing Services & Integrated Marketing Intelligence,
　Nabisco Foods Company
Jerry Noonan, Chief Marketing Officer, 1-800-flowers.com
Missy Park, President, Title Nine Sports
Terry Patterson, former CEO, Frederick's of Hollywood
Willa Perlman, General Manager/Sector Head, Shared Services, Hasbro, Inc.
Jim Postl, President/COO, Pennzoil-Quaker State
Terry Preskar, Vice President Health Management, Merck-Medco
Joseph F. Prevratil, President/CEO, *The Queen Mary*
Judi Roaman, President, J. Roaman Ltd.
Robert Rogers, President, The Great Outdoors
Ken Romanzi, President/CEO, Balducci.com
Stephen I. Sadove, President, WWBC, Clairol, Inc.

Andrew J. Schindler, Chairman/CEO, R.J. Reynolds Tobacco Company
Wolfgang R. Schmitt, Retired Chairman/CEO, Rubbermaid, Inc.
Lisa Schultz, Executive Vice President, The Gap, Inc.
Pattie Sellers, Senior Writer, *Fortune* Magazine
Aliza Sherman, President, Cybergrrl.com
Todd Simon, Senior Vice President, Omaha Steaks
Mary Springer, Founder, SWAN
Gloria Steinem, Author, Co-Founder, *Ms.* Magazine
Isabel Carter Stewart, National Executive Director, Girls, Inc.
Susan Thomases, Esq., Wilkie Farr & Gallagher (retired)
Bernadette Tracy, President, NetSmart-Research
Kenn Viselman, Chairman, the itsby bitsy Entertainment Company
Aaron Waitz, President, AANets, Inc.
Sheila Wellington, President, Catalyst
Rick Welts, formerly, President NBA Properties, NBA
Caryn Wiley, President, Wiley and Associates
Marie Wilson, President, Ms. Foundation
Peter Wolf, Director Operations, McDonald's Corporation

Contents

Acknowledgments / ix

BrainReserve TrendBank / xix

BrainReserve Glossary / xxi

Introduction: EVEolution: What It Is, How It Works,
Why Your Business Can't Survive Without It / 1

Chapter 1: Connecting Your Female Consumers to Each Other
Connects Them to Your Brand / 17

Chapter 2: If You're Marketing to One of Her Lives
You're Missing All the Others / 41

Chapter 3: If She Has to Ask, It's Too Late / 79

Chapter 4: Market to Her Peripheral Vision, and
She Will See You in a Whole New Light / 105

Chapter 5: Walk, Run, Go to Her,
Secure Her Loyalty Forever / 133

Contents

Chapter 6: This Generation of Women Consumers
Will Lead You to the Next / 153

Chapter 7: Co-Parenting Is the Best Way
to Raise a Brand / 175

Chapter 8: Everything Matters—You Can't Hide
Behind Your Logo / 195

Chapter 9: The Truths Can Set You Free:
Revlon Reborn / 219

Chapter 10: In Conclusion: Making the
World Safe for EVEolution / 239

Appendix / 247

Index / 255

EVEolution

BrainReserve TrendBank

Anchoring: A reaching back to our spiritual roots, taking what was secure from the past in order to be ready for the future.

AtmosFear: Polluted air, contaminated water, and tainted food stir up a storm of consumer doubt and uncertainty.

Being Alive: Awareness that good health extends longevity and leads to a new way of life.

Cashing Out: Working women and men, questioning personal/career satisfaction and goals, opt for simpler living.

Clanning: Belonging to a group that represents common feelings, causes, or ideals; validating one's own belief system.

Cocooning: The need to protect oneself from the harsh, unpredictable realities of the outside world.

Down-Aging: Nostalgic for their carefree childhood, baby boomers find comfort in familiar pursuits and products from their youth.

EGOnomics: To offset a de-personalized society, consumers crave recognition of their individuality.

EVEolution: The way women think and behave is impacting business, causing a marketing shift away from a hierarchical model toward a relational one.

Fantasy Adventure: Modern age whets our desire for roads, real and virtual, untaken.

FutureTENSE: Consumers, anxiety-ridden by simultaneous social, economic, political, and ethical chaos, find themselves beyond their ability to cope today or imagine tomorrow.

Icon Toppling: A new socioquake transforms mainstream America and the world as the pillars of society are questioned and rejected.

99 Lives: Too fast a pace, too little time, causes societal schizophrenia and forces us to assume multiple roles.

Pleasure Revenge: Consumers are having a secret bacchanal. They're mad as hell and want to cut loose again.

S.O.S. (Save Our Society): The country rediscovers a social conscience of ethics, passion, and compassion.

Small Indulgences: Stressed-out consumers want to indulge in affordable luxuries and seek ways to reward themselves.

Vigilante Consumer: The consumer manipulates marketers and the marketplace through pressure, protest and politics.

BrainReserve Glossary

The following is a glossary that will familiarize you with Brain-Reserve's language of the book and language of the future.

Blamestorming: A negative non-productive ideation session that prohibits creative thinking. Never employed at BrainReserve.

Brailling the Culture: Monitoring cultural signals—magazines, newspapers, books, videos, movies, TV, music, events, food, fads, the Internet, shopping channels—in order to "feel out" the Trends.

BrainJam: A BrainReserve ideation session that uses the Trends as a springboard for generating ideas. A proprietary "ThinkTank."

BrainReserve: Faith Popcorn's company, founded in 1974; a future-focused, Trend-based marketing consultancy. See Web site via FaithPopcorn.com or BrainReserve.com

Brand-Me-Down: The generational passing-down of a brand, based on its good performance and reputation.

Brandwagon: All the positives that a brand rolls in front of the female consumer, moving the product into a visible, comfortable, familiar place in her home and heart.

Brandwidth: The applicational capacity of a brand.

Children's Crusade: A coming social and cultural phenomenon in which children are the driving force to save the planet.

ConsumerSpeak: A language used by consumers that needs special interpretation—because they rarely say what they mean. You need to ConsumerListen to come up with their Truths.

Corporate Soul: A decency positioning for any company that wants to establish an EVEolutionary relationship with its consumer, based on trust. It means full public disclosure of its political and environmental stances.

CreativeThink: A step in BrainReserve's proprietary 36-step consulting methodology. An ideation session, held with carefully screened TalentBank members or highly articulate consumers, to generate a brainstorm of concepts.

CriticalThink: A step in BrainReserve's proprietary 36-step consulting methodology in which the BrainReserve staff evaluates the results of BrainJams and CreativeThinks. We screen ideas through the Trends and our clients' corporate culture to determine their value.

CultureScan: An ongoing audit of traditional and electronic media; of consumers; and of thought and opinion leaders.

Decency Decade, The: A timeline to create an EVEolutionary relationship with the consumer that's based on trust by being or doing good.

e-llennium: The big bang of the little e—an era where e-commerce dominates the way consumers access their goods and services.

Emotional Content: The Eighties represented the absence of negatives (i.e., no fat). The Nineties were about the addition of positives (i.e., plus calcium). The 2000s will see a bonding to a company or brand through an emotional connection.

EVEollennium: The millennium in which EVEolution will be preeminent.

EVEolution: The new marketing theory for the millennium, based on the premise that men and women are different, so why do we market to them in the same way? See BrainReserve TrendBank for definition, p. xix.

EVEsdropping: Listening in with a woman's acute sense and sensibility of hearing.

Female Realism: Marketing without hype.

Foodaceuticals: Food enhanced with medicinal qualities to improve the dynamics of the body and mind.

FutureCorner: Predictions just around the bend of time.

FutureScape: A future-focused landscape of the consumer marketplace. Included in every BrainReserve assignment, it provides a positioning statement, marketing strategies, and concepts with clearly defined long-term competitive advantages.

Girlcott: A new way of female participants leveraging purchasing power by "boycotting" a product or company.

ImagiNation: The space where one can play, laugh, work, dance, worry, argue, make and spend money, and live.

Mouse Potato: Lolling in front of the computer instead of lounging in front of the TV.

NanoSpan: The extra-short attention span of today's ultra-busy 99 Lives female consumer.

Perfessional: The melding and blending of the personal with the professional life.

Pharmacopia: Great demand has created an abundance of alternative medicine offerings.

Shop-o-logical: The inherent difference in the way women and men approach shopping, perceive shopping. Although not biological, it's the DNA of going marketing. For women: Daily, Nomadically, Absorbed. For men: Do Not Ask.

SocioQuake: A series of seismic societal events that transform the global culture.

TalentBank: BrainReserve's global computerized network of 6,000 experts.

Techno-Isolationism: A condition caused by too many hours spent alone in front of a computer.

Three "E's": The main concerns for the future: Environment, Education, and Ethics.

TrendBank: The repository of BrainReserve's Trend information, creating a database made from our culture monitoring and consumer interviews.

TrendProbe: A highly-structured Trend-based interview technique used with carefully screened, articulate consumers or experts; designed to uncover motivations, desires, and disconnects in the consumer culture. Hypno-TrendProbe: Under hypnosis.

TrendSalons: A once-a-month Thursday evening meeting where experts from the TalentBank, friends from the Fortune 500, and BrainReserve staff discuss issues that will confront us in the next one hundred years.

TrendTrek: A market check or "field trip" to cutting-edge locations in order to stimulate fresh thinking about new products and services. May be focused on a specific Trend/market theme, or broadly conceived to explore a range of unconventional retail environments.

TrendTrek, Virtual: An Internet check or "field trip" to cutting-edge Web sites, as above, only virtually.

TrendView: The seminar presentation of BrainReserve's Trend-Bank, with applications from the current marketplace. Brain-Reserve's Trend-identifying process is described and discussed during the 60-minute session, including Q&A.

Ur-Club: From "Ur," meaning the pinnacle, the best, the first.

EVEolution:

What It Is, How It Works,

Why Your Business Can't

Survive Without It

A Pop(corn) Quiz:

Go ahead. Explain it.

- Explain why the Web has a long list of successful "Women Only" sites—and why there are no comparable communities for men.
- Explain why the take-out-foods industry (home meal replacement, to marketers) has changed the eating habits of Americans over the last five years.
- Explain why home spas and other pampering products have gone from a niche for the rich to class for the mass.

- Explain why industrial appliances and professional cookware are the "must haves" for the home kitchen.
- Explain why door-to-door selling is booming, with over 7 million female salespeople, more than double the total employee base of the top ten companies in America.
- Explain why kids don't dress like kids anymore.
- Explain why women have created a $9.8 billion pharmacopia of alternative medicines.
- Explain why organic foods have moved from an esoteric sliver position to become a major force in the marketplace.

Is there any unifying explanation? I have come to realize that there is. One fundamental reality underlies all these marketing phenomena.

A single canopy insight explains it all: EVEolution. And marketers don't understand its power and its inevitability.

EVEolution is a series of marketing axioms built around the reality that women and men are as different shop-ologically as they are biologically.

It's a profound realization. And it makes EVEolution the essence of successful marketing to females for the decades to come. Ready or not ready: EVEolution means that all you've learned, studied, and thought was sacrosanct will be replaced by a new marketing mantra.

We've organized EVEolution into Eight Truths that reveal how to understand, reach, motivate, and sustain the loyalty of the female customer.

And that is the force behind this book.

I'm convinced, based on everything I know and believe, that EVEolution is the most powerful marketing principle ever developed for understanding and motivating women.

EVEolution guarantees success, if you get it right. Or your biological blueprint for disaster if you mess up. EVEolution will change forever the way products and services are developed, marketed, and distributed, period. Beginning (and end) of story.

In short, these Eight Truths represent the foundations that will define the new marketing to women. Each Truth was identified and defined and enriched through an ongoing dialogue with thousands of women (and men) across the globe. Individually, the Truths are powerful. Together, they can change your world.

I recognize that EVEolution will encounter some resistance. Habits die hard. Traditional business defaults to the familiar; it's easy, comfortable, and bonus-building to rely on old business models, outdated templates, yesterday's strategies. That's why every market-shifting idea I've had that ran against the tide, from the Trends of Cocooning (my prediction in the disco-dancing '80s that people will be returning home) to Pleasure Revenge (a defiant turning away from guilt and self-denial) was originally poohpoohed, laughed off, and otherwise dismissed. Now, these identified societal Trends are accepted marketing dogma that are studied at business schools around the world.

I'm used to skepticism. But even so, all the business leaders I've talked to know that somewhere, somehow something is very wrong with their marketing approach to women. I can see it in their body language (pulling back, fingers tapping, eyes shifting). They recognize, deep down, that women are different from men. They know it's true from their real lives and their experiences. But they keep on marketing to them in the same old way because they don't know exactly how to change, what is needed, or where to begin.

This book will show the how, what, and where of marketing to women. And it will make it crystal clear why American business, and in fact, global business, needs to change. It will demonstrate why the traditional approaches for reaching women must be:

1. dragged into the Recycle Bin (today's computer metaphor of choice) or
2. tossed into the Circular File (the quaint paper-based metaphor of my youth)

As the EVEolutionary Truths challenge conventional thinking, you'll find something invigorating washing over you. It's intellectual refreshment. You'll be inspired to explore the new marketing pathways. To redefine what a brand is, what it represents, and what it can be.

I've worked hard to bring the Eight Truths alive with case studies and real-life examples of EVEolution in action (or inaction), as well as future-focused examples of just how powerful and effective EVEolved marketing can be. If your brand is a poster girl for counter-EVEolution, I'll apologize in advance for being tough on you. But won't you want to know before it's too late?

Those of you who've read my other two books, *The Popcorn Report* and *Clicking*, know that I tend to be pretty direct (it's my style). And I've learned that sometimes, most of the time, it's the only way to make a point.

So if you think EVEolution is something your company can relax about and put off for a while, I've got some important news for you. YOU CAN'T. EVEolution won't wait. Understanding EVEolution and implementing it (the most difficult part) means the difference between building healthy brands and profitable relationships with women . . . or building a flimsy, fluffy foundation with no future. And the latter inevitably leads to decreasing market share, eroding loyalty, plunging earnings, unhappy shareholders, early retirement.

Women Don't Buy Brands; They Join Them

If I had to summarize the Eight Truths of EVEolution in a single sentence, it would be this: A customer of the moment is the one who buys your brand; a customer for life is the one who joins it.

Think about it. The things we join—clubs, political parties, organizations, even religions—are the institutions in our lives that really matter. The ones we stick with through thick and thin. The ones we cherish and value and grow old with.

These institutions that women join are also a vehicle for meeting people, building relationships, finding like-minded people. We all know how women are gifted at finding the common ground, at identifying the ties that bind rather than the differences that divide.

Is it over-reaching to think that a brand . . . your brand . . . can fill an EVEolutionary role? Not at all. In our blurring, shifting, spiraling society, all roles are up for grabs. And I believe that in this, the twenty-first century, the dominant brands with women will be the brands women join.

It's a mind-altering experience. You'll need to think about your brand more expansively, more deeply than ever before. It isn't a tweak. It's a tornado. But you don't have to cope alone. This book will help you construct an entirely new framework for brand-building. It's not a book about theory, but a practical solution for understanding and implementing the Eight EVEolutionary Truths.

There's something else really important that I want to reinforce. Most mainstream marketing books are about the One Big Idea, the Global Solution. The 115 mph ace that spectacularly ends the tennis match. EVEolution works differently. You'll soon see that EVEolution isn't about a single corporate overhaul. It's not a magic bullet. It's a systemic redefinition that leads to dozens and dozens of subtle shifts and fine alterations.

EVEolution is about a cascade of changes. It reminds me of F. Scott Fitzgerald's definition of "personality" in *The Great Gatsby* as "an unbroken string of successful gestures." The sheer depth and breadth of EVEolution makes it a revolution with profound implications—not just for marketing, but for the way your business is structured, financed, organized, and managed on a minute-to-minute basis.

How to Please a Woman

At one time or another, all men (including John Gray in all his *Men Are From Mars, Women Are From Venus* books) have railed at the heavens, trying to figure out what would make women happy. Most of the time, their plaintive questioning is used to underscore the issue that pleasing women is an amazingly difficult, almost impossible task. We are, or so it appears in the popular press, impossible to satisfy in our capriciousness and emotional volatility.

Beyond being insulting, it simply isn't true. I'm not a psychologist or even a pop-psychologist, so I am not a licensed expert about what women want out of life. But I am tenured in interviewing, positioning, and marketing to women. I'm secure in my knowledge and understanding of what women want out of the companies and brands they share their lives with.

Women want a brand to extend into their lives in as many ways as possible. They want a brand to speak to their heads and their hearts. To understand them. To recognize their needs, values, standards, and dreams.

They want a brand that doesn't say, "Tough luck, that's not our strategy," but that says, "Tell us what you want and we'll make it our strategy."

And what women don't want is just as important as what they do. They don't want to do business with an organization, a company, or a brand that condescends to them. That inconveniences them. That makes them wait, argue, or defend themselves. They don't want one that establishes the wrong role models or exploits the wrong kind of imagery.

Do men want the same things? Not necessarily. While many men—particularly younger ones—are becoming EVEolved, it is the differences between women and men that are at the core of EVEolution. And the Eight Truths are based on this fork in the evolutionary road.

The EVEolution Moment:
The longer you wait, the farther behind you'll fall

Two forces—one economic, one biological—have come together to make the next two decades the onset of the EVEolved Era. The first is the economic power of women. Let's face it, if we were back in the warm bath of the Ozzie and Harriet 1950s, and women represented a small portion of the economy, no one would pay attention. But it's the next century, and women are the dominant economic force in the country. You've probably heard some of these statistics individually. But their power as a group is exciting—and chilling to those in EVEolutionary dinosaur-land. So here goes:

- Women buy or influence the purchase of 80% of all consumer goods. That includes 51% of consumer electronics and 75% of over-the-counter (OTC) drugs. Women also influence 80% of all healthcare decisions.

- Automobiles are no longer the male bastion they once were. Women actually buy 50% of all cars and influence 80% of their sales. While once it was men who drove the computer market, now women buy 50% of all PCs. And in perhaps the most powerful symbol of economic clout—stock ownership—consider that 48% of stock market investors are women. Half of all women own mutual funds. By the way, by the day, these numbers are zooming. And in families where both spouses work, wives outearn their husbands in 22.7% of these households. Did you realize also that 40% of households with assets over $600,000 are headed by women? So ignore at your own risk.

Even though I'm sure you get the point, here are a few more statistics. Women start businesses at twice the rate of men (every sixty seconds), for a total of 9.1 million of them. Female-owned and female-run businesses generate $3.6 trillion annually and employ 27.5 million people—more than all the Fortune 500 companies combined, in America.

This is a ton of purchasing power. An influx of influencing power. Which is why marketers want to lock in on their female target. Except there's one major stumbling block: Although they know they should *reach* women, they don't know how to *market* to them. Big problem? Big opportunity.

The second reason that EVEolutionary marketing is so critically important is the biological one. Women are different from men. Very different. Like all the great truths, it's simple but complex. Women perceive the world through their own gender. It's a matter of genetic imprinting.

The point is that women process information differently because our brains are wired differently. We hear, acquire, and use language in our own way. Which accounts for the fact that girls generally speak earlier than boys, articulate their feelings more easily, and see themselves more as links, not as loners.

This isn't just interesting cocktail party patter. (Try it and you might get a very dry martini in your face.) It's wild in its implications. Yet it's a subject that never comes up in any marketing plan or strategy session. And that's not surprising. Tell a marketer that he needs to develop a program based on the neurological differences between women and men and he'll get a panicked look in his eyes.

This book will turn that blink of panic into a long and hard stare of opportunity.

Women are different and they have money. So, what do I do?

Here's the world as it stands. We know that women have greater economic traction than ever. And we know that women can't be approached by using the same traditional strategies that have worked with men.

But what's next? How does a company, a brand, a service, turn its business around and become more relevant to the women who will decide its fate?

This book, with its Eight Truths, will provide you with the keys to unlock your EVEolutionary future.

Remarkably, even shockingly, this subject has been virtually ignored by writers and business journalists. This has been one of the biggest business gaps (and gaffes) of the decade. Drop by your local Barnes & Noble (or check out their Web site) and you'll see what I mean. You'll find a vast acreage of books about the ways women differ from men. You'll find fields and fields of books on marketing theory. But never do the twain meet. Marketing to women is a big and echoing void.

Publishers are not the only ones who overlook the subject of marketing to women. There isn't a single course at Harvard or Stanford Business Schools or the Kellogg School of Management on the subject.

The answer is simple: Fear. After years of listening (or at least partially listening) to the Women's Movement, men have become hyper-paranoid about anything that smacks of gender stereotyping. It just hasn't been politically correct to think about, talk about—or worse, capitalize on—the differences between women and men.

Things are about to change. It will become safe (safer, anyway) to identify, analyze, and celebrate the distinctions between women and men. And to develop products and programs that women will need and want and relate to and own.

The truth is that the failure to explore the EVEolutionary road has set marketing to women back about two decades. It's time to make up for lost time. And lost business.

EVEolving to EVEolution

As many of you know from my other books, I am a futurist. A trend-spotter. A cultural detective. My detective agency is BrainReserve, a marketing consultancy like no other. I started the company in 1974, many futures ago, with a Creative Partner (and Art Director), Stuart Pittman.

Our idea was to help companies understand the future, so that they would be able to build and secure a place for themselves in it. It seems so basic: How can you build a successful strategy unless you understand the world that is evolving? Unhappily, with the time it takes companies to develop products, most end up marketing to the past.

In 1978, Lys Marigold joined us as our Creative Director, and thanks to her analytic acumen and uncanny instincts, we began to name and frame our Trends. Soon after, we developed a 36-step proprietary methodology that enables us to create a vision of the future. This broad vision, which we call a FutureScape, is built through the careful execution of the BrainReserve process, and allows us to position or reposition global brands.

We use tools like our TrendProbes, highly imaginative ideation sessions where we encourage consumers to think beyond the moment. We also rely on our computerized, global Talent-Bank, 6,000 female and male experts who represent the best and the brightest and the brainiest—from bio-engineers to Indian chiefs to great chefs to political leaders who help us Braille the Culture and anticipate SocioQuakes long before they make the national news.

It was through BrainReserve's work with the Fortune 500 that I began to realize how neglected the female market truly was. On one hand, I watched as the stories and the statistics that tracked the economic power of women kept going through the roof. On the other, I would sit in meeting after meeting where women were described as a "niche market" or as a "segment" or a "special interest group." What an upside-down, inside-out take on the world, I thought.

I began interviewing thousands of women, exploring their thoughts about brands. The technique that we used was to ask them to personify their favorite companies and brands (being candid about their strengths and their weaknesses), as if they were good friends. We also probed for any differences between the way women shop vs. the way their husbands or boyfriends or brothers do.

These TrendProbes unearthed surprising insights, interesting twists, and unexpected flashes of clarity—the best of which we used to build this book. Because women love to share their experiences, and are committed to making their world a better place, these interviews were revealing and rewarding.

Read EVEolution front to back. Or back to front.

Most books—it's safe to say almost all of them—are written to be read front to back. (Except in the Middle East and Asia, of course.) EVEolution can certainly be read that way. But that's not the only way. In the spirit of women, who are nonlinear and approach the world (and problems) from every possible perspective, EVEolution was written to be read in virtually any order you want.

There are eight main chapters that cover the EVEolutionary Truths, and they can be read in or out of sequence. The Truth is the Truth, from any angle.

Each chapter will explain the essence of a Truth, giving you examples of brands that flopped because the marketer misjudged it . . . or triumphed because they grasped it early on. To give "in-real-time" applications, we go through BrainReserve case studies showing how we took each Truth and used it to help build our clients' businesses. My personal favorite section in each Truth chapter is "Around the FutureCorner," which imagines the EVE-olutionary future in categories as divergent as healthcare to fast food. I think you'll find "Around the FutureCorner" helpful, because:

WARNING

THE FUTURE IS ALWAYS CLOSER THAN IT APPEARS

All in all, this book is a marketing to women wake-up call. To grasp the enormity of what we're saying, you have to understand the Eight Truths of Marketing to Women. Here they are.

1. Connecting Your Female Consumers to Each Other Connects Them to Your Brand.
2. If You're Marketing to One of Her Lives, You're Missing All the Others.
3. If She Has to Ask, It's Too Late.
4. Market to Her Peripheral Vision and She Will See You in a Whole New Light.
5. Walk, Run, Go to Her, Secure Her Loyalty Forever.
6. This Generation of Women Consumers Will Lead You to the Next.
7. Co-Parenting Is the Best Way to Raise a Brand.
8. Everything Matters—You Can't Hide Behind Your Logo.

The Answers to my Pop(corn) Quiz

■ Explain why the Web has a long list of successful "Women Only" sites—and why there are no comparable communities for men.

Answer: The First Truth: Connecting (we're calling the Truths by their shorthand names). Because women love sharing ideas, feelings, dreams, fears and most of all, information—forming spontaneous communities, whether it's in the playground, gym, or out in cyberspace. That explains why women-geared dot.coms are so EVEolved, including: ivillage; oxygen; oprah; chickclick; women; hipmama; wiredwoman; womanconnect; hersalon; igc; journeywomen; she-net; and coffeerooms.

■ Explain why the take-out-foods industry (home meal replacement, to marketers) has changed the eating habits of Americans over the last five years.

Answer: The Second Truth: Multiple Lives. Women are hard at work and yet are still responsible for getting food on the table (or, at least, in the fridge). Hence, breakfasts, lunches, and dinners come in pre-packaged, complete "square meals" (think of Lunchables). That explains the success of Happy Meals at McDonald's drive-thrus; the popularity of chains such as the Boston Market; the emergence of hot food counters in every deli and supermarket.

■ Explain why home spas and other pampering products have gone from a niche for the rich to class for the mass.

Answer: The Third Truth: If She Has to Ask. Oh, our aching backs. Anticipatory marketing follows the formula: X (more stress) and Y (more cash) equals Z (more ways to relax). This category includes huge Roman-like tubs with Jacuzzi jets; steam showers; bidet toilets; massage tables; aromatherapy products; richer, more complex creams, lotions and potions.

■ Explain why industrial appliances and professional cook-ware are the "must haves" for the home kitchen.

Answer: The Fourth Truth: Peripheral Vision. There's a good reason why home kitchens have gone from avocado-green stoves to six-burner stainless-steel Viking ovens. From an odd assortment of pots and pans to matched sets of heavy-gauge black Calphalon®. And it has nothing to do with cooking. A woman looks at such state-of-the-art appliances, over and over—in the open kitchen of her favorite Tuscan restaurant; in the editorial pages of *Architectural Digest*; on B. Smith's TV show or the Food Network. The point is, if you gently sur-round a woman, instead of attacking her head-on, she'll notice and she'll buy.

■ Explain why door-to-door selling is booming, with over 7 million women salespeople, more than double the total employee base of the top ten companies in the Fortune 500.

Answer: The Fifth Truth: Walk, Run, Go to Her. Marketing that goes to the home is marketing that hits home. Shopping in the comfort of the living room saves one more trip on crowded roads to the crowded stores. Time and stress savers—from the Avon lady to the manicurist to delivery of almost everything— are the necessities of life today.

■ Explain why kids don't dress like kids anymore.

Answer: The Sixth Truth: This Generation Will Lead You to the Next. Fashion retailers are on to what mothers have always known (and what I, as the mother of an almost-two-year-old nicknamed g.g., am fast learning): Kids can't wait to grow up. Creating Mom-alike ways of dressing will lock in the loyalty of a whole new generation of consumers. Early on. Mini-trend-setters, as young as 18 months, are decked out in beaded, flared jeans; cropped sweaters; long wrap skirts; platform shoes; and your basic black, instead of baby pink and blue.

(How come "one-sies" don't come in black, navy, and gray and we have to hand-dye the plain white ones?)

■ Explain why women have created a $9.8 billion pharmacopia for alternative medicine.

Answer: The Seventh Truth: Co-Parenting. Women are turning away from traditional doctors and healthcare (for treating them as second-class citizens), and instead embracing alternative medicine. About 65% of the market in herbal remedies, vitamins, minerals, and amino acids are women—who like this opportunity to mix-and-match such things as anti-blues St. John's Wort with resistance-enhancing Echinacea tea, a get-aligned chiropractic neck adjustment with a flu-fighting vial of Boiron Oscillococcinum. The issue is control. Of bodies, of self. Being involved in basic decisions makes a woman stay involved.

■ Explain why organic foods have moved from an esoteric sliver position to become a major force in the marketplace.

Answer: The Eighth Truth: Everything Matters. Women will now pay $5.49 for a pound of Horizon organic butter or $3 for a small container of Fresh Samantha tangerine juice because they know they're better for their families. Watch out—all you hormone-pumping, pesticide-wielding, big league marketers. There is not a spot on the supermarket shelves that's safe from the Everything Matters woman.

That's EVEolution.
That's our future.
Our Female Future.

Chapter 1

The First Truth of EVEolution:

Connecting Your Female Consumers to Each Other Connects Them to Your Brand

When it comes to women, we all know it's time to forget *pink think*.

For too many years, the decision makers who ran the business world thought the way to connect with women consumers was by appealing to old-fashioned notions of femininity: powder pink, sweet hearts, and bouquets of roses. Froufrou products would appear . . . and vanish.

It's 2000.

It's time to *think link*.

A woman steps into an elevator, hits the button for the

tenth floor, and before she reaches her destination, she's busily chatting with some woman standing next to her.

A woman sits down to dinner in a restaurant, and by the time the glass of wine arrives, she knows the name of the waiter's acting coach and the next play he has a bit part in.

A woman knows all about who in the office, who on the school board, who in the book club, who on the softball team, is seeing a therapist, dating a former boyfriend, being investigated by the IRS, or thinking about changing jobs.

How come?

The uninitiated may call it *gossip*.

I call it *connecting*. Making a spandex stretch between people. Looking for the threads that weave us together.

Women cross-pollinate. They take the powdery-fine residue from one story and dust it on the next. Deborah Tannen, author of *You Just Don't Understand: Women and Men In Conversation*, points out that women naturally reinforce their bonds by freely and clearly dispensing information, directions, or heartfelt help. Dr. John Gray, of *Men Are From Mars* fame, claims that the behavior is encoded in our very chromosomes: Men retreat to "their caves" to solve their problems while women "get together and talk openly."

Whether you call it an urge, a desire, a need, or merely a playing out of some genetically pre-written script, the female connection behavior is the foundation on which the First Truth of EVEolution is built: Connecting Your Female Consumers to Each Other Connects Them to Your Brand.

To anyone in the business of marketing to women, the Connection Truth means that you must rethink what women want from brands. Your brand must be differentiated, not in the way you *bring the components together*, but in the way you *bring women together*.

To get a hook on this, compare the woman-link approach to traditional brand-think. Look back to the '60s, the era of the marketing one-night stand, when companies basically sold isolated products, and brands were simply trademarks built around hyped claims and slick comparisons.

Over the next decades, marketers came to realize that, beyond the simple arithmetic of product superiority, other powerful influences swayed brand choice: Emotional appeal, aspirational image, and character. Such intangibles required deeper target understanding on the part of the marketer and more frequent exposure on the part of the consumer. The answer was to seek longer-term relationships with consumers. Be it kicky or kinky, odd or honest, whimsical or heavy, jelling was key.

We are now entering a higher plane of this new marketing phase—an EVEolutionary age. From now on, if marketers stick to tired, conventional marketplace practices, they can only hope for the best when it comes to reaching out and touching women consumers.

But those marketers who EVEolve will learn to facilitate one of the most basic female urges—the urge to merge.

In this new age, brands will serve as connecter-uppers for women seeking links with others; brands will "host" relationships among their consumers, just as brands sponsor chatrooms today. Brands will be the fulcrum for connecting; women will bond over brands, find their friends through brands, form clans and clubs and communities around brands.

Why is the need to connect so acute today?

The connection desire has grown explosively since entrepreneurial female baby boomers and mommy-tracked and downsized working women started leaving on-site corporate jobs to create off-site home businesses, or opted to work remotely. One result of this exodus: Women let their fingers do the talking. Nearly 70% of all the long-distance calls dialed from home phones are made by women.

Crucial to this, most of the traditional connection conduits for women have either been transformed drastically or have disappeared completely. Think about *The Saturday Evening Post* covers: the coffee klatch, the typing pool, the beauty parlor, the supermarket aisles. Many of these ghetto-ized women, so we're glad they've vanished into the ether. But where was the substitute? Women needed to find a new direction for connection.

Enter the Internet.

Today, women make up a full 50% of the on-line population.

Ironically, early on, hordes of naysayers expressed their firm belief that womankind, as a group, would shy away from the Internet, due to a "lack of affinity" and an underlying mistrust of technology. Others expressed the opposite fear: that women who got wired would become the new hermits, stuck at home in a vacuum of Techno-Isolationism. In fact, both predictions were way off the mark. Women are amazingly comfortable with the Internet (after all, how much different is it, skill-wise, from being a crack typist?). And the Net offers women the best thing ever: a limitless conduit for connection to bring us closer to each other. To e-mail our faraway friends, relatives, kids, and grandkids. To

Going to Saturn—Together

Women love company. And they love to talk. So they meet . . . at the deli counter, in parking lots, on the bank line, outside their kids' classrooms. When is the last time you saw two guys get up from the table to go to the bathroom together?

The people who sell Saturn cars understand that. That's why they started their well-publicized parties for all Saturn owners. It was a sure bet that their women customers would bring other non-Saturn-owners—boyfriends, husbands, parents, children, friends—along for the ride. And that's just what happened. Women's urge for connectivity brought a herd of potential Saturn buyers to the gathering, making it a marketer's dream for introducing potential new buyers to the brand experience.

A Circle Around Her

Pulitzer-prize-winning journalist Anna Quindlen once said, "I only really understand myself, what I'm really thinking and feeling, when I've talked it over with my circle of female friends. When days go by without that connection, I feel like a radio playing in an empty room."

Quindlen also recalled meeting the First Lady, Hillary Rodham Clinton, for the first time: "She showed me a bracelet she had just been given for her birthday. Her nine closest [female] friends had bought it for her, and the initials of each were engraved on the links."

Late in President Bill Clinton's first term, Quindlen met the First Lady again. "I asked how she managed to survive the maelstrom and continual scrutiny in the White House, and she showed me the bracelet once again. It was her circle of friends that kept her equilibrium constant."

buy cars and sell our Heisey glass. To check out the correct dosages of Ritalin for ADD or what's the latest on Vitamin E for wrinkles.

The Connection Truth is deeply woven into the texture of my life. Case in point: I often walk my sister Mechele the two blocks to her home at night. If we're not done with our conversation by the time we've reached her building, then she walks me back to my home. If we're still not done, I turn around and walk her home again. Then she walks me home. Finally we cut the cord and separate halfway between our abodes. This is not typical male behavior. As always, with women, it's the journey and not the destination that is the point.

The Connection proclivity in women starts early. When asked, "How was school today?" a girl usually tells her mother every detail of what happened, while a boy might grunt, "Fine." Harvard professor Carol Gilligan, an authority on girls and young women, says, "People used to look out on the playground and say that the boys were playing soccer and the girls were doing nothing. But the girls weren't doing nothing—they were talking. They were talking about the world to one another. And they became very expert about that in a way the boys did not."

Starting in the playground, females begin to establish connective behavior that can become a life-support system later.

Joanna Bull runs Gilda's Club, a support group for people living with cancer founded by the late actress and comedian Gilda Radner. When Bull was diagnosed with leukemia, her connection clan quickly gathered.

"It meant everything in the world to me," she said, "that there were ten women who came from across the country just to nurture me. . . . Some of them I rarely saw in person and mainly kept in touch with by telephone. Most of them had never met one another. But all of them wanted to come right away and . . . We sat in the hot tub, and we ate and drank and laughed and cried and talked and talked and talked."

In the late 1890s, Freud was the first to identify the technique of free association as a "talking cure."

Women beat him to it by about umpteen thousand years.

For businesses, this all adds up to an EVEolutionary opportunity.

Why?

Women's recent behavior in the marketplace already indicates that they're ready for a change in the way products are marketed to them. According to marketing expert Lori Moskowitz Lepler, founder of the Intuition Group, women are three times as likely as men to recommend brands when they know friends are looking for a particular product or service. And Yankelovich, an international marketing research firm, did a survey showing that 70% of women believe they learn the most about a new product from someone who already owns one. That's brand-passing at its best.

Make these statistics work in your favor. Get EVEolved.

EVEolved marketing will be all about how you help women connect the individual dots, and how you handle the post-connection opportunity. If you provide the connective network that women need, women will form a stronger bond with your brand.

Let me be clear:

This is *not* word-of-mouth marketing.

This is *not* relationship marketing.

This is *not* a simple sign-up-a-pal program.

This is *not* business as usual, one-on-one marketing.

And most of all, this is *not* a quick hit—a short-term promotion that catapults women together, as a gimmick. It's not about inserting two coupons into a women's magazine and labeling one "for a friend." Women instinctively recognize a bad connection. And when they hear one, they shut down faster than you can repeat "EVEolution."

Talking Over the Cyberfence

Women need to connect. But all over the world, there's been a weakening of community, the original connective tissue of family life.

The backyard fence is a symbol of what we've lost. It's also the image that inspired Mary Furlong to found Third Age Media, a warm and fuzzy cyber-community. Furlong is EVEangelical about her Web site aimed at the first wave of baby boomers and explosively successful with 45- to 59-year-old women.

"Institutions aren't as pervasive as they could or should be," she explains. "Third Age wants to be a place for sharing and for growth. I believe all women have an inborn need to communicate, plus a strong curiosity. That's what the backyard fence represented when I was growing up spending summers in the south."

"We want to be a backyard fence that's there twenty-four hours a day for anyone who needs us. We care."

Fence me in.

In the end, it *is* about building and supporting a community of women—a healthy place where your brand is a prominent, helpful, active, fully contributing member. It *is* about creating a geometry of growth for your brand that Legos up steadily, exponentially.

At first, it may feel like you're running in circles, scattershot. Yes, I am saying that *the strongest route to your customer may not be a straight line*.

"You mean that I have to connect one woman customer to the next before either one will feel truly connected to me?" Yes, I am saying that you will have to take a little more time than you did in the past.

Forging solid relationships requires an extra push. But if you can become a part of her clan, a link in her bracelet of support, you've earned yourself a deeply loyal customer (don't forget what we mentioned before: Women are three times as likely as men to learn about a product from other women).

Let's look at Oprah Winfrey—the undisputed Queen of Connection. Before Oprah, daytime talk-television had mainly revolved around conflict. Fists and four-letter words. She reversed the formula. Oprah brought women together in a network around higher values, sharing common ground. Oprah, the diet buddy; the book reviewer; the gospel guide; the public defender; the environmental scout. This is how she created the first brand in the talk-show universe, a carefully planted groundcover capable of spreading out into additional areas. Oprah's power lies in her fundamental understanding of the need that women have to be emotionally bonded to each other. Is it any accident that her own book is entitled, *Make the Connection*?

Connections have begun to be established in unlikely territory. Mucho-macho Harley-Davidson strived to connect up employer, employees, and consumers, turning all of them into rabid Harley fanatics. Harley sought to build a lifelong relationship with its customers by creating H.O.G. (Harley Owners

Group) back in 1983. An offshoot, "Ladies of Harley Group," is now 63,000 members strong. (Overall, women account for nearly 25% of first-time new motorcycle owners). Not only do the bikers connect with each other through the Harley Web site and robust rallies, they also connect with the community-at-large by sponsoring the highly visible annual "Bikers Against Breast Cancer" convoys.

Weight Watchers International is what I would call an accidental EVEolutionary. Well, let's just say that the company provides both an example and a warning. Weight Watchers embraced the Connect Truth when it transformed dieting from a solitary, hush-hush ordeal into a positive and, yes, enthusiastic group activity. The tell-all stories, shared agonies (how to get through Thanksgiving dinner, etc.), semi-public weigh-ins, and cheers for reaching goals held stressed dieters on track. Even beyond the bathing suit, any successful watcher-of-weight will tell you that what kept her motivated was the support of the other women in the weekly meetings.

But when H. J. Heinz bought the company, Weight Watchers veered slightly off their proven course, becoming more of a food provider than a service provider. Instead of mainly gaining the women's trust, there was a stronger thrust: Namely, promoting the Heinz line of diet cuisine. Weight Watchers group leaders' commissions were determined, in part, by the amount of Heinz food they managed to sell to the dieting believers.

Many of the veteran group leaders left the company, disillusioned by the newer emphasis on sales over service (read: Selling vs. Connecting to women). Many loyal customers followed them out the door.

By and by, Weight Watchers and Heinz wised up and realized that they were on a starvation diet. In just a few years, sales had become sluggish, and worse, the brand was losing its coveted franchise for success: Satisfied, thinner customers. Result: Heinz sold off the Weight Watchers service business, keeping only the manufacture and distribution of the branded food products. Weight Watchers, in turn, hired the high-profile, flame-haired Fergie, the Duchess of York, for its spokesperson and refocused its efforts on again serving women in a supportive group atmosphere.

The Connect Truth has far-ranging implications, not only for the aforementioned business, but also for all businesses.

Just around the FutureCorner . . .

- What would happen if women, who by a factor of 5-to-1 research genealogy on the Internet, were connected to one another by a drug company who does research on genetically transmitted diseases? Imagine

Rosie's Rehab

Rosie O'Donnell has used her TV talk show to create support for diverse women's issues, but none takes on a weightier challenge than the "Chub Club" she started in January 1999.

As America heads toward being the most obese nation (23% of the population) on this rotund Earth, Rosie is trying to reach out to the huddled masses (huddled, that is, over a feeding frenzy of pizza, nuggets, fries, chips, chocolate cereals, and sugar-laden soft drinks). She's beaming out her message of self-acceptance through marketing tools such as a newsletter, a Web site, and viewer call-in polls.

Instead of crash diets and scary drugs like phen-fen, Rosie has shed over twenty pounds by eating sensibly and treadmilling an hour a day. Her rosy vision? Get a healthy attitude, and you'll get a healthy body—eventually, gradually, finally. Her mission? For women to rely on themselves and each other as they face the issues that are all too familiar to Rosie herself. The driving force behind the battle of the bulge is a collective, somewhat reluctant, realization that we've all, in the end, got to take care of ourselves. No one else is going to do it. Rosie is using her effervescent energy to toughen our tortured souls and pare down our ever-thickening bodies.

the loyalty engendered in anyone searching for information on such illnesses.

- What if Hallmark, whose cards are predominately purchased by women, turned their Web site into a "feelings exchange?" What better way to recapture the communications high-ground lost to the chat rooms and Internet communities. And Hallmark might just get some heartfelt new lines to add to their collection.

- What if Johnson & Johnson took the innovative step of taking over the charge of the ladies rooms at many of the fast food restaurants? (Maybe changing the universal symbol for Rest Rooms at the same time. Aren't you tired of the silhouette with that old rigid triangular skirt?) J&J could transform bland or messy places into sparkling, sanitary, social spaces as well as provide an opportunity to sample J&J products.

- What if American Express made a concerted effort to connect up female empty-nesters through on-line and off-line programs, geared to help women re-enter the workforce with today's skills? Once a woman gets earning power, guess which card she'll be constantly using?

- What if ExxonMobil or Shell dipped into their credit card database to help commuting women interview and make a choice of car pool partners? The big fuel companies can then donate back an incentive of, perhaps, 25¢ less a gallon to those car poolers who display a special "In the Pool" sticker . . . and lock in the loyalty of multitudes of happy women. Added pluses: Fewer cars, less pollution on the highways.

- What about the 11 million widows who collectively control $8 billion in buying power? Often in charge for the first time in their adult lives, many feel isolated and insecure about money and finance. Why isn't one of the large financial centers, such as Citigroup, thinking about bringing these women together around someone like respected business columnist/TV reporter Jane Bryant Quinn? Isn't that a more compelling approach than aggressively selling to women by direct mail or those obnoxious cold calls? (I've always wondered if they're called "cold calls" because they leave the person who answers the phone cold. A marketing icicle for women.)

- When will MCI stop focusing on allowing people to talk for less money? Instead, they could inspire customers to use telephone communications more like Internet communications. Offer seminars on an 800 line about how to talk to your teenager or your elder-parent. Or maybe test the popularity of foreign language chats and "English as a second language" tutorials.

Are you beginning to see the EVEolutionary patterns in connecting women—and the varied ways of providing them with information and support in a branded environment? Connecting the links while keeping quality and function intact.

It takes a village—an iVillage, that is—to showcase the techno-power of EVEolution. Few Internet companies are riding the first wave with as much know-how. Warm-as-cashmere and immensely welcoming, the iVillage site has become one of the most talked about (and targeted) Web destinations.

What's their secret?

iVillage lives and breathes *think link*.

Founded in 1995 by Candice Carpenter and Nancy Evans, iVillage.com is widely recognized as the leading women's community on-line, attracting at least 7.1 million visitors a month.

Like most Internet start-ups, iVillage has yet to show a profit. But its managers (and investors who poured $1.6 billion into the 3/99 initial public offering) are betting that profits will follow as iVillage expands its number of on-site merchandisers (approximately one hundred at any given time) and starts raking in its share of their sales revenues.

What's the attraction? iVillage.com offers their advertisers a way to connect on an emotional, tingle-the-nerve-ending level through content developed specifically for the site. Advertisers don't just market *to* women, they actually become a part of the bonding process. In effect, marketing *with* women. A smart move, a right move toward EVEolution.

When we interviewed Candice Carpenter, she talked about her belief that women consumers "need a lot of information, and they actually consider it a service to have it all mapped out for them. Of course, we hope a woman will buy off our site—and we certainly don't offer any product we don't believe in—but a one-shot sale is not our goal. We're building relationships, not making sales. Our primary goal is to connect women to each other."

Every sponsor and marketer on iVillage.com shares this EVEolutionary credo.

"We're very selective about whom we partner with," Carpenter says. Only those companies that, as Carpenter puts it, "seriously get it" are chosen. Given this, I was very flattered when

Connect.com

Cyberspace is a natural for connecting women. Too often, though, I come across dull, tough-to-maneuver sites. Who has time to navigate all those nooks and crannies?

Here's a hint on how to get on the right path: Start with a little EVEsdropping. Log on to successful woman-specific sites and find out what the participants are talking about, worried about, passionate about. Try to figure out how your brand might fit into that kind of mix. Click into iVillage.com, hissyfit.com, disgruntledhousewife.com, or Women.com. And some of the health/medical ones: Medscape.com, womens-health.org, wellweb.com, or wcn.org (Women's Cancer Network).

she invited me to give an on-line seminar on EVEolution. The idea behind the screen? To help bond the connections between the members of the audience and (Duh!) cement their connection to the site.

It's interesting to look at one of iVillage's corporate alliances to see how it was done.

Renova. Ask any woman who's over the age of thirty-five what she'd like to hear about and you'll get an earful on anti-aging, or more accurately, looking your best . . . longer. So there's a ready group at attention. To introduce the wrinkle-fighting cream Renova, iVillage put together an on-line chat with a well-respected dermatologist. Participants asked "lots of fantastic questions" about skincare and aging during the session. That archive of personal information was then turned into a permanent place with an on-line resident expert. The abracadabra-selling point is that the viewers' own chat-inquiries were the basis for long-term content.

For the future? Carpenter says her immediate goal is to make iVillage a household brand. And with her firm grasp of both the power and the promise of EVEolution, I have no doubt she'll succeed.

• • •

Business travel used to be a male domain. No more. In fact, recent research shows that by the year 2002, half of all those business travelers on the wing will be women vs. 1% in 1970. For the business travel industry it's also important to know that women bring a spouse/friend 32% of the time—vs. men's 12%—and are much more likely to extend their stay to include some personal extras.

Wyndham Hotels & Resorts is EVEolved and ready. They were smart enough to see it coming, and smarter still to put 18 businesswomen on their advisory board.

The centerpiece of the effort is Wyndham's "Women on their Way" Web site. It compiles tips shared by women travelers,

Fore!

This statement is not going to come as a shock: The fastest-growing group of golfers is women. And no drum roll either: Businesswomen are using the game as businessmen did before them—for networking, for entertaining clients, and for making business deals right on the links—but with their own female twist. Talk during the game is more personal and self-revealing; winning is secondary to winning a new friend or ally. (Generally. Don't think about or tell me of the one cut-throat woman you've encountered.)

That spells EVEolutionary opportunity. What do you do with it? Here's one wise businesswoman who's teeing up.

Georgeanne Skelley, owner of a women's golf apparel and equipment franchise in Las Vegas, Nevada, was fed up with golf being such an unwelcoming sport for women.

For starters, she offered golf togs that made sense. "I tried . . . to select clothing women could use more times than just on the golf course," she said. "Very functional things that could be worn for a work day or a lunch date."

More to the point, she turned her store into a place where female golfers could come to talk golf, practice their swings, or learn from the store's pro. Besides the always-friendly atmosphere, there's a regular come-together time called "Golf Tip Tuesday."

"You don't have to buy a thing," Skelley says. "Just come in and share your golfing experiences. I want to create a comfortable, non-pressured atmosphere where women can explore their love of the sport. Where they can make connections with each other and learn something new."

And that's the (Connect) Truth.

plus has interactive sections for exchanging opinions on various cities, hotels, restaurants, airlines, and business news.

Wyndham puts out an on-line newsletter filled with great advice and travel information from its advisory board of big-deal

Home Away from Home

If you're a mother and have the kind of job that requires you to travel, once a week or more, what do you tell your child? Sometimes, it's "Let's pack your bag, you're coming with me." Children were brought along on about 24,000 business trips in 1996, up from only 9,100 in 1990. In response, some business hotels are customizing their rooms to fit the needs of working travelers with children. The New Jersey–based chain Travelodge has installed "Sleepy Bear's Den" rooms with everything an away-from-home family would need: Microfridges, VCRs, appealing sleepy bear bedspreads and curtains, low-to-the-ground chairs, small drinking cups, and . . . a cuddly stuffed animal. A library of children's videos is waiting at the front desk. And in answer to a working woman's prayers, many offer (or can line up) daycare and baby-sitting to cover appointment times and business dinners.

Some nights, after a brutal day of travel delays and long meetings, who wouldn't feel better with a sleeping baby and a sleepy bear? Count me in.

businesswomen. You can also find a potpourri of other tips that will be useful for the virtual community. For example, a handy list of what fabrics travel well without looking like a wrinkled mess (I rely on Issey Miyake's already-crinkled clothes) . . . or what hotels can ferret out a reflexologist for your tired feet when you arrive at two A.M.

The Web site isn't Wyndham's only *think link* program. Feedback has indicated that many women—even though we may long to relax with a glass of wine after a hard day of meetings—don't feel comfortable going into a hotel bar alone. So the hotel chain invented the concept of "libraries:" Inviting (un-pick-uppy), laid-back, book-lined rooms where women can hang out and have a drink/light snack, connect with others, or simply have a quiet moment to themselves. That's definitely an EVEolution edge.

Alice in Womanland

Working solo, playing solo. It seems as if couples aren't glued at the hips anymore. Here's a trend-to-watch: When women travel for a brief bit of R&R these days, a growing number are leaving the men in their lives back at the homestead.

Some of the fem-member trips can be found mentioned in the Web site, journeywoman.com. Or the tour operator, Wild Women Adventures, from Sebastopol, California, now offers 25 different women-only trips a year, up from 10 only five years ago. The Women's Travel Club, an Aventura, Florida, company that also packages all-women tours, reports similar increases. Aruba Sonesta Resorts just created its first female travel package with the sassy name (if you say it with "attitude") of "Go, Girl!" And the Hilton Jalousie Resort & Spa on Saint Lucia has a new "Diving Divas" scuba package, designed to cater to the 40% of divers at the spa-like resort who are women.

Why so many women-only trips? Phyllis Stoller, founder of the Women's Travel Club, generalizes that it's because men and women have such different travel styles. Women tend to prefer the snail's pace (wandering, studying, reflecting, finding little out-of-the-way places, meeting the locals), while most primal guys want to sprint and keep moving. Women would rather eat a sandwich or yogurt (and pay less), while most men would never dream of skipping their lunch. And, of course, women like to discover-shop, exploring even the native fruit-and-vegetable markets in hopes of finding some divine handicrafts. While, frankly, most men simply don't give a damn.

When it comes to travel, either alone, by twos, or in troops, a woman-based plan can be fun for a change of venue. If you can add color, spirit, laughs, and life to the EVEolved soul of trips, I say buckle up and get going.

What about your brand? Can you hot-wire a connection between women by reconfiguring a physical space?

Case Study: SnackWell's

Speaking of pioneer EVEolutionaries, consider Snack-Well's. In 1998, when Nabisco asked us to work with the company, annual sales of its wellness brand had slid from $270 million to under $200 million in just two years.

Why had the cookie crumbled?

In this new age of size 2 for grown waif-women (look at model Kate Moss, *Ally McBeal*'s Calista Flockhart, and *The Practice*'s Lara Flynn Boyle), pencil-thin (around 100 lbs.) equals beautiful. With jutting ribs, knife-sharp hipbones, pointed collarbones. And that's proving to be a problem for a large number of women and girls with normal curves or ample proportions. We asked: Could SnackWell's connect its female consumers to each other in order to talk out feelings about body issues, and could SnackWell's be recognized for its stewardship?

Our first step in the discovery process: Internal BrainJams, lots of heated discussion among the BrainReserve team, then again with our SnackWell's client.

BrainJams are great. That's how our company refers to the formal technique of "brainstorming" a topic. This differs vastly from the negative, nonproductive meetings that I call "blame-storming," where new ideas are shot down and fingerpointing is the group's main form of exercise. We stick only to the positives and creatively, joyfully, brilliantly (okay, my opinion) build on each other's ideas. Our BrainJams are an informed form of collaboration—my university of choice. In this case, we set out to pigeonhole the product category defined as "cookies," and then uncover the emotional attachment to SnackWell's in particular. What were the target audience's unmet needs? What needs did SnackWell's meet? What needs could it meet in the future?

Our next step was to build on the resulting insights from the BrainJams by bouncing the hypotheses off some consumers and experts from our TalentBank.

During the next step in BrainReserve's methodology, the CreativeThinks for SnackWell's, we asked our participating TalentBank members for the most powerful memories, experiences, and emotions they associated with cookies. Were there "cookie-enhanced" events in their childhood?

More than one TalentBank member reminisced about the first time her child baked cookies for Mother's Day. Memories of family moments poured out from those gathered: About when a child sprouted tall enough to put a hand in the cookie jar, about buying favorite cookies, about everyone sneaking cookies at night

Tap your own TalentBank

All of us have our own personal TalentBanks: Peers and mentors, co-workers and neighbors, a reliable vendor or customer, family and best friends.

We rely on our personal TalentBanks for a spreading of news, reviews about the latest film, tidbits about the new family on the block or a firsthand report about the best brand of detergent. Of course, we expect to have our brain picked in return. And most of us relish the constant give-and-take.

Sometimes I'm asked how BrainReserve recruits its TalentBank. The assumption at first is that busy people won't want to be bothered. That it's only the sloughers, the down-and-outers that will have the free time to give. Totally wrong. Most everyone likes being asked for an opinion, or gets a charge out of advancing some outlandish theory in a "non-office" meeting, or feels good about contributing to a future vision. And our TalentBank members say they welcome the chance to connect with people in dissimilar fields who they normally wouldn't meet with (or even more bizarre, direct competitors) during our BrainJams.

continued . . .

I think of my TalentBank as an Ur-club of global experts who, like all of us, want to talk and think, do mind exercises, and talk some more. Reporter friends back me up on this phenomenon. They know that when investigating a story, they can call up almost any stranger and probe for views on everything from spies to spices. Almost invariably, the voice-at-the-other-end cheerfully obliges.

And the BrainReserve TalentBank is a two-way communication. Members are free to call us up and ask a question any time they like. More often than not, these questions lead to more questions that lead to new ideas, new conclusions, and the discovery of new Trends.

In the course of our assignments, we've talked to everyone from CEOs, Virtual Reality experts, astronauts, and artisans to writers, politicians, hobbyists, and househusbands. And the best part is that our CreativeThinks are an exercise in pure EVEolution (and especially the First Truth): By communicating and networking, I've had a chance to learn something truly unique, unusual, and new from every single one of them.

with cold glasses of milk. The ultimate conclusion: Cookies represent a deep-rooted, early-seeded symbol of a healthy connection between mothers and children.

SnackWell's, we reasoned, could build on this foundation and become a conduit for the delivery of wholesome treats. Secondly, they could get involved with the passing on of good eating habits. The very name suggests a healthy relationship to food: If you snack well, you're eating properly, not gorging or junk-fooding. We decided to narrow this focus even further, to do something specifically about helping mothers and their daughters feel good about themselves.

At what age are daughters most receptive to input from their mothers, ready to listen, to consider advice, to learn comfortably from them? To a large extent, the experts cited and the girls we interviewed concurred, it's in the pre-teen years that

Mom's voice cuts through the clatter of friends and media. It's when a girl's future attitudes and beliefs are formed. It's a time when connection is critical.

We saw that SnackWell's could become an integral part of a positive body-image message. We believed SnackWell's Brandwidth had unused capacity; that the brand could be relaunched as one of the nation's foremost supporters of female self-esteem, built through the mother-daughter connection.

It was a tall order—to strengthen the mother-daughter bond in a SnackWell's context (although early EVEolutionary Rick Lenny, President, Nabisco Biscuit Company, was ready for the challenge). But it had a big payoff—they could capture a unique positioning with this kind of underlying mission: A rallying point for all customers, mothers, and everyone associated with the brand. Our shorthand message: "SnackWell's—nourishing a woman's self-esteem."

Our shorthand strategy. The First Truth of EVEolution: Connecting Women to Each Other Connects Them to Your Brand. (Snackwell's also was a perfect fit with our Sixth Truth, as a Hand-Me-Down generational brand.)

We went to work to implement this connection with the SnackWell's team at Nabisco. The launch started in January 1999, when SnackWell's announced in major newspapers that it was donating $250,000 to Girls Inc., the largest girls' advocacy group in the U.S. SnackWell's set up an 800-number to call for information on their new series of Mother/Daughter Workshops. It was a three-way partnership. With SnackWell's at the helm, BrainReserve created the format and Girls, Inc. facilitated the seminars.

Six weeks before Mother's Day, SnackWell's ran ads in major newspapers offering a Mother/Daughter Journal for three proofs-of-purchase. The Journal, which sold out, was a unique Mom's Day remembrance with spaces for photos and places for favorite quotes. Advertisements for the Journal also laid out details of the more than one hundred Mother/Daughter Workshops to be held in SnackWell's markets coast-to-coast. The undisguised point: SnackWell's is participating in getting mothers and daughters together, linking them with other mothers and daughters, and introducing all participants to tools that nurture self-esteem.

So far, hundreds of mothers and daughters have attended the workshops, covering discussions where Moms remembered what it was like to be their daughters' age, and topics on careers and ways to communicate. The seminars connected mothers and pre-teen daughters from a variety of backgrounds.

No surprise, the response from workshop participants was overwhelmingly positive. One Mom wrote: "This was a first, but hopefully not a last. I learned a lot not only about my daughter, but also about the other mothers there and was pleasantly surprised at how alike we really are!" Another mother e-mailed, "I'm still in touch with several women from my workshop; so much so that we've each brought in our own friends and meet twice a month to talk about our relationships with our kids and other life-shaking topics."

SnackWell's path to EVEolution also found its way to a Lifetime TV documentary about the first test workshops, called "Mothers and Daughters: A Lifetime Bond," which aired in April 1999.

Simultaneously, the smart people (Sandy Greenberg, Terri Meyer) at SnackWell's agency, Foote, Cone and Belding, captured the strategy in their elegantly simple tagline—"Live well. Snack well." May I add, "Connect well?"

The SnackWell's seminars provided a shining example of the best of women's abilities to meet and talk. No matter where the workshops were held, no matter what age, ethnic, or economic background, these mothers bonded with an "instant connection." SnackWell's, in turn, made many new "friends" and benefited from this closeness and conviviality.

Close your eyes . . .

Here's a sampling of an exercise for the mothers in the Snack-Well's Workshop. Do you understand our point?

"I close my eyes and imagine that I'm traveling back in time to the age my daughter is today. What I see is . . . "

- *How I looked and where I lived.*
- *Who my best friends were and what we did together.*
- *What I was told was okay for girls to say and how to behave.*
- *What messages I received about food.*
- *What messages I received about being a girl (from TV, magazines, teachers, parents).*
- *What messages I received about work.*
- *What I imagined I would be doing with my life as an adult.*
- *What I saw as my job . . . or my work at home.*
- *Whether I thought I'd ever have a daughter and what she'd be like.*
- *How my daughter's life is the same or different from mine.*

Here's what we asked of the daughters.

"I close my eyes and imagine that I'm grown up. What I see is . . . "

- *How old I am and what I look like.*
- *Where I live and whom I live with.*
- *What I like to eat, snack on.*
- *How much education I have.*
- *What I do for fun. Favorite sports? Hobbies?*
- *What kind of volunteer/community service work I do.*

Confirming that: Women don't buy brands, they join brands. That's EVEolution. It works. It has here. It always will.

• • •

All of the businesses I've talked about in this chapter have been impacted by the First Truth of EVEolution: Connecting

Your Female Consumers to Each Other Will Connect Them to Your Brand.

Ask yourself, "What should I be doing now?" Here are some questions to help you apply the Connect Truth to your own business.

- Do I really know enough about my customer to connect her to others like her?
- Are the women in my own company really connected to each other? Because if they're not, they won't have a clue how to connect my female customers to each other.
- When is the last time I took the women in my company out for lunch/drinks/dinner and just listened and listened?
- Am I qualified to connect women to each other, or do I need a dedicated female marketer on staff to lead the way?

I know how hard a prescription this is, and how much it goes against deep-seated business practices. You just have to trust me on this one.

But most of all, you have to trust women.

And until you do, you'll never EVEolve.

Connect women with each other in a brand-identified setting and you'll set the stage for them to join your brand.

So *think link* and you'll think ink . . . that is, the black ink of success.

Chapter 2

The Second Truth of EVEolution:

If You're Marketing to One of Her Lives, You're Missing All the Others

Recently I was told by a doctor friend that maybe I had some kind of disorder where I can't filter out distractions. Sensory Integration Dysfunction. I'll be sitting in the office deep at work when I suddenly realize that someone is giving out the wrong number over the phone. Or when it seems a little too warm, I check out the thermostat and hear from three floors above that my little girl is fussing. And notice that the paint is chipped on the corner of the stairs. And the radio from the construction crew next door is playing my favorite song from the '60s, "Oh Donna."

Without stopping what I'm doing, I manage to fix, repair,

take care of, and listen to, each and every thing. I don't think it's just me. I think it's being a woman. The ability to multi-task and do everything at once . . . extremely well.

Why is this important to marketing? Because women lead multi-lives, and a marketer, concentrating on only one of them, will miss out on all the others. The answer is to help women integrate their lives more seamlessly. Only then can you tap into the power of EVEolution.

Natalie Angier, in her book, *Woman: An Intimate Geography*, mentions that '80s icon, rocker Chrissie Hynde of the Pretenders, prefers "playing with the boys." Angier goes on to quote Hynde as saying, "I work with men. They're single-minded, straightforward and they can rock."

I mostly agree with the "Chain Gang" diva: Men *are* more direct and more single-minded than women (although women *do* rock-around-the-clock). Men have the ability—or maybe the need—to tune out all but the one thing they are doing at the moment, while women can meander to a different drummer.

Helen Fisher, in her book, *The First Sex*, discusses this difference insightfully and at length, calling "men's . . . compartmentalized, incremental reasoning process, 'Step Thinking.' " She contrasts this with the observation that "women tend to think in terms of interrelated factors, not straight lines." She calls this manner of thought, "Web Thinking."

Fisher goes on to say, "As a general rule, men tend to focus on one thing at a time—a male trait I first noticed in my twenties. At the time I had a boyfriend who liked to watch the news on television, listen to rock music on the stereo, and read a book—presumably all at once. In reality, he just switched channels in his head. When he was imbibing from one modality, he tuned the others out. Not I. The flashing of the TV screen, the throbbing music, the printed words: All of these stimuli swamped my mind." Fisher relates what all women know to be true: Men do one thing at a time, while women do many things at the same time.

Where does this gender difference come from? According to a recent article in *Men's Health*, men have fewer connections in their cerebral cortex, making them less coordinated than women. Maybe more women should take up juggling for exercise.

And regarding the female/male difference in magazines, did you ever notice that the ones aimed at women cover a broad base of subjects (life profiles, food, fashion, beauty, babies, travel, love, home, hearth, health, and the best of Heloise)? While men's magazines concentrate mainly on two areas: pecs and sex.

Possibly the reasons are biological: Natalie Angier traces this multi-tasking ability to "a woman's mosaic brain" and tells women, "No wonder nobody can figure you out. No wonder you're so damned clever." Or possibly the reasons are genetic: Helen

Which Way Is Up?

Haven't you noticed that when men are lost, they need to turn off the car radio to concentrate on navigating? But if a woman has strayed off the beaten path, she'll probably be talking on the cell phone with her office, drinking a cup of coffee, and brushing her hair while pulling into the nearest service station to ask for directions.

I'm not trying to make the gender battle worse, but in Dr. Warren Farrell's book, *Women Can't Hear What Men Don't Say*, the jokes are funny.

Q: Why is it a good thing there are female astronauts?

A: So someone will ask for directions if the crew gets lost in space.

Q: Why does it take a million sperm to find one egg?

A: Because men can't ask for directions.

And so on. You can either find these differences annoying or amusing.

My point is: Men have an astounding ability to focus. Maybe too astounding an ability.

Fisher says that "50% of all women are genetically better equipped than all men to coordinate multitudinous bits of information."

A product that I always thought was accidentally EVEolutionary is Advantix film. After developing a roll, you get one neat little sheet, showing all your photographs, only in miniature. Instead of the old way of having to hold strips of negatives up to the light, you can instantly see your whole Disney World trip or birthday party or family reunion laid out before your eyes in one-inch squares. I see it as a metaphor for the way women snapshot their lives. Not in strips, not unfocused, but total and fully focused on everything at once. Sharp and clear.

Certainly since pre-Stone Age, a millennia of conditioning has placed women in multiple positions. With their original responsibility being caretaker for the offspring, every other responsibility became an add-on, a simultaneous set of "to-do's." After all, if you put the baby down so that you can turn your attention to rubbing sticks together for a fire, a hungry mountain lion might just make the most of the opportunity. Can't do one thing; must do both. As if a life depends on it.

Society has also factored into making women take on many (too many?) parts. Women have finally won the right to try out for any role they want. But there is a problem: The tasks just keep piling up. Women can't abandon one role to assume another. Whether they want to or not. Just because they own a business doesn't mean they aren't the head of a household. Just because they are wives doesn't mean they aren't feminists. And just because they are compassionate volunteers doesn't mean they aren't committed to their corporations.

I know firsthand, as mother, businesswoman, corporate board member, author, volunteer, friend, sister. The house still needs to be kept up, the social schedule still needs to be maintained, my little girl still needs to be read to, the dog still needs to be walked, and the car still needs to be serviced. *In our quest to have it all, somebody still has to do it all.* Multi-tasking has become a woman's survival response.

As some observers believe, have we as women allowed men the luxury of single focus? Have we done this to ourselves? Maybe. Natalie Angier blames much of the complication of the female condition on the pressures—like guilt and perfectionism— which women allow themselves to feel. She states simply that

EVE Talk

After working together with my best friend (and co-author), Lys Marigold, at BrainReserve for 12 years and on *The Popcorn Report* and *Clicking*, I observed an interesting occurrence: She could really write in my voice. While working on this book, I realized that when she was writing "in my voice," I could anticipate what she would say and jump in with comments in "her voice being my voice." As we were sitting at the computer, I was thinking that a perfect example of a woman's multi-dimensional existence happens when I listened in on my own conversation with Lys. I heard:

FP: What's a good word for "chance?"

LM: How about "opportunity."

FP: What time is Skye Qi coming home?

LM: Six, I think. Lynne (Skye's caring daycare-giver) is dropping her off.

FP: If she could get here by 5:45, we could all have dinner at Sam's before g.g. has to go to bed.

LM: Did you see the article in the *Times* about the Miss Boo Web site?

FP: It's like having Virginia (Lys's mother) say to you, after you're all dressed, "Is THAT what you're wearing?"

LM: No, it's worse than that. Sort of an S&M fashion moment. But it's also kind of nice to have a personal shopper. Although she can be brutal.

continued . . .

FP: What chapter would that go in?

LM: The Fifth Truth, Go to Her. Obviously.

FP: Have you booked your trip to Petra yet?

LM: Not yet. My dig isn't until the spring. But look at these pictures of me last year in the Nabataean tomb.

FP: Wow. But shouldn't we get back to work?

LM: Isn't it interesting how the Advantix system shows you all the pictures on one small sheet? It's like Trip-At-A-Glance.

FP: Shouldn't that go in this chapter?

LM: Yes. It's perfect mosaic brain.

What might seem like idle small-talk to the corporate listener (or most men), is, in actuality, the rich field of a woman's creativity. Skipping from topic to topic to topic, we can leap from the mundane to the mind-bending.

"Men have still not habituated themselves to babies as readily as women have to paychecks."

Women still function as the final backstop for most of the domestic responsibilities in their households. Men's "to-do" lists are usually monopolized by work-related things (with a wife-compiled, Saturday "honey-do" list thrown in—mainly clean the garage, rake leaves, fix toys). Women's tasks are rarely that one-dimensional. Proof? How many men remember who they are having dinner with on Saturday night? Or how many check to see if there is lunch for the kids in the fridge? Or know whether Woofus is up on his shots?

The multi-dimensionality of women's lives goes beyond the obvious blurring of home and work. It goes beyond the physical roles of busy, busy beavers, with so many tasks to do. That phenomenon has been covered by women's magazines for the last decade. What we want to explore is something different, something deeper. How a marketer should be tuned into the emotional side of women. Without fear of the tears. With an understanding that it can lead to unlimited EVEolutionary marketing opportunities.

A woman's role is to be the command center of all information for the family. She's the mediator for all complex negotiations between family members, or friends, or business associates. The United Nations ambassador, the balancer. A woman is also called upon to handle the emotional tug of career against personal responsibility—like being unable to leave the bedside when a beloved parent is sick, even though she just landed a big case. Or being the dedicated employee who stays late to finish the last paragraph of the proposal, even when she has twelve guests, all her husband's business associates coming for dinner.

As Judy Sheindlin of "Judge Judy" fame says in her book, *Beauty Fades, Dumb Is Forever*, "I sometimes joke that within the family structure, what men do best is breathe. They inhale and they exhale. Male bashing? No. Truth. Women do everything. Work, shop, cook, clean, do laundry, take care of the children, arrange social functions, the whole *megillah*. Men breathe."

I think she's only half-joking. I would have put it differently: Women do everything and men mostly work and work and work. In their minds, still shouldering the weight of the family.

Whether you, as a business person, employ one woman or many, you will find this multi-dimensionality in your female employees' lives every day. Look closely. In reality, there is no place where a woman's Multiple Lives are more apparent than in the workplace.

And no better place that can serve as a "greenhouse" for growing great ideas on how to market to her many lives.

Maybe it's such fertile ground because the relationship between a company and its female employees mirrors the relationship a company has with its customers.

If you view your female employees only as employees, you are missing the opportunity to bond deeply with them. And over the course of a long relationship, to learn from them. Look at the statistics: Women are much more likely to stay with a company for the long haul if that company makes their lives richer (in all senses) and easier. Or helps them attain personal goals outside the workplace.

Look at the criteria *Working Mother* magazine uses to develop its list of "100 Best Companies for Working Mothers" (it's kind of nice that they have such a list at all. And it's doubly nice that a magazine called *Working Mother* even exists). What do they see as critical to a female-friendly workplace? Their six most important ratings are: Leave for New Parents, Flexibility, Child Care, Work/Life Balance, Advancing Women, and Pay.

Over the fourteen years of compiling this list, *Working Mother* has "watched new work/family challenges and solutions develop, and once-unique benefits quickly become the norm." If only this were totally true. Employers still feel that these rated items are special and exceptional perks for which their female employees should be grateful.

We're saying that with the growth of female entrepreneurship, companies will have to EVEolve to keep the talent on board. "Perks" will become as standard as free coffee and a donut. What I have suggested: Giving blocks of stock in the hot IPOs as an incentive to take a job. That's a variation of what the new CEO of Compaq, Michael D. Capellas, did. As reported in *Business Week,* Capellas immediately "gave each employee 200 shares of Compaq stock . . . It's the quickest way to convince employees they have a stake in any turn-around."

We thought it would be interesting in this chapter to more closely examine EVEolution in the workplace. This is the perfect place to address how to reach a woman when she's doing her multiple-tasks. Your female employees are a captive (so to speak) audience, and represent a critical constituency that should be marketed to. You have scores of opportunities to interact with her, to learn more about her and how she behaves.

Because the first and best place to get women passionately involved with your brand—to get women to join your brand—is at your brand's birthplace, your workplace.

In an attempt to describe this EVEolutionary marketing to women at work, we coined a new word: *Perfessional*. Meaning the ultimate blurring of the personal and the professional.

When a woman plans her family's vacation, where is the travel agency that also meets her business needs? Notifying clients and contacts that she will be away and where she can be found. Or conversely, what travel agency when booking her business trip (kids included), lines up daycare, baby-sitters, numbers of local pediatricians, playgrounds, and playdates?

Think of the other companies that could get in the *perfessional* act:

- Office Depot could become Life Depot, offering a selection of last-minute items for the hard-pressed, female small-business owner. "Besides the ream of fax paper and a package of black ink cartridges, send me a case of Coke, a large-size Shout stain remover and a chili dinner for four with cornbread. But first, and fast, a computer repair person." By phone or via Web site.

- Timex could become Time(x) Management, going beyond watches into a time-planning system designed for the complex lives of women. Beyond the Franklin Planner (what did Ben know in 1776 about working women?), *this* business planner would have an integrated calendar that included space for school pickups, hockey drop-offs, ballet recitals, choir practice, facial appointments, T.J. Maxx stops, GAP returns.

- Weight Watchers could extend out to Family Weight Watchers. Overweightness tends to run in families; everyone from the chubby baby to the chunky Mommy to the hefty husband to the generous Gen-Xer . . . to the rotund Rover or flabby Tabby. What a format to go beyond diet advice and food to marketing to all their Multiple Lives. Set up diet meetings at offices, factories, pre-K's, schools, veterinary hospitals, parks. As the expert, Weight Watchers could advise other companies about making targeted products—everything from comfortable, cushy cars (a new positioning for Cadillac?) to wider toilet seats. After all, at the average of two pounds per week, it can take a year for the extra-tubby to get to goal (plus, there's only a 50% success rate in keeping the weight off for two years). And for the family pets, what about formulating their own WW low-fat dog and cat foods and treats? And selling a little treadmill so that their little legs can jog next to yours?

In the *perfessional* arena, there are thousands of examples of women who are successfully blending their Multiple Lives. Technology is making it easier today. In an AT&T television spot, a mother feels the pull of her two kids who want to go to the beach, on a day she has to work. Solution: She takes them to the seaside and they play in the sand while she uses her cell phone to conduct a critical business call. Thus, AT&T shows empathy for two of her lives and sells their service, EVEolutionarily.

Denise Ilitch, Vice Chair-woman of Little Caesar Enterprises, created her own work solution. "I have a thirteen-year-old girl and an eight-year-old boy, and know as a parent, you are pretty much always worried about your kids. So I started on-site child care here," she said. "I think the employees are much more productive now and it's a fabulous recruiting tool."

That's one answer for having your sweeties . . . and working too. So is the multi-life of a typically atypical woman, Lucy Fisher. She's the Vice Chairman of Columbia TriStar Motion Pictures—a noticeably female female in a noticeably male world. Her 16-plus-year career has resulted in credits such as *The Fugitive, The Color Purple,* and *Malcolm X.* When Columbia TriStar experienced a slump several years ago, Lucy was the one to revive it with some serious hits: *Jerry McGuire, My Best Friend's Wedding*, and *As Good As It Gets*. She even helped set a Hollywood record for money-making, grossing $2.3 billion in 1997.

With successes like these, Lucy and her commitment to her career are impossible to question. But she insists on limiting her work week at the studio to four days. She wants time for her husband, Doug Wick (who is also a film producer), and their three daughters. She wants time to mentor the growing, but tiny, number of women breaking into the executive ranks of the studios. So she has turned down promotions and job offers that would have jeopardized the arrangement.

"I love Lucy," director Steven Spielberg once said, "because she won't take my calls on Friday." There aren't a lot of people in the Hollywood Hills who won't take calls from Steven Spielberg, no matter what day it is.

Apply the Multiple Lives Truth to the workplace, and the results are a highly satisfied and productive staff: Employees who have joined your company brand. Loyal and true. And that return on loyalty can be measured in dollars and cents. Consider this: Two independent consulting companies—Hewitt Associates and The Saratoga Institute—have estimated that the cost of replacing a worker runs between one and two-and-a-half times the salary of the job. And the more skilled the job, the higher the cost.

So what do your female employees need to stay and never stray? Here are some ideas just around the FutureCorner:

- What if a large-scale employer like IBM radically redefined "employee benefits" to include a menu of options? Flexible packages that offered choices: Dry cleaning, house cleaning, gardening, accounting, legal services (or any service that the company already uses to service itself), tutoring or day camps for employees' children, in-home emergency care for an elderly parent. Or, maybe they could have courses in caring for housebound loved ones, giving guidance for administering

Niftier Fiftier

Overlay the peak of the baby boom with the fact that more women are in the workforce than ever before, and what do you have? A "change of life" of massive proportions.

Seventeen million working women will be turning 50 by the year 2005. That's a lot of hot flashes. "That many women over 50 is going to impact us medically and economically," says Marie Lugano, President of the American Menopause Foundation (AMF).

Some forward-thinking companies are preparing. The AMF, backed by a grant from Eli Lilly in Connecticut, has started to offer menopause seminars to companies in that state. Such menopause management programs are designed to answer any questions, clear up any misunderstandings and offer practical information on the various options, either natural or medical. A healthy understanding of the subject results in reduced healthcare costs, increased productivity, seasoned employee longevity, and a better corporate image.

Very smart, very EVEolved.

medications and personal care. The company could also stipulate "family days" as part of the allotment of sick days/personal days, or tardy days to help an employee adopt a pet. Or at least health insurance could insure the nanny/babysitter/housekeeper. Employees could elect to retain a "guidance counselor," trained as a career, social, and familial advisor. Employees could also choose financial/retirement planning as one of their benefit options. What an improvement over the "do you want Point of Service or Preferred Physician Organization coverage" benefits-turned-hassles offered in most large companies.

- What if companies that focus on "family" encouraged a religious/spiritual life at work? I'm not suggesting a support of cultism (or church over state), just envisioning resources for female employees to nurture their spiritual lives, if they choose. A minister, priest, and rabbi (depending on makeup of employees: an imam, Brahman, Buddhist priest) on call. A quiet room or garden to reflect or meditate in, for a few minutes before, during, or after the day. A library of reading materials. What about forging a closer link to local churches? And encouraging female employees to take time off work to help out in soup kitchens (by providing a shuttle bus) or teach Sunday school (by donating craft materials)? What about communion and confirmation and Hebrew classes offered at your offices? What a profound level on which to bond with your employees.

- What if a top-of-the-line limousine service, like Fugazy in New York, who normally ferries executives to meetings, made Multiple Lives use of their cars' "dead time" while those executives meet? If the time falls between 2:30 to 4:30, the limos could be made available to transport employees' children from school to home or to a friend's house. The families know they can trust the service—after all, the drivers are professionals, screened and bonded. Mothers who have become family chauffeurs will be forever grateful. Such a company will have solved a major juggling dilemma, and will have picked up a community service pat-on-the-back along the way. This could be expanded to work for cab or local car services, or even smaller school buses.

But how does this EVEolved view of your female employees' world translate to your female consumers? What does If You're Marketing to One of Her Lives, You're Missing All the Others mean to you as a marketer?

Some companies out there are on the EVEolutionary forefront. One might surprise you: mega-male Merrill Lynch.

In 1996, Merrill Lynch became convinced that if they could resolve the push-pull of professional-personal conflict, they could develop a more loyal workforce. They also understood something that most businesses didn't (and still haven't). That there are fundamental *economic* reasons to make life better for their employees—especially their female employees—who were trying to balance long commutes, family responsibilities, and work. Reasons like increased productivity. Decreased turnover. Fewer sick days. (And happier faces.)

In answer, Merrill Lynch created a group called the Alternative Work Arrangements Group that set up the practice of telecommuting. A full 60% of participants are women.

Merrill knew that you can't just give an employee a desk, a computer, and a phone at home and say, "You're on your own." They set up a training program in telecommuting and a two-week, work-at-home simulation lab, helping employees fix the unexpected but unavoidable glitches in their new life—before they began. And before little problems became catastrophes.

This Early EVEolutionary now invests nearly $5,500 per telecommuter to make sure its off-site workers have the technology and support they need. Merrill has seen a clear payoff: Employee retention is up, turnover is estimated to have declined by 6% and the telecommuting employees themselves feel their productivity is up 10–20%. These employees are successfully living their Multiple Lives, enabled by their employer. To quote one of those telecommuters at Merrill, "The telecommuting program has dramatically improved the quality of my life by giving me the flexibility I need to balance work and family responsibilities."

For all the numbers of women who are working out of their houses these days, it's amazing how little thought has been given to the home-working environment. Thinking about this and the obvious "fit" with the Trend that I identified (in the 1980s) and named "Cocooning," I decided to see if I could design a home work center in the same spirit: comfy, orderly, calming.

To get a better picture of what was out there, I sent disposable cameras to hundreds of work-at-home women and asked them to take photos of where they worked. Of what their desks looked like. What was on the walls. Where was their equipment. I hate to say it, but the results could give new meaning to the phrase, "What a mess." It was stressful just to see the chaos. Stacks of papers piled on computers and fax machines. Books falling every which way.

Several commonalties ran through the multitude of images: A perching of coffee cups, an earring removed for phone comfort, rickety pitchers of flowers, pictures of kids push-pinned into the walls, and in many cases, a smaller makeshift desk so a child could "work" alongside. It was amazing that women were generating billions of dollars out of these nooks, corners, and ramble-scramble places.

Bring Help to Work (She'll Pay You Back)

As an employer of 28 women (at BrainReserve, our entire workforce is currently made up of double-X chromosomes), I am very sensitive to the multi-tasking needs of my employees. This means helping them manage their time and their lives in a way that makes sense for each of them. And for BrainReserve.

Solving the lumps and bumps of our Multiple Lives doesn't make me tense—just very, very alert. Four of my most senior staff work remotely. I have every possible service brought to the office for those of us who are here every day. A variety of bagels with cream cheese for breakfast; and soups, salads, and sandwiches for lunch (plus endless snacks: melon cubes, cookies, chips, and a daily bowl of freshly-popped popcorn). As well as a steady stream of hairstylists, manicurists, grocery and drugstore deliveries, dry cleaning pickups and drop-offs, an accountant, and, sometimes, a masseuse. I make sure that appointments are

continued . . .

made for everyone around me—calling doctors (and diagnostic centers for yearly mammograms), dentists, and veterinarians. To make life easier all the way around, I even help set up those necessary license, registration, and passport renewals.

Any of my staff (and spouses) are welcome to a guestroom on a late work night. And there's a nursery upstairs that my daughter is happy to share with any of my employees' kids. This saves us all time, reduces stress, increases our productivity, and makes people feel considered and secure.

I know this bonds employees to my company. I work very hard to attract gifted people, and I spend a lot—in time and money—teaching them the BrainReserve way. By supporting them in the non-work areas of their lives, I am helping ensure that they'll stay forever.

P.S.: The group happens to have shaken out to all women. But we've had male employees in the past, and I'm currently interviewing a very bright guy to be our new Trend Director.

After pondering how this info could be translated into a more organized workspace, I came up with the design for "Faith Popcorn's Home Office Cocoon." And under the guidance of Carl Levine (my Home Furnishings Licensing guru) of CLCL, we brought the blueprints to the Hooker Furniture Company in North Carolina. Third-generation Chairman/CEO of the company, John Clyde Hooker, Jr., understood my Cocooning concept immediately and gave the project his stamp-of-approval to go to production. At 80-some years old, Clyde has more vision than most marketers less than half his age. So did his VP of Marketing, the very patient, very persistent Hank Long.

My home-haven has places for everything: a BrainReserve-logo embossed coaster for your coffee cup; a jewelry tray in the drawer; a big recessed V-shaped glass vase; cork board for photos; and child's step-stool that opens to a mini-desk. The back panels of the credenza part can stay wood-paneled or, something every woman would like, can be matched to your room décor. And it comes with a hangtag laid out by BrainReserve's visual designer, Johanna Busch, that explains my philosophy on Multiple Lives.

To my delight, the Home Office Cocoon will be in stores to start the millennium right. Here's to Home (Neat) Home.

After the positive response of the Home Office Cocoon, I narrowed the concept down to a Cocooning Chair. The spark came from an article in *The New York Times* about the popularity of "movable" upholstered furniture. I immediately started thinking about everything I would ever want in a really comfortable recliner that could be a virtual center for a woman's life.

It would have a swing-out tray table that I could compute on and snack on. It would have big, roomy pockets on its sides and back, where I'd be able to stuff a month's worth of magazines and books. It could warm up on a chilly winter's night at the flick of a switch, much like my car's seats (or maybe cool down, on a hot summer's day). It could have an optional, attachable baby seat so that a little one could also Cocoon up close.

Of course, my cozy chair would recline, but not too far back, because women are always having to pop up and down for quick errands. It would have a leg rest, not too big or broad, yet strong enough for a toddler to sit on and color her Elmo book. In one armrest, there would be a set-in well for a small vase of flowers. The other could have a tiny DVD player mounted on a pull-up tray (for intimate movie-watching), similar to the First Class seats of planes. Built into the headrest would be an optional speaker system for listening to music or get-us-going motivational tapes. There would be an aromatherapy system where you could pour in your favorite healing fragrance—chamomile for relaxation, bilberry for easing eye strain.

My Cocooning Chair would come with two cuddly blankets, one large and one baby-sized with plenty of pockets to hold everything from tissues to small toys. The chair would swivel, of course, and have sturdy wheels so that a woman could easily roll

THE HANGTAG

Home office furnishings inspired
by the life and Trends of Faith Popcorn,
noted "Nostradamus of Marketing."
Similar to Faith's own Home Office Cocoon,
each detail has endured the test of a true visionary.

The Satellite and La Cocoon collections have been
created to lift you into your best future.

WARNING:
DO NOT USE THE
Faith Popcorn Home Office Cocoon
FOR ANYTHING BUT:
working at home, managing your
portfolio, going public, applying for a mortgage, signing a
contract, surfing the net, starting a business, balancing a
checkbook, planning a board meeting, conducting an
interview, creating holiday cards, filing your coupons,
managing your child's and your parent's lives, researching
your family's genealogy, designing a resume, returning
voice mails/e-mails and snail mails, learning a language
and eating lunch.

To learn more about Faith Popcorn
and the Trends that have
inspired this design, please visit:

www.faithpopcorn.com
www.hookerfurniture.com

it from room to room, or even outside to the porch or patio. Again I turned to my Furniture Licensing expert, Carl Levine, and he enthusiastically recommended going directly to High Point, NC (center of the Home Furnishings market in America), to meet with his many associates.

We are in the process of refining the details and testing the design options with hundreds of women across the country (your thoughts would be welcome by e-mail: ideas@faithpopcorn.com).

And if you're working in a Cocooning Home Office and reading in a Cocooning chair, what's missing? You guessed it. We have one more project in the works—Cocooning Lamps, with Hank Bowman, President, CEO of Stiffel. Some of the EVEolutionary concepts to be incorporated: Ophthalmologist-tested lighting; reusable, biodegradable packaging; ethical ingredient labels; washable, pink-glowable, seasonal-switchable shades; built-in timers; body-sensor activation; and a Cocooning Collection Club Web site. Nice.

There are already a few stellar examples of companies that are working on understanding how to develop consumer products to help make a woman's Multiple Lives easier, such as:

- Classroom Cameras: One EVEolutionary industry understands that when a mother happens to be at work, she doesn't leave her parenting life at home. Companies such as watchmegrow.com, kinderview.com, and toddlerwatch.com offer Internet-based systems that link Web cameras installed in over 150 daycare centers nationwide to special software installed in a mother's office computer.

    For a price ranging from $15-$20 a month, a mother can observe her children periodically throughout the work day. For an average of six times for about fifteen minutes at a time, she can be with them in spirit and comment specifically (and honestly) on the day's activities. Because an observant mother feels relatively

A "Brass Ceiling"

The New York Times ran a front-page feature on November 29, 1999, highlighting the Multiple Lives struggle of women in the military. It featured Lois Beard, "youthful-looking and energetic, with an officer's unflappable discipline, who seemed headed towards becoming the first mother promoted to Army general"—but instead of getting her stars, she quit.

Beard had held every job needed to become a general. She had completed every educational requirement. She had the support of her peers and her superior officers. But what she did not have was the endorsement of her three children, who felt that she wouldn't be there when they needed her. And ultimately, when she examined her life, she realized that the Army hadn't ever shown her the deep support a mother needs. In fact, military life wasn't set up to help a woman cope with the pressures of being both an officer and a mother. It does nothing to reconcile a female's many lives.

Yes, you could guess that the venerable U.S. military might be one of the last institutions to get EVEolved. But shouldn't a front-page article in the *Times* at least make someone in the Pentagon snap to attention . . . and salute the complex lives of women warriors?

guilt- and worry-free, she can actually concentrate better—so that any time lost to an employer is more than made up for in productivity.

If this strikes some as a bit "Big Mother is watching," there is another good reason for these cameras. Complaints about daycare centers have diminished as mothers can see for themselves their giggling or napping or being-read-to kids and that a good job is being done there.

- Workout Strollers: The Baby Jogger, invented and made by Phil Baechler, finally allowed a mother to do two of her favorite activities at once: Fast-walk or run for some aerobic exercise and keep her child with her, in a lightweight, sleeker stroller engineered to race. Happily zipping along together in the fresh air. The best is being able to enter a 10k and, as a fast family duo, maneuver well and pass the competition. Other new kid ideas that we'd like to see made: My weekend nanny, Sonia Trulli-Zaki, was wondering why children strapped in their strollers have to be so low-slung to the ground? In other words, wouldn't it be nicer if the stroller wheels were sized like standard bike wheels? No more bending over for the caregivers. And kids don't have to look up to see the world. I would go even further and ask for some secure place on a stroller to keep my wallet, my car keys . . . and my tiny, light-weight Sony Vaio notebook.

And why should Lys Marigold have to go all the way to the land-of-bicycles, Holland, to bring back the perfect young child's bike seat? One that has her daughter, Skye Qi, sit in front of her, not in the back, letting Lys protect her from brambles and branches, but more importantly, hug, whisper, sing, and point things out to her—birds, bees, butterflies, blue sky, flowers, clouds, leaves, and the lovely people of East Hampton.

- One-Hand's-On Tools: When the Oxo® company developed its ergonomically designed kitchen hand tools—vegetable peelers, can openers, and corkscrews, among other things—they thought they were developing products for an aging and increasingly arthritic clientele. Little did they guess that serious and not-so-serious cooks who wanted to multi-task in their kitchens would use these fatter, softer, easier-to-use products for one-handed food prep. When using the Oxo® garlic press, for example, a woman can prepare an aromatic clam sauce for her linguine dinner while finishing up a conference call with the office—without dropping the phone into the olive oil.

- Freeze-Ease: Balducci, New York City's #1-rated (by *Zagat's*) gourmet food store, uses its one-of-a-kind capability to flash-freeze and deliver fresh food to a woman's doorstep (plus offering the convenience of ordering from its Web site, Balducci.com). According to Ken Romanzi, President and CEO of Balducci.com, "If a woman has a successful career, a full social life, and no time, all she has to do for a top restaurant-quality meal is order online and press the enter key."

    Tah-dah: A delicious disaster-proof answer for Multiple Lives.

Such companies help a woman to manage more than one role at once. Winning her love . . . and loyalty.

Case Studies: Four Small Companies

This book isn't only about Big. It's also about the little, ambitious, hungry, young, start-up, middle-of-start-up, even old-timey, female-run and -focused businesses.

When working on the very foundations of EVEolution, we asked ourselves: Can a Truth be really "true" if it doesn't work for the small, the entrepreneurial, the underfinanced, the non-MBA'd? Those of a size that talk about bookkeepers and not Annual Reports; staff dinners, not Board-of-Directors meetings. Truths shouldn't only be for the Fortune 500. They must apply equally to the un-Fortune ones, as well.

To test the width and breadth of our Truths, we turned our sights on four small businesses. Too small for BrainReserve's full-scale consulting (and consulting fees), we treated them as friends and took them through a zipped version of our methodology. We found out amazingly that each company best fit the Second Truth: If You're Marketing to One of Her Lives, You're Missing All the Others—plus a light overlay of the Eighth Truth: Everything Matters. This foursome each has a different approach to understanding, reaching, motivating, and sustaining the loyalty of their female customer—in all her Multiple Lives.

J. Roaman: Customer-Wise

The first is a clothing store whose owner has an uncanny focus: Figuring out what women will want and putting it together for them. Retailer Judi Roaman absorbed the in's and out's of the fashion "biz" in New York City—especially after years of being a buyer for Bloomingdale's—but then decided that she wanted to be her own boss, set her own standards, follow her own vision.

Utilizing her expertise in marketing and design, Judi opened the easy, sportive Jane Fonda's Workout, off Main Street in East Hampton, NY. She then moved to a busier location and opened Confetti in 1985, offering a sophisticated selection of women's clothes—everything from sweaters to stretch pants to scarves to evening wear. Judi started building up her loyal customer base, made up of women who have come to rely totally on her personal taste and conviction. In 1990, another space on Newtown Lane became available, giving Judi the opportunity to expand into more casual "jeans" and related accessories.

But in 1993, Judi made a strategic decision, based on what she understood to be a Truth for her customers (a mix of weekenders, summer folk, and increasingly, year-rounders). More and more of the women were working and they didn't have the time or the energy to go through all the rigmarole of shopping in a large department store (getting to the right floor, looking through racks and racks, finding a salesperson). Knowing this, Judi closed her other two shops and opened the first, free-standing (her idea) DKNY store in America. And two years later, a second DKNY in her second hometown: Aspen, CO.

What separates her way of selling from many others? Judi

caters to her customers' Multiple Lives. She gets messages, phone calls, and faxes with specific requests, such as: "Thanks for sending me those perfect Client Meeting suits. But help! I have to go to Florida for a family wedding and need one outfit for Friday night's dinner, another for the afternoon ceremony and reception. Oh, and I have to meet an old college buddy for an informal lunch on Sunday."

Then there's the Size 2 customer who special-ordered fifty-five pairs of stockings because she was tired of scouting for her small size and wanted a year or two's worth to take her through every occasion—from charity balls to school events. Or when Judi answered an SOS from this office—to help dress some of our very own BrainReservers, following the requirements of our particular brand-look (see page 111).

In the area of extra service, consider these measures. If her store is out of a certain DKNY item, she tries to track it down, even if it means purchasing it retail from another store. Though her stores carry the DKNY women's line, Judi smartly, thoughtfully, stocks some sweaters and tees in men's XL and XXL for her heavier female customers to feel comfortable in. And speaking of comfort, she places large sink-in-able armchairs and ottomans (and local newspapers) for patiently waiting husbands or friends. For a place with clean, all-white interiors, she's extremely kid-welcoming, having extra-wide door openings for strollers and offering, at any given time, dishes of jellybeans or Christmas ribbon candy.

Considering the relatively-small spaces of the stores (East Hampton: 1,500 sq. ft. and Aspen: 1000 sq. ft.), Judi goes beyond the usual one or two in sales-help, to keep her store highly-staffed for focused service at the busy times. Four or five are around to assist, especially on an overcast August day in the summer height-of-season in East Hampton; as well as four workers for both winter's glory and the fresh-aired July festivals in Aspen.

J. Roaman is overly-committed to being generous to charities: Supporting the Susan G. Komen race in Aspen, selling stacks (or giving away copies) of *Portraits of Hope: Conquering Breast Cancer* by the photographer Nora Feller, donating gift certificates, merchandise, you name it. In these small resort communities, it's a visible and welcome demonstration of the Everything Matters Truth.

For Judi, we envisioned a future-focus that suggested an East Hampton-Aspen newsletter to hand out (or snailmail or e-mail) to customers that had stories, and maybe even photos, of their Multiple Lives. For example: A montage showing which one of the DKNY winter looks BrainReserve's President, Kate Newlin, was sporting on the Colorado slopes and how easily it was changed for après-ski at the Jerome bar.

This idea of a foray into communications came after watching Judi work. That's when we uncovered her most EVEolved trait: Within minutes of meeting a customer, the gregarious Ms. Roaman finds out all about the woman. Where she's from, what she does, the ages of her children, who her friends are, her habits and hobbies, her favorite restaurants, her stock investments and . . . any problems, major to minor. Judi doesn't merely sell an article of clothing. She networks with each customer, makes a new friend, and ends up putting together a wardrobe for that particular woman's lifestyle. That's being mindful of Multiple Lives-style, at its best.

Hollywood Wings: Ready to Fly Again

If you rent one of the movie classics, *Sunset Boulevard,* you can catch a look at film legend, Gloria Swanson, playing an aging Hollywood star who is frantically trying to look younger in order to make a comeback. What are those wing-shaped things stuck all over her face? Hollywood Wings, an age-old answer to getting rid of wrinkles—but one that still works and works well.

The small, female-run company was started in 1937, with

one of the original owners being Mary Roebling, the first woman Treasurer of the United States. The kitchen-table beginning was in the hope of finding a way to erase those deep frown and forehead lines (especially) that even most surgeries can't tighten up. It works like this: A patented moisturizing glue backs a linen-like fabric (hypo-allergenic) that's cut in an elongated angel-wing shape. These spreading wings are left on while sleeping (some women use 4–5 each bedtime), both adding and trapping moisture, hence plumping up the woman's own skin cells. The next day, her skin looks smoother, fuller.

Pleased with the results, most women get hooked on this nightly regimen. Rose Kennedy ordered the little aqua blue boxes until she was well over 92 years of age. Most of the new sales happen by word-of-mouth. A Southern female gospel minister used to stand at her pulpit and praise Wings to the heavens (prompting her parishioners to order the face saviors by the dozens). Also, the Wings name was routinely "revealed" in newspaper articles around the country, whenever the topic covered "Best Beauty Secrets of . . ."

In the late '80s, the book, *How to Be Wrinkle-Free: Look Younger Longer Without Plastic Surgery* by Carlotta Karlson Jacobson, mentioned Wings under the guise of "Stop expressing yourself at night." It seems to be a common problem, now more than ever, that if one is stressed, the unwitting response while sleeping is to wrinkle the brow under tension. The author suggests a glass of warm milk, a hot bath, soothing music before bed, or just ". . . apply adhesive-backed Wings anywhere you don't want lines to form at night (forehead, laugh lines, or crow's feet)." She goes on, giving directions: "You simply massage your wrinkles for a few seconds, splash them with cold water to stimulate circulation in the area, dry your skin, and place moistened Wings over them, pressing until they stick firmly."

Most of the customers are stuck on Wings for life. Maybe because the sample box is only $6 for 50 Wings (Box 680, East

Hampton, NY 11937). Among the mail-order letters and scribbled notes from all over the world, there are more than the law-of-averages from . . . law firms (do lawyers frown more than other women?). And mothers frequently pass them on to their daughters (for their jobs . . . or more likely, in hopes of getting them married), in the form of presents or as in this quote from a note: "My daughter is 34 now; it's time I shared my faithful Wings with her." That could be because deep forehead creases are quite often due to heredity.

This simple, remedial, one-product company has one female owner (in the spirit of full-disclosure, it's Multiple Lives Lys Marigold) and one helper (Susan Ceslow), both being mothers and both working out-of-home.

The future-focus: Deeply aware of the growth of the new aging population that is still vibrant in the workplace, BrainReserve recommended developing an Internet catalog (for 50-plus), featuring other products that Wings had been investigating. Products in the same genre as Wings—not gimmicky, not avant-garde, not rip-offs. Such as a really terrific stain remover that finally takes out the indelible; something that lightens those old-age spots on the backs of hands to the imperceptible; and an eyebrow stain that's nontoxic yet covers the give-away gray. Leveraging the bond of trust built up between Wings and its users. As well as building upon the Wings' research that showed a consumer is actually shocked when a product lives up to its claims.

Wings has EVEolved into a company that has something that every business envies: Customers that are loyal for all of their Multiple Lives.

Lorin Marsh: Inner Resources

Sometimes the clichés of a culture tell the deepest Truths. Look at all the phrases tossed around in the corporate world that sound tough, even squirmy to women, such as "You scratch my back, I'll scratch yours," or "One hand washes the other." It's been men (mostly) who have used this buddy system to help each other. When everything's green and rolling saying, "Let's work together, old chap." Or deployed as a safety net, to call someone up when times are tough, asking (without embarrassment), "Throw me some business." Women are just learning the value of buddyship, and how to profit from the give-and-take of working together on a business-to-friendship-to-business level.

Very good at the best, the noblest, the most fun aspects of networking, mixing friends with clients, clients with friends, are the women who started Lorin Marsh, a high-end decorative showroom of furniture and objects (both antique and custom). Founded in 1975 in New York by Lorraine Schacht and Sherri Mandell (and now ably partnered by Lorraine's daughter, Caryn), the company immediately made a reputable name for itself by noticing a niche in the decorative accessories market. At that time, there were plenty of antiques, but very few great-looking contemporary accessories.

To fill that void, Lorraine and Sherri designed and created objects of style that definitely made a statement. No little busy-body things to stick on shelves, but boldly attractive accessories that shouted, "Here I am." And the women backed up what they offered by filling their city and country homes with examples of their products and entertaining with the same *largesse*. Hosting dinners and parties to display and network at the same time.

Today the business has widened into an eclectic boutique, selling everything from 19thc. antiques to French Thirties furniture to yards of Swedish leather books (for instant "old" libraries) to making fine reproductions in Italy. Even though Lorin Marsh isn't dealing with the stratospheric "priceless" category, Sherri personally tries to track down the provenance of the antique pieces they have in their showroom, researching in-depth in a library that specializes in the decorative arts. But very appealing to the Multiple Lives of women is, as Sherri explained, the commitment behind the concept: "Of course, the product is of utmost importance, but we believe in backing it up with service."

Since the owners of Lorin Marsh are so adept at integrating their business contacts into their Multiple Lives (something, by the way, most women just haven't done enough of, unless it's to help out their husbands), they get a chance to hear what their clients have to say—in a more relaxed atmosphere. But once or twice, this close blending of *perfessional* (personal with professional) has gotten sticky. Lorraine told a story about how, at one party at home, she was stopped by a designer who was perturbed about the late delivery of a table. Lorraine sweetly explained that it was coming in from the South of France and the week's delay was out of her hands. Nevertheless, hearing that the designer's client was getting upset, Lorraine sent over a huge bouquet of flowers the next day. Her two-pronged philosophy: "Show that you care; and flowers soften the blow." In fact, at Lorin Marsh, they mostly try to avoid these conflicts ahead of time, calling the customers if an ordered piece is late and arranging for a "loaner" piece to be sent over.

Following intuition like that is a sure sign of women's EVEolution.

Elizabeth Dow Ltd.: Cutting Edge

Wallpaper had almost gone out of fashion until Elizabeth Dow began a business that lifted it from the realm of stripes and flowers, moved it away from being a kitchen/bathroom staple, and attached the word "handpainted" to the art of wallcoverings.

Elizabeth started the Soho-based company only seven years ago, working out of her bedroom (do you see the pattern here?), washing her paint buckets in her kitchen sink. Her wallpaper studio now employs thirty full-time workers and had an astounding number of international interns in 1999 (75 chosen out of over

500 applications), all responding to a small insert placed on a job opportunity-based Web site.

Trained as a fine artist, Elizabeth worked for years restoring and documenting historic houses around America. She personally blended and applied up to fifty colors a day and executed elaborate design motifs, fixing up such notable places as South Church in Nantucket, Matthew's Mansion in South Norwalk, CT, and the City Opera House in Traverse City, MI.

On her own, however, she turned to wallpaper, calling it, "The fastest way to change the feel of and add richness to a room." Elizabeth has developed technological innovations in the field: Her own formula for glue, as well as new collage methods of incorporating Nepalese ferns or hand-torn papers or newspaper fragments within subtle layers of her metallic paints.

ED Ltd.'s first real commercial space was at 580 Broadway in New York. It was there that Elizabeth worked out a very EVE-olved solution for a modestly funded, start-up venture: Sharing resources with two women who ran a small textile business, Yoma, on the same floor. The three of them chipped in, renting an empty office between the two companies for a mutual showroom, using the same sales rep, and exchanging such information as the best software or a good place to get a letterhead made.

Now in a light-filled Sixth Ave. commercial studio, Elizabeth runs her company to fit with her co-workers' Multiple Lives. They all have flex-hours, to allow for one physically-impaired worker to get to therapy, or for another to leave twice a week at 3 P.M. to serve hot food to the homeless. Her busy atelier was recently filmed for a how-to segment on Martha Stewart's network television show.

Elizabeth also designs for the *perfessional* lives (personal/professional) of her clients, from Gwyneth Paltrow to the Estée Lauder Spa in Tyson's Corner, Washington, D.C. to the Chart Room and private suites of the Soho Grand Hotel. Her own Internet page is elizabethdow.com.

BrainReserve made a future-focus recommendation that Elizabeth use that Web site to let everyday, regular women share part of the same joy of creation, letting them choose from a palette of design elements to further customize her papers for their own Cocoons. Even to the extent of being able to incorporate favorite names, items, icons, or symbols into their wallpapers. For instance, instead of using the ED Ltd. ferns within a soft coppery background, a woman could choose clematis vines on a dusky rose background. Or well-designed versions of black toy poodles on slate gray.

Her success story is an inspirational woman-as-entrepreneur source for study. Carving out a unique niche and setting a higher industry standard. Tapping into a female-inspired set of needs, values, and dreams. Slowly, gradually, planning a strategy of company growth that's structured, organized, and managed with sensitivity and care. Proof of the how and why EVEolution works.

● ● ●

The multiple aspects of Multiple Lives can be found working well in small, female-run companies. And here is the larger company that BrainReserve worked with that so aptly illustrates the Second Truth: If You're Marketing to One of Her Lives, You're Missing All the Rest.

Case Study: Hasbro

Some toy companies are in for the short haul, grabbing a fad by the mane and riding it until it stumbles, but not Hasbro. This toy company runs its business in the old-fashioned way, constantly building on its classics, yet solidly backing its exciting new entries.

In addition to its vast target audience, Hasbro is a future-forward, highly EVEolutionary company, respecting women's lives—all of her lives. Unlike others who attempt to bypass the mother, Hasbro considers her as a conduit to her child's creativity.

When Hasbro came to BrainReserve, it was to help it envision the future of play and determine what part of that future Hasbro could shape. Hasbro's challenge was to look into ways to develop (going far beyond the first purchase) and sustain the relationship it has with its consumers—including the children, the parents, and the ever-widening circle of friends and family.

It was a fun assignment for BrainReserve to be able to investigate the "power of play," instead of the more usual corporate powerplays. As one of our TalentBank experts told us, "Play leads people to be more creative, more productive, and happier in all parts of their lives." Based on all our EVEolutionary knowledge of a woman's long hours, Moms need to play more. And certainly entrepreneurial and executive Moms need to play more. In fact, don't we all need to play more?

Hasbro, a multi-faceted business today, actually started in 1923 as Hassenfeld Brothers, a company that sold textile remnants and later manufactured pencil boxes covered with fabric. It didn't take long for them to expand beyond that line of manufacturing, soon offering pencils and other school supplies.

In the 1940s, Hassenfeld Brothers made its first foray into the toy market as a manufacturer of play doctor and nurse kits and, by 1952, it had introduced an amazing hit, the lovable, playable Mr. Potato Head. Hasbro, in an innovative marketing move, advertised Mr. Potato Head on the then-beginning medium of television.

Alan Hassenfeld, Chairman and CEO since 1989, is the third generation to run the company (and he reminds me somehow of Tom Hanks in *Big* in that he's an innately smart businessman who has been able to retain the open directness and enthusiasm of a child). Hassenfeld quickly went about the business of furthering the company's aggressive acquisition strategy and expanding its reach into the global market. He explains his philosophy, "We've invested considerably in projects that are designed to instill the Hasbro name with the values of family, quality, fun, and benevolence. We make products that offer the excitement of play to consumers of all ages, but Moms are key customers for our core brands."

In 1998, Hasbro scored a major home run with the launch of its Furby line. Boosted by tales of being "the hottest, must-have toy of the year," Furby-frenzy intensified right before Christmas when stores had long lines of frantic shoppers and shelves were empty. Unbelievably, charities were auctioning off the little critters for up to $5,000. Now there are little Furby Babies to collect by the dozen.

Part of the attraction is that Furbys (clearly addressing Multiple Lives) let a busy mother work or accomplish something else while the child plays with a pal who speaks hundreds of words in Furbish (*may-may* means love) and can be taught to talk back in English. Little girls love to "mother" their Furbys, often asking for a larger family to nurture. And smart mothers also love Furbys, not only for their cuteness, but as increasing-in-value, highly-sellable collectibles.

Understand the significance of these interactive creatures to EVEolutionary marketers: Toy as baby-sitter; toy as educator; toy as emotional-relationship maker; and toy as equity-builder.

Alan Hassenfeld has always been a leader in recognizing that great play patterns can come from anywhere on the globe. He has always been a strong proponent of Japanese play (that's where he found Pokémon), eagerly pushing forward new concepts (many fast-action, tech-driven) from non-American sources. To help him achieve his expanded vision for the company, he brought in a visionary partner, Herbert M. Baum, as President and COO, who was formerly Chairman and CEO of Quaker State and BrainReserve's very first Trend-seeking client when he was President of Campbell's Soup Co. North and South America.

In 1999, Alan and Herb hired BrainReserve. We plunged in

immediately, setting the wheels in motion for our 36-step consulting methodology. Our first visit to their home office in Pawtucket, RI, reminded us of a child's fantasy of where toys come from (it was Santa's workshop and *Alice-in-Wonderland* rolled into one). Even the executive nametags are made with building blocks.

Getting from there to here was an interesting EVEolutionary trek—meeting with key thinkers from all over their far-flung toy empire, and having 19 management interviews. We probed, listened, and talked to lots of people, conducting a total of four management CreativeThinks, two TalentBank CreativeThinks, three TrendTreks, ten TalentBank expert interviews, and eight internal BrainJams.

At BrainReserve, we felt as if we had been through the looking glass and back, finding Hasbro's future would fit in with our Second Truth: If You're Marketing to One of Her Lives, You're Missing All the Others. As with other very successful companies, Hasbro also fits neatly into two other basic Truths: This Generation Will Lead You to the Next (as the mother connects to the brand, so the child will imitate) and Everything Matters (with their Children's Foundation).

Through the use of our proprietary TrendProbes (the way we gather consumer insights without the pitfalls of traditional research), we began to explore a world that we called the Imagi-Nation (as you can see, at BrainReserve, we like to make up names). ImagiNation is a space where one can play, laugh, work, dance, worry, argue, make and spend money, and live.

BrainReserve "brought" experts and consumers to that imaginary place and learned that the best aspect of play and the best of work share a common trait: Each allows us to lose track of time and self. A tremendous benefit to women in today's multi-tasked, time-pressured world—and an even more important one as we EVEolve in the 21st century.

Women who work are being rubberbanded, being caught

up and pulled every which way—until they snap. As author Beth Wilson Saavedra wrote in *Meditations for New Mothers*:

> ". . . . we are often too burned out to play. When we want rest, even play feels like work. We forget how rejuvenating it can be. Play refreshes our minds and bodies. If our relationship with our spouse is strained, play helps us to soften and let go of unnecessary grudges. Children love it when we let down and play with them. Play brings us close and it lets our kids know that no matter how busy we get, we always have time for them." Ending with the meditation: "I must not forget to play. I need it and my children do, too."

Hasbro wanted to go further in its relationship with its consumers. To go beyond the "feature" side of toys (meaning "wow," "bang," "she talks/cries," "he walks/leaps buildings") to the toy's "content" (what it really provides). Very EVEolutionary—to build up a long and loyal relationship.

After all of our reading and research, as well as many intense discussions with Alan, Herb, and the Hasbro management team, we all realized that the company has an unprecedented opportunity. It could own this strong EVEolutionary position: To Children and Their Mothers, Hasbro Is the One Company That Brings Play to Everyday.

Here was the thinking behind our positioning. Every time you reach a mother, you get her kids, her mother, her father, her husband, their parents, friends, neighbors, co-workers—and more. They're the sum total of the players in her Multiple Lives.

The beauty of Play Everyday from a woman's perspective is that it frees her from the reality of self, allowing her to escape, to imagine, and to create. To spend time with the people who are important to her.

Playing Everyday creates 365 selling occasions. Adding Play to the Everyday makes the mundane fun. Play lets a woman be freer, happier, more adventurous, and more productive in all parts of her Multiple Lives.

Hasbro's new logo, new look, new promise—"Making the World Smile"—is now used in their packaging and in their marketing communications, as a happy reminder of the benefit of play. Interestingly, it's exemplified on the back cover of their 1999 Annual Report with a beautiful little *girl*, smiling.

Toys are not just for tots. Along with the newer Furby fever, women often cling to memories of childhood favorites, either wanting them back as keepsakes or seeing their value as collectibles. How much would an early Monopoly board fetch? For clues, Hasbro has initiated its own Web site, HasbroCollectors.com, which not only offers rare and hard-to-find toys for purchase, but also provides helpful information on what's hot to collect, and what's not.

Although Hasbro is known far and wide as being on the forefront of action games and the latest gadgetry, strategically it has more than its fair share of non-tech toys, even promoting a "family game night" in its advertising and marketing efforts. In fact, we found that some women (especially those with very young girls) are pleased that the company makes some simple products for playtime needs. Among its stars: the Easy Bake Oven and Koosh. And the unprecedented winner: Pokémon cards. We don't have to tell the world about their over-the-top, sold-out success.

Willa Perlman, one of Hasbro's senior executives and a mother herself, explained the beauty of most of these Hasbro toys for the Multiple Lives woman. She said, "Let's call it Play Fast: You can jump in without too much set-up and not too much take-down." Hasbro also is known for having easy instructions and an 800-number that's handled by patient people.

However, for others, technologically-based toys are the way to go, teaching such skills as eye-hand coordination and getting girls ready to enter the computer world. We predict that by 2010, the distinction between real and artificial will be eroded, giving access to a universe of play possibilities.

A girl will be able to play Scrabble with Raggedy Ann, fly a space craft with *Star Wars'* Queen Amidala, buy Park Place from Tiffany Trump, and go through the Florida Everglades with Frogger.

Mothers will be sure to join this brand when they discover the good works of the Hasbro Children's Foundation. During just this past year, the Foundation gave grants to help over 160,000 disadvantaged children. As one example, the Hasbro National Resource Center for Boundless Playgrounds advises communities, municipalities, and individuals on how to build "universally accessible, sensory rich, and developmentally appropriate playgrounds."

Good works, goodwill. That's the strength of our Eighth Truth: Everything Matters, and you'll see how much this means when a woman has to choose one product over another.

But the real power behind Hasbro's EVEolutionary strategy is this: Everyone wins when every one of a woman's Multiple Lives becomes more playful.

What can your business learn from the Hasbro model? That women's lives are varied and complex and you can become instantly indispensable if you help them handle their multiplicity of needs. And you can find unlimited opportunities if you look beyond the first life you see.

• • •

So start by asking yourself *three* critical EVEolutionary questions:

- When is the last time my marketing group has closely observed, analyzed, and been sympathetic to a woman's 24/7 life?
- How many women's home offices have I visited lately?
- What could I do personally to help a woman manage her Multiple Lives better?

Again and again. Marketing to her Multiple Lives is a multi-layered marketing Truth. Start with one of her lives and circle out to all the others. You'll meet a lot of her friends, family, and business associates there and find a cadre of brand evangelists that will sing out your praises worldwide.

That's the gospel Truth (number two).

Chapter 3

The Third Truth of EVEolution:

If She Has to Ask,

It's Too Late

To successfully market to women, you have to understand what would please a woman. I had once read this little bit of folk wisdom that captures it well:

A girl doesn't say what she wants,
But you're somehow supposed to know,
If she wants to do this or do that,
Stay here, stay there, or just go.

Men have been wondering about this for eons, wringing their hands, clenching their fists or crying out to the starry sky, *"What do women want?"*

Even the noble Sigmund Freud was bewildered, declaring this to be "the great question that has never been answered and which I have not yet been able to answer, despite my thirty years of research into the feminine soul."

And if you wait for women to tell you what they want, guess what? You're in danger of being dumped. Whether you are a boyfriend, husband, boss, subordinate, or brand.

Because women will *never* tell you what they want. They'll utter a phrase like, "It's not the same if I have to tell you." This is a deeply familiar female sentiment that's completely unfamiliar to males. Unless it's said during a fight, a break-up, or in couple's therapy.

As the Calvin Klein ad for the fragrance "Contradiction" states: "I'm just a simple complicated woman."

Between a Rock and a Beach

Here's the marketing joke that I tell at the part of my seminar that sums up the female dilemma:

A man is walking down a beach on the East Coast when he kicks a bottle and, lo and behold, a genie pops out, saying what else but "Your wish is my command."

The man thinks a minute and asks, "Well, I'm deathly afraid of flying and since the major part of my job is on the West Coast, I need you to build me a bridge so that I could drive back and forth."

The genie strokes his beard and says, "That's an awfully difficult request. Don't you have an easier wish for me to fulfill?"

The man says, "Let's see. Well, as I market to women, it would be really helpful to know what they want."

The genie answers, "About that bridge, two lanes or four?"

Maybe our reticence to express our needs is part of a learned behavior, honed in the classroom: Girls start shutting down in the Sixth grade, according to a recent study by the American Association of University Women (160,000 members), and drop to minimum levels of participation by the Seventh and Eighth grades. Or maybe we pick up signals even earlier, learning from our mothers that saying "I want" or "I need" seems unladylike and unattractive.

Or maybe the reasons are even more serious. The extreme view: Carol Gilligan, in her book, *In a Different Voice*, summarizes her interviews with several women by saying, "Describing a life lived in response, guided by the perception of others' needs, they can see no way of exercising control without risking an assertion that seems selfish and hence morally dangerous."

Whatever the reason, women have learned not to speak up. In so doing, we have developed an unwritten, unspoken code of behavior, characterized by subtlety, innuendo, inference, and, at its worst, manipulation. And we have become comfortable living by this code. But men are not. In their book, *What Do Women Want: Exploding the Myth of Dependency,* authors Louise Eichenbaum and Susie Orbach observe this phenomenon: "Rarely does a woman confidently report that her husband is able to anticipate and pick up the signals she emits about her emotional state and what she might be needing."

The bottom line: What seems normal in a man's universe sends women into orbit. It is brutally obvious to most women that the men around them don't notice such basics . . . as the fact that they never wear orange . . . or that they left a Tiffany catalogue on the bed with a page or two strategically turned down . . . or that a "That's r-e-a-l-l-y N-I-C-E" comment while passing a store window means "I'd like it for my birthday present."

It's puzzling and frustrating to women that men don't tune in early to our needs. Because it's first nature for us to tune into theirs.

Darwinian logic says that women are conditioned not only to determine why the baby is crying, but also to prevent him from crying in the first place—by anticipating and meeting his needs even before he experiences them.

But men just aren't wired that way. Unless they have been carefully trained, like Pavlov's dogs, by the electric shock of a woman's disappointment.

Think I'm painting a picture here of shy, mousey, shrinking-violet women, those unusually unable to express themselves? Think these must be women "somebody else" lives with, works with, markets to? Yes, I'm sure most of the women you know don't retreat from battle in your home, your family, your health club, or especially your office. And what about that crazy woman driver who guns the car and cuts you off? I'm sure you're surrounded by New Millennium females: Do-it-all women who have a hardcover copy of Sun Tzu's *The Art of War* on their desks in place of the old air fern and a small canister of Mace in the drawer.

Won't these kung-fu women tell you what they want? In a focus group, won't they pound their fists on the table and demand the products and services they need? Won't they call your 800-number ten times a day and log on to your Web site 24/7 to let you know what they need? Right? Right?

Wrong. Really wrong.

Because marketing is different from life.

You have a well-staffed 800-number and a sexy Web site for her to reach you on, you say? Not good enough. That's the business equivalent of saying, "Hey, she's got my phone number, she can call *me*."

If women have to go out of their way to track you down . . . if you make them jump through hoops to get service . . . if your attitude is take-it-or-leave-it . . . well, they'll leave it—and take their billions of dollars elsewhere.

The Third Truth of EVEolution says it all: If She Has to

Ask, It's Too Late. And also keep in mind the critical corollary: It's easier to keep her than to win her back.

In this world of consumerism, if a product is disappointing, another option is immediately available, waiting to snatch her soul. Why bother complaining, she asks? Why not just quietly divorce the brand and remarry?

Another way to think of such an abrupt exit from a brand is to compare it to the last time you tried a restaurant that was just "okay." You didn't complain to the manager about the sloppy service or send the overcooked salmon back. No, not you. You paid the bill, left a generous tip, and skipped the unwrapped mints (no longer on your acceptable-for-health list) on your way out the door. For the first and last time.

In most cases, women act the same way when they break up with their brands. "Ninety-six percent of female customers never complain," said Lynda Smith, a consumer-satisfaction consultant. "They just never go back." (But if women get mad enough, as a group, they'll "girlcott"—read, stop buying in a protest—your service, your brand.)

We're talking Anticipatory marketing here. Remember the fact that women control 80% of all household spending. Overlay that with the fact that women keep their needs to themselves. Then you'll see that a radical shift in the way businesses operate is necessary. It's time to get serious about *Anticipating what women want.*

All of the traditional techniques have been responsive and slow, not Anticipatory and ahead of the game. None of these work today: focus groups and weekend omnibus studies. Internal company policies on change, R&D, advertising copy development. They're responsive and slow.

"Responding" creates marketing that's based on putting together some ideas, then going out and asking consumers what they think and getting a thumbs-up or a thumbs-down. This technique is reactive. It can't Anticipate a good idea for the future.

Consider the development of the telephone. If you'd asked every woman on March 9, 1876 (the day this transformational device was patented by Alexander Graham Bell), what they really needed to improve the quality of their lives, I doubt you would have heard back, "Funny you should ask, but I'd like a black box which would allow me to talk to my mother every day. To be precise, I'm looking for a way to reach out and touch someone." But if you knew how much mother-daughter conversations really meant, you could anticipate the need for a new product, a new technology.

Worse yet, "responding" means "selling" her. It means finding a way to convince her that what you have made is what she's asked for. That you've given her what you think she needs. Now.

But "Anticipating" means understanding your female customer well enough without having her draw you a diagram. It is pre-need marketing. Fulfilling future-future wants. Creating products, services, and technologies that women may not yet even know they need.

Businesses always say they do long-range planning. But five-year plans become eighteen-month plans become make-the-quarter plans. Businesses have steeped their employees in making the numbers, not in making their customers happy. How often do businesses bemoan the fact that they can't implement any Anticipatory marketing because they are "trying so hard to sell today?" If they learned to Anticipate, building ten-year plans—that they actually stuck to—they'd be ready to fit into her future.

One large company that learned to Anticipate, with big results, was Sony—or more accurately, Akio Morita. He realized in the 1960s that the nature of life at-home was changing, and that one day we would all have a TV in every room. And that the nature of life out-of-home was changing, and we would want to take entertainment everywhere with us. And so he created one ground-breaking gadget after another (small and female-friendly Walkmans, Discmans, kitchen TVs, and so on). As Morita states in *Made in Japan*, his "plan is to lead the public with new products rather than ask them what products they want. The public does not know what is possible, but we do." That's Anticipatory marketing (by the way, Sony's marketing plans project 25 YEARS OUT).

Other EVEolutionaries do exist, but on relatively small terms. When a woman buys Enfamil baby formula from Mead Johnson, her shopping habits are captured in store scanning data. As her child gets older, the mother will receive mailings and coupons for Next Step and EnfaGrow for toddlers. Sending this kind of advance information, before she knows she needs it, helps to keep her brand-loyal. Kimberly Clark is on the same track, sending Huggies Pull-ups Training Pants home to Moms at their kid's eighteen-month-or-so mark, and toilet training guides at the two-year date.

Safeway, in the United Kingdom, is a pioneer in Anticipatory technology with its new "Collect and Go" pre-ordering system. The supermarket is giving scores of its customers Safeway-branded Palm Pilots that come loaded with their personal buying history (past four months), as well as bar-code readers, to take home. Every time you take a product out of the refrigerator or off the shelves—say, open a can of Campbell's tomato soup—you would scan in the bar code, creating a new shopping list.

Look how easy this makes a woman's life. She simply plugs the Palm Pilot into her phone and goes to the store to pick up her pre-packed order. (I'd suggest one more EVEolutionary move: Why not deliver the groceries to her home?)

There is more to this technologically-advanced system. After all the data about a woman's particular shopping habits is

Finding Shopping's "Center"

From our close Dutch friends, we've heard tell about a few supermarkets of the EVEolutionary future already in operation in the Netherlands. One, located in Haarlem, part of the Ahold chain, is laid out in concentric circles, instead of only linear aisles. At the center, you'll find a wide variety of ready-to-go meals.

Otherwise, products are organized by times of day, making shopping a more rhythmic process. For example, typical breakfast items—eggs, bacon, muffins, juices—are presented together. Similarly, all products that would go into making a spaghetti-and-meatball dinner—a box of pasta with tomato sauce, ground meat, parmigiano cheese, spices, and garlic bread—are displayed together. Shoppers are given handheld personal scanners at the entrance to the store. As each item is selected, it's scanned and totaled before being put in the shopping cart. At the checkout counter, customers pay up, making the process so fast, it's almost instantaneous. (No more fully loaded, and sometimes abandoned-in-frustration carts facing a long, slow checkout line.)

This will be the model, based almost purely on Anticipation, if supermarkets are to continue to exist.

Another example of an EVEolved food establishment is eatZi's Market and Bakery, started in 1996 in Dallas, TX; also now in Houston, TX; Atlanta, GA; Rockville, MD; and Manhattan's Macy's Cellar. Modeled after a European market, it prepares some 1,800 signature items daily, set in a centrally focused Chef's Case. This core is surrounded in circular fashion by the rest: Breads, desserts, even cheese, wine, and flowers—so you work your way out from the center—right to your table.

gathered off the Palm Pilot, the system can actually suggest "impulse buys" it thinks that she might like. It's like putting a Personal Shopper in the palm of her hand.

There is a big future for this. Think of all the possibilities. Marketing links can be made with financial services, travel companies, and airlines to Anticipate a woman's needs in areas beyond the grocery aisle.

Kraft Foods has formed a partnership with a company called Net Perceptions to solve the perennial problem: What's for dinner? On the Kraft Web site, a Recipe Recommender will make real-time menu suggestions that match the consumer's food preferences. According to a November 1999 press release, this site can "predict relationships between individual customers and products based on the customer's past and current behavior." This means that if you like to serve your family Italian-style chicken, Kraft will provide new recipes for your chicken dinners, incorporating the ingredients you like. Maybe suggesting a mozzarella cheese topping or a broccoli-and-rice (risotto) side dish. Anticipating more and more Kraft sales.

The Phoenix, an EVEolved hotel in San Francisco that is particularly popular with a female clientele, is run by the good-at-picking-up-Trends Chip Conley (he followed *The Popcorn Report*, *Clicking*). Conley gives guests a checklist when they register. Want 30-SPF sunscreen? A favorite magazine? Computer discs? Baby formula? A masseuse? You check off your choices and by the time you're unpacked, *voilà*.

Finally, a hotel that Anticipates what a woman wants—without that first frantic search through closets and drawers. Provided: a powerful hair dryer, lots of soft hangers for women's softer suits and sweaters, your choice of down or allergy-free pillows. Notice that it's the hotel management, not the guest, who's doing the asking.

One of the most advanced early EVEolutionaries I've found is 1-800-flowers.com, where the Third Truth of EVEolution is in full bloom. Not counting Valentine's Day (the biggest day for men to send roses), 1-800-flowers.com has a customer base that is predominantly female.

Chief Marketing Officer Jerry Noonan tells me the company practices Anticipatory marketing throughout its business.

Great examples? 1-800-flowers.com encourages women to register important birthdays and anniversaries, then reminds them a week or so beforehand with a note: "Last year, you sent poppies to Emily. What would you like to send this year?" Their Web site automatically links with your on-line calendar to remind you of a gift-giving occasion. It then registers information about the recipient so that 1-800-flowers.com can tailor its gift recommendation.

They have also developed a "gift concierge," based on researching choices appropriate for different cultures, religons, and ethnic groups. "This will include a pro-active marketing outreach to inform customers when a certain gift choice may not be appropriate," according to Jerry. For instance, since white is the color of mourning in China, it would be considered offensive to send a white bouquet (even worse, signaling a deceased mother) or a white scarf to a Chinese woman on her birthday. "The idea here is to make you a more successful gift-giver, and that is increasingly difficult in today's global village." Very forward thinking.

Famous for having changed the sales and marketing paradigm in the flower delivery world, CEO Jim McCann is now expanding the site's gift-giving focus. His mission: To become "your sole resource for thoughtful gift-giving." Is that because this company is beginning to Anticipate women's needs better than other gift-giving resources? I think so.

One venue desperately in need of an EVEolutionary makeover is any store that sells women's clothing. It is Anticipated, even in smaller men's shops, that a customer will need some alterations to make his clothes fit. There's always a tailor on staff or nearby, with chalk and pins. Most women, however, have to take their recently-purchased clothes to their local dry cleaner to get sleeves shortened or hems lifted. And usually not a quality job—not to mention the inconvenience. Of course, in a higher-end women's store, such as Armani, a tailor (Maria Calabro, in

New York's main store) can totally reconstruct any suit, fitting it to just about any body shape. Even so, the very honest Armani manager, Ellen Hopfinger, once told me that all six suits I tried on were simply the wrong cut (even beyond alterations) for me. Anticipating a woman's need for honesty. Creating a relationship, not just a transaction.

To quote Germaine Greer from her book, *The Whole Woman*: "The sharpness of contrast between the genders when it comes to shopping can be seen in the marketing of clothing. By and large, men's clothing is constructed to last; women's clothing, though not at all inexpensive, is instantly obsolete. Menswear represents very much better value for the money than womenswear. What is more, the clothes are expected or altered to fit the man; women have somehow to try to fit the clothes. There are few male fashion victims; all women are victims of fashion."

Department-store shopping perpetuates these inequities again and again. Rarely fun, never leisurely, shopping in a large store is more a necessary evil. So why can't department stores make the experience more painless, even productive for women?

It takes a little imagination, a little empathy, and a lot of serious, focused, Anticipatory thinking about the stress of shopping. How about taking some of the legwork (and later, lugging) out of parking by running a continuous shuttle bus from the far reaches of the lot? Or free valet parking? How about a baby-sitting service run by trained professionals, not just some dumping-off room filled with battered toys? How about employees in the children's departments who really understand children, even have child psychology training, to help women steer their kids into the desired choices?

How about e-mail access in dressing rooms? And lighting (a version of Banana Republic's) that simulates where you'll be wearing it—a keypad on the wall could change the overheads to bright sunshine (for bathing suits), night-time (for formal wear), or the merciless fluorescents of so many offices (for suits). How about an Estée Lauder makeup sampler in dressing rooms so you can pick the best makeup to go with a new outfit?

And just in case you forgot your own cell phone (or God forbid, don't have one), what about cell phone rental by-the-day in the store or the mall, so that friends and family can stay in touch while you're shopping? Why couldn't a store send its best customers video or e-mail previews of back-to-school clothes, holiday outfits, and gift ideas?

What would happen if stores opened at 6:30 A.M.—or even on demand—so a woman could stop in on her way to the office? Last year, I was in a last-minute panic: I needed invitations for a friend whose birthday party was in less than a week. Dashing over to the Ocean Copies in Bridgehampton, I got there at 6:00 P.M.— only to discover that closing time was 5:30. The owner, Mary Fehrenbach, was inside tallying the day's receipts, saw my face in the window, and opened the store just for me.

Who doesn't appreciate that kind of attention and empathy?

The big idea here? Figure out unexpected ways to surprise a woman. You simply can't afford to wait until she asks. By then she's annoyed. At you.

e-merchants have an extraordinary opportunity to reinvent this wheel. And one of the spokes must be the Third Truth of EVEolution. How can e-commerce Anticipate women's needs— not only in traditional retailing, but in healthcare, diet, fitness, romance, parenting, education, in fact in every facet of a woman's life? This is one of the most important challenges facing companies today.

So why aren't companies uncovering the unarticulated subtext of their female consumers' lives (the "story untold") and doing something about it—like marketing to it?

Because most marketers aren't able to switch gears and think in terms of having a relationship, rather than forcing the transaction. This is pivotal. You need to establish a relationship. Relationship. Relationship.

The answer lies in developing a women-centric mind-set, culture, and strategy. It requires a methodical examination of women's lives. It requires listening—really listening—to real women. And finally, it requires offering Anticipatory solutions.

How does a company begin the move from being reactive to being Anticipatory?

Hint 1: Women must be in on the planning every step of the way.

Hint 2: Talk to consumers in ways that inspire innovative thinking. Scramble their brain cells a little, as I like to say. Ask

Bad News Bank

All women have experienced some real crass-from-the-past behavior, at one time or another. Here's a personal "favorite" of mine.

I parked in my bank's spacious (and almost empty) parking lot in East Hampton, dashed in, made my deposit, and then ran a few errands in town. When I got back fifteen minutes later, there was a note on my windshield informing me that since parking was for bank business only, the Bank of New York had noted my license plate number and the next time I parked there, I would be towed.

I went to the door and spoke to the manager, who wouldn't even let me step foot in the building. He told me that if all the bank's customers showed up at once, there wouldn't be enough places to park. Then he ended the conversation by saying, "I'm sorry you're not happy." That was it. Didn't matter if I had $10 or $10 million with the bank. Didn't matter if I had been a customer for ten minutes or ten years. Didn't matter what I needed from that bank at that moment or in the future.

Why not Anticipate the problem in car-choked East Hampton? How about privileged parking once-a-week for long-term, good clients? (Even 777-Film gives one free ticket for every ten tickets.) Or a keydrop, so that if the lot suddenly got clogged up, someone could take a moment to move my car to the town parking across the street? In a gesture of
continued . . .

> overwhelming service, the bank people could even offer to run a few of
> my errands (dropping off film, a video)—on their off-time.
>
> The unEVEolved opposite of "membership has its privileges."
>
> Meanwhile, Lys had to make a deposit at the Bridgehampton
> National Bank in the other parking lot. What a difference. Where the
> previous bank is old-think, cold, and, I might add, empty, the tiny
> branch of the BNB is new-think, warm, and thriving. Although physically
> one-eighth its size, BNB glows in its female-orientation: Three vases of
> fresh flowers, baskets of hard candies, posters of local people and their
> testimonials about dealing with this bank, and framed photos of the
> tellers' kids, facing out toward the customers.
>
> You don't have to ask: Which bank is more EVEolved? And where
> is my money going?

questions in your market research that may seem somewhat
removed from your brand or business. An example: Instead of
asking consumers for new ideas for a kind of soup, ask them
whether they would consider eating soup for breakfast (oatmeal-
raisin, egg drop-noodle?) or buying soup for their dogs (beef
broth-and-rice?). Really fresh insights will emerge.

A helpful exercise is to imagine that your woman consumer
is a specific person. Picture your sister, mother, grandmother,
wife. What could your company possibly do to Anticipate her
needs, to surprise and delight her, to raise her comfort level?
Invent some scenarios:

Say your mother arrives at the airport in a strange city and
goes to pick up her rental car. Wouldn't it be wonderful if the car
was equipped with a just-in-case umbrella; pre-ordered CDs; an
amenities kit; no horrible scent trees; a bottle of Evian; and an
apple? Or how about the radio being pre-tuned to the traffic-and-
weather station so she can immediately find out what sort of driving conditions she'll face? Also, clear warnings about tough

neighborhoods to be avoided? Why not offer to confirm her hotel or make a restaurant reservation while she waits in line to pick up the car? And how about the route planned with some terrific stops (museums and galleries) taken right from those MapEasy guidemaps that clearly chart landmarks, hotels, retaurants, retail shops and roads of 64 cities and locations? Very right-brained, very EVEolutionary.

But the best way to Anticipate what a woman will want is to envision just around the FutureCorner.

No Free Lunch

e-tailers, too, have to toe the mark if they want to attract and hold woman-share. A recent study by BizRate.com, a Los Angeles firm that tracks customer satisfaction with e-commerce, outlined the many problems with customer service. They're not as simple as an easy exchange and return policy. Up to 50% of consumers fill their "carts," then click off before completing the on-line buy. There's no patience. Another study by California-based Zona Research calculates an on-line shopper will only wait 8 seconds—you read it right, 8—before abandoning a purchase on a sluggish Web page download and moving on.

Web merchants are just starting to get the drift, though, says Nicole Vanderbilt, an analyst at Jupiter Communications, a research firm in New York. Customer satisfaction will keep declining as long as e-tailers' investment in infrastructure and service lags, she says.

e-commerce must become Anticipatory. The customer-service phone number is often hard to find on Web sites, and you can spend anywhere from 10–20 minutes on hold before you actually get to speak to a service rep. And although e-mails can travel in a split-second, they often sit unanswered for days.

My advice to all e-commerce Web sites: Master the Third Truth of EVEolution. Or blow an historic opportunity.

Once you start seeing what the future looks like, you can look backward to see what you need to do to get there. Believe me—I've made a career based on it.

Here's my vision of a tiny piece of tomorrow: the way we'll all start the day. Read what I think and figure out the products that could become an integral part of a woman's future rituals. I've italicized the categories that I believe have unleveraged opportunities.

This day will dawn sooner than you think . . .

It's 6 A.M. and my wake-up electrodes gently urge me into consciousness. Fifteen minutes earlier, my Intel smart home has started to waft a scent of vanilla with ginger *aromatherapy* into my room. To lift my spirits on a day that was forecast to be gray and overcast. Extra ginger has been added today because my *pillow sensors* (developed by Sun MicroSystems, marketed under the positioning, "Start your day with a little Sun,") detected a low-immunity condition in my blood, early signaling of an oncoming cold. In the background, *my automated closet dresser* is picking out my clothes, based on the weather report and any suggestions that have been picked up from *my pillow dream analyzer.*

As I enter the bathroom, my Sony *customized morning report* delivers a panoply of local and global news (selected for my areas of interest), spoken e-mails, and my day's "to-do" list. My morning report includes carefully placed product messages as well:

- A gentle FYI from Amazon.com tells me that my favorite jazz artist, Chet Baker, has been rereleased on a new CD.
- A message from United Airlines tells me to check my e-mail during the day because my afternoon flight to California might be delayed due to fog.
- A reminder from TwinLab tells me to take my immune-boosting vitamin and herb formula, based on my overnight pillow scan.

All of this is interspersed with my *customized music selections,* chosen to fit my mood, the time of year, the weather, and my level of REM sleep.

In this bathroom-of-wishes, I find that my *automated Personal Control Center* is preparing the morning's *fresh supply of essentials*. This includes *custom-blended soaps,* created overnight in the Dove soap dispenser, formulated to counterbalance the effects of the outside humidity and temperature. *Fresh Crest toothpaste* is also prepared, based on my pillow sensors' detection of the acid and alkaline factors in my mouth. And depending on what I ate last night.

Sensing my presence, my *shower goes on automatically* set to my favorite temperature. The water itself is supplied by a *private reservoir*, one of many that was created after the public water supply was polluted beyond redemption. In addition to drinking water, even the water for showering and dishwashing is branded and delivered by the companies that own the private reservoirs. The old public water supply's incoming pipes have been drained and are now used for the *pneumatic high-speed transmission of mail and small packages.*

Meanwhile, in the next bedroom, my daughter, g.g., is getting ready for school. Her *Internet appliance* presents her customized morning report, including her day's schedule and homework reminders, courtesy of Disney. She can also track the path of her school bus so that she can get to the bus stop at exactly the right time.

While g.g. and I are getting ready, down in the *Preparation-and-Control Center*—what used to be the kitchen—my *Robotte*, a joint venture between Panasonic and Merck, is preparing breakfast. Merck created the "gen-electronics"—short for genetic electronics—that makes Robotte possible. My and g.g.'s blood chemistry, which was analyzed non-invasively by our pillow sensors, was sent electronically to Robotte's "brain." With this knowledge, she can whip up a morning meal to feed us the right levels of vitamins, minerals, and antioxidants. Even give us a dose of those safe hormones that "up" our creativity and inspire optimism.

The whole day's meals are planned out under the umbrella, a *BioDeficit Supplement Program*, developed by my *Wellness Insurance Policy*. Wellness Insurance is sold by women who work for a new entity, jointly-owned by the government and MetLife.

After breakfast, g.g. walks to the bus carrying her *Smart Backpack,* made by Apple. When she first picks it up, a little voice reminds her, "g.g., you don't have physics today, so don't take that heavy e-book unless you want it for study hall at 2 o'clock. And, by the way, you've forgotten your karate belt."

In my car, a single unit, made by a start-up called HAL (named after the upstart *2001* computer), functions not just as a cell phone and Internet appliance, but as a video conference facility and a link to my own *Personal Computer Server* that routes all voice data to the various hubs and nodes of my life.

By this day in 2006, the Personal Computer Server—engineered by Cisco—will be emerging as the next killer technology. An individual form of the intelligent network will weigh the importance of each message and know how to handle it. A message from the school nurse would get top priority and be delivered instantly to wherever I am, car, or home, or office. On the other hand, a message about the book fair in two weeks will show up on my customized report the next day.

It's 8 A.M. and g.g. and I are facing the day with surety and joy. And with this clear vision of the future, so can you.

● ● ●

A key ingredient of the Third Truth is guts. Since we aim to Anticipate what women want, there's an element of educated guesswork involved. You won't hit the mark every time—but women will credit you for trying. In fact, a sincere attempt will touch her and strengthen her bond with your brand.

One group that has guts and is paying attention to Anticipatory marketing is—and this might surprise you—condominium builders. The male-dominated construction industry would seem like the last place to look for sensitive types willing to cater to

Sexy Secrets Revealed

Terry Patterson, the female former CEO of Frederick's of Hollywood, inherited a brand that was known for a tawdry, dated, male-driven approach to skimpy lingerie. Understanding that women today want to be in control of their own underwear (and are doing most of the buying), it was important to Anticipate what that female customer would be needing. To shift the company's focus, she used innovative research techniques to uncover women's most intimate feelings about sex. With these insights, she Anticipated—and offered—what the contemporary woman could expect from Fredericks.

Daughter of an Army colonel, graduate of Purdue University, and mother of two children, the 45-year-old Patterson took the old Frederick's leer and turned it into a sly wink.

At first, she tried the typical focus groups, but soon found that women were too shy to talk about what turns them and their partners on. The most provocative information she was able to get out of such groups was the shape women prefer for perfume bottles. Phallic.

Only later, in one-on-one interviews, did women open up and reveal what was exciting to them. In an exercise using magazine photos to create cut-and-paste diaries, they revealed even more about their everyday sensual thoughts and actual experiences. This information helped Patterson understand, for example, the stimuli that stir a feminine response: how important smells are, what color palettes make a woman feel relaxed or feel sexy. The result: sensual undergarments that speak first to the woman. And then to the man.

By conducting ongoing—and highly original—market research with women, Frederick's is able to stay a step ahead of what they want and Anticipate their EVEolving turn-ons.

women, but *there it is*. Of course, it may help that construction is the third-largest growth arena for female business owners. And that single women account for 25% of high-rise sales.

Builders are putting in amenities that often surprise female homebuyers. An extra room perfect for a home office; double dishwashers; bathrooms with big tubs, big shower stalls, big "rain" showerheads, even big enough for a treadmill; dressing rooms designed for a working woman's wardrobe; an extra mini-washer and dryer; a niche for a home altar for meditation; lots of cabinets, closets, and storage space.

But perhaps the biggest change is the emphasis on security. Concerned with safety and aware of their greater vulnerability, women want secure parking areas, 24-hour door attendants, and camera surveillance. Knowing that If She Has to Ask, It's Too Late, designers and builders are Anticipating the desire for these features and providing them.

However, the auto-service industry is a font of *faux pas* as far as woman-share is concerned. Risky business considering that 65% of customers who take their vehicles to a repair shop are women. But rather than visualizing what she might need to make her life easier, these are the guys who require you to drop off your car for repairs by 8:00 A.M. and pick it up by 5:00 P.M.— that is, if they've managed to complete the work. If not? Your problem, lady.

This kind of attitude is what makes the exceptions so exciting.

Case Study: Jiffy Lube

One company whose EVEolutionary ingeniousness and zeal leaps out is Houston, Texas–based Jiffy Lube International, Inc. (a part of mega-merged Pennzoil-Quaker state). They service over 23 million vehicles a year in their nearly 2,200 fast lube oil change stores nationwide.

The fact is that auto maintenance is almost always a woman's job if she's married, and for the 40 million single women in the United States, there's no "almost" about it. So if you're still marketing car care and maintenance to men, you're absolutely focused on the wrong market.

Add in the atmosphere of a need-it-now world, a business like Jiffy Lube, which specializes in the 10-minute oil change, has a ready-made appeal for women with too much to do and no time to spare. That is precisely what we told Jiffy Lube when it came to us recently for help in re-creating its image and outlook for the first decade of the new millennium.

How does a company that presents a male face (most Jiffy Lube employees are men) in a male category create a relationship with women?

BrainReserve's 36-six-step consulting methodology EVE-olved into this new positioning statement for Jiffy Lube: To all women with cars, Jiffy Lube is the neighborhood automotive resource that *installs* confidence.

Then we focused on putting the If She Has to Ask, It's Too Late Truth to work.

In practice, while many women take on the responsibility for arranging for car maintenance, they typically don't give much thought to what's going on under the hood. Out-of-sight, out-of-mind. But when something goes wrong, more times than not, their reaction is anxiety. One respondent to a TalentBank survey said that when she heard the first rattle or squeal, "It felt like I had a time bomb ticking."

Flashing red dashboard light. Clunk-clunk engine noise. A car that takes a notion to die on the Interstate. When there are kids in the car, or she's alone and vulnerable, a breakdown can suddenly turn into a real disaster for a woman.

Jiffy Lube's problem, we proposed, was too much Jiffy and not enough Lube, meaning that it had been concentrating on delivering fast service without bothering to form long-term bonds with its female customers—or even recognizing them as different from men. Arguably, the real, underlying value of Jiffy Lube wasn't fast service at all. Rather, it was the company's ability to "install" confidence.

What a woman wants is a protective relationship that makes her feel safe. One where she knows the belts have been checked, the oil's been changed. There's coolant in the radiator and air in the tires. She's got peace of mind. She's got confidence—installed by Jiffy Lube.

First things first, though, and that meant helping Jiffy Lube establish an immediate empathy with women customers when they brought in their cars. We had to help Jiffy Lube get women's positive attention.

We found that women have complicated feelings about their cars, and are admittedly insecure about them. What adds to the stress is that when a car needs service, women have to deal with men who all act like they're on the Formula One team. Many women report feeling that mechanics take special delight in making them feel stupid.

And in the midst of what feels like a general put-down of their overworked, overwhelmed selves, women get queasy, uneasy feelings that they're being taken to the cleaners by disreputable auto technicians.

Jiffy Lube was under-leveraging its role as a confidence builder by failing to form trusting, comfortable relationships with its women customers.

In the male mold, Jiffy Lube was going all-out to deliver quick, efficient service. But, in the female mold, women were being turned off by the "let's get it fixed fast, no conversation required" experience. And Jiffy Lube waiting areas had absolutely no female orientation either. *Guns and Ammo* is hardly preferred reading—reinforcing feelings of being a stranger in a strange land.

That all changed when Marc Graham took over as President of Jiffy Lube, and, as this book is being written, he's helping forward the EVEolved vision for the company.

It's Jiffy Zen!

When we took the too-much-Jiffy, not-enough-Lube concept to Jim Postl, Pennzoil-Quaker State's President and Chief Operating Officer, he immediately understood our EVEolutionary recommendation. After all, he had built his career by selling to women—from Doritos to Snack-Well's—and demonstrated an uncanny empathy for and an understanding of women's needs.

"EVEolutionize Jiffy Lube and make it a serene, safe environment," we suggested.

It's "Jiffy Zen," he said.

I loved his right-on-target connection.

Now, as soon as a woman drives into the shop, an employee introduces himself without making her get out of the car. (We learned that women don't like to leave the security of the driver's seat. Whether a baby is napping in the car seat, a dog is curled up and calm, or her handbag/packages are there.) If she wants, she can be brought a cup of coffee or water, and be left alone to relax safely inside her car while the attendants do everything they need to do under the hood.

Jiffy Lube's new attitude is based on the four If She Has to Ask, It's Too Late cornerstones we identified in the EVEolutionary process:

- *Control* over her environment.
- *Comfort* in the service setting.
- *Trust* that her car is being serviced properly and for a fair price.
- *Respect* for her intelligence and ability.

It's almost as if Jiffy Lube's reassurance is in the car with her: a guardian mechanic.

Every piece of the program we designed for the company

helped Jiffy Lube create a relationship with the woman, instead of one with the car. Focusing on the customer is an enormous shift for a company in the automotive market.

The whole change in operating manner was in itself Anticipatory—Anticipating her needs and her fears.

But we've thought of a few more Anticipatory ways to enhance her positive experience.

- Why doesn't the mechanic—whose name she knows by now—personally send her a reminder of when the car is due back for its next visit?

- Why not make it a policy to inspect children's car seats to make sure they were installed properly—no need to ask. And instead of reinstalling the child's seat for the customer, show her how to do it herself—build her confidence.

- One of my favorite suggestions for Anticipating her needs was to have Jiffy Lube service available in the parking lots of large companies. Can you imagine coming out of work to find that your car has been serviced on schedule? That you didn't have to wait days for an appointment? And that you didn't have to take time driving to an out-of-the-way location? And why couldn't the cost be automatically deducted from your paycheck?

How about similar Jiffy Lube service linked up with malls, movie theaters, clubs, stadiums, we wondered.

It almost goes without saying that when you bond with a woman customer, you bond with the whole family. And anything you do to Anticipate the family's needs wins you points with her.

• • •

The Third Truth of EVEolution. It's perhaps the most difficult. To really understand what a woman wants is complex enough. What we're asking is that you understand what she *will* want. And how you are going to create it.

Ask yourself, when is the last time you sat your customers down and set out to discover:

- When she dreams of a perfect brand or service in your category, what would it offer her that it's not offering her now.
- What does she think her family configuration will be in the next five years?
- What does her home of the future look like? Where is it?

Remember, If She Has to Ask, It's Too Late.

Fail her once, and she'll forgive you.

Fail her twice and she'll blame herself.

Fail her a third time and you are out.

But if you don't lose her in the first place, you won't have to worry about getting her back.

Chapter 4

The Fourth Truth of EVEolution:

Market to Her Peripheral Vision, and She Will See You in a Whole New Light

All day, every day, your television screen pulses with endless in-your-face commercials.

Our car is sexier.

Our beer is better.

Our clothes are cooler.

It's all the concentrated work of traditional marketers, hired to hit throngs of viewers between the eyes. Since television's earliest days, advertisers have sworn to appease Madison Avenue's two sacred gods—Reach and Frequency. They long believed "If you're loud, splashy, and repetitive," the masses will be seduced to buy your brands. Communications assaults like the '80s "Battle of the Burgers" and "Cola Wars" propagated such adver-centric beliefs.

Even with today's more subtle strains of image advertising and the buzzwords of Visibility and Recency (short for "landing" on the spending window-of-opportunity), the game is still won by He Who Has the Most Cash behind the celeb athlete, spokes-model, or ever-so-suggestively-placed logo. Exposure trumps every tested approach in the advertising world.

This I believe: It's time to rethink that tired old wisdom. When it comes to marketing to women, Reach and Frequency are false idols, incapable of answering today's prayers. And Visibility and Recency only work if you've chosen the right way to be visi-ble and recent to a woman.

The fact is, women don't bond with brands that market to them in an overly aggressive way. A full frontal attack just isn't the way to turn a woman on. (We particularly hate being whiffed in the face with fragrance, either from a magazine fold or on a department store floor.) Nor do women respond to the too-obvi-ous subtlety of "I've listened and made my logo smaller than our old, all-caps logo." Nor are women impressed when you've spent a gazillion dollars on an ad (thinking instead of all the social ills a sum of money like that could have helped). Clearly, these mar-keting approaches no longer body-snatch today's aware women.

Try as you might, you can't browbeat a woman into buying something she either doesn't want or doesn't need. In fact, you can't browbeat a woman into much of anything—unless it's kiss-ing your product good-bye.

Why not?

Look again at the basic differences between the sexes.

Men and women differ in the way they receive and evalu-ate information. Women don't just look at the center ring of the bull's-eye—we look around it, walk around it, circle around it. Women have retractable antennae that tune into multiple channels—scanning, hearing, and seeing the world on all levels. We pick up clues, weave together threads, intuit and infer the inner meaning.

These differences between the sexes are well documented. Long ago, Charles Darwin wrote, "in woman, the powers of intuition . . . are more strongly marked than in man." Dr. Mona Lisa Schultz states in *Awakening Intuition* that, "in women, as a general rule, information tends to be processed by the left brain, the right brain, and the body, all working together as a whole . . . men may have less of their intuition network available at any one time to make a correct decision based on insufficient physical information." Dr. Joy Browne says, in her book, *It's a Jungle Out There, Jane,* "male and female brains are wired differently. Male brains tend to process information in an either/or way . . . guys tend not to see as many gray areas as women do."

Women are able to take in information quickly from many levels, but we are not necessarily quick to make decisions. We like to weigh the various inputs before making up our minds and hearts. We are also more wary of impulsive responses.

These discrepancies are attributed to the level of two key neurotransmitters, or messengers, in the brain: Dopamine, which motivates people to action, and serotonin, which discourages impulsive action. Women have less dopamine and more serotonin than men. (This may be the real explanation why women can sit and watch a movie from start to finish on television, and men scan all channels every three minutes.)

Researchers like Ross Goldstein, a California psychologist, have found that women also pay more attention to the texture of relationships, the details. "Men tend to think in a much more macro way," he says. Women see not only the forest but also the trees and the underbrush and the twigs underfoot—the nuances and specifics that make up the whole.

A *New York Times Magazine* article featured an interesting theory on socialization in parks by the noted author of *The Orga-*

nization Man, William H. Whyte, which stated that "men seek out the front row—and if a park has a sort of gate or entrance way, they will assert themselves as guardians of it. Women tend to congregate in more secluded places."

I guess this can be distilled down to gate-keepers vs. con-gre*gate*-keepers.

What's interesting is the wealth of undeniable physical *and* anecdotal evidence that women and men respond to entirely different stimuli, and they also respond differently to the same stimuli. Any way you look at it, the physical and psychological differences

Truth in Humor

Telling jokes is not my thing, but I find it fascinating in a socio-pop way that so many married women (seemingly happy) are busy e-mailing each other with endless, "sharing-a-secret" scenarios. This one that made the rounds was given the subject/title of "Ain't It the Truth":

HOW TO IMPRESS A WOMAN

Respect her, Honor her, Compliment her,

Cuddle her, Kiss her, Caress her,

Listen to her, Care for her, Comfort her,

Wine and Dine her, Stand by her,

Love her. Go to the ends of the earth for her.

HOW TO IMPRESS A MAN

Show up naked. Bring food.

Men, too, like to send around self-deprecating jokes, positioning themselves as the underdogs, the hen-pecked fodder for a giggle of girls. Exhibit A: This one that came from an Alpha-guy who works on Wall Street. It goes like this: "A dear friend suggested a book for me to read to enhance my relationship with women. It's entitled, *Women Are From Venus, Men Are Wrong.*" Same source, same theme, different e-mail: " Question: If a man says something in the woods and there are no women there, is he still wrong?"

between men and women are clear and substantial. Women pick up on and respond to things men can't and don't.

When Dan Rather shows up on the nightly news in his new camel cardigan sweater, do American men stream into department stores the next day in search of a similar sweater? No. In fact, most men are so busy listening to the news that they don't ever even notice Rather's choice of sweater.

Women do. When Diane Sawyer runs through the latest headlines, the women watching aren't just following what's going on in the world. We can be listening intently, but also noting the great collar and tighter cut of Diane's jacket. Plus whether the color is good for her eyes. Whether her haircut/color/style looks the same as before. Are those earrings diamond studs? Whether she's looking tired. Thinking about the poor family we just heard had lost their life savings. Pondering what we should feed our family. Musing, "Hmm, would that jacket look good on me?"

You might call this phenomenon: Female observation.

You might call it: A woman's roving antenna.

I call it: Peripheral Vision.

It's a surround-sound branding opportunity that drives the Fourth Truth of EVEolution: Market to Her Peripheral Vision, and She Will See You in a Whole New Light.

Women hone in on Peripheral branding in a glance. Uniform style/good taste creates an impact; a solid sense of power. At Louis "The King of Color" Licari's new salon, everyone's in uniform. The top managers, like Enid Schneider-O'Sullivan (creator of the Enid O' makeup line), wear gray jackets and long skirts; the next level has the same jackets on with pants; and the assistants sport all-black Asics running tops, pants, and shoes.

I stop in there every ten days to re-highlight my red hair, mostly with a shock streak of Poppy Pink, sometimes with added feathers of green or blue. Louis mixes the formula according to how I feel, saying that the color changes are my "mood ring." He further explains his own creative philosophy: "Hair color should

BrainReserve Branding

As my company, BrainReserve, grew into an all-women firm, I decided that we should have a "brand look." So that when clients, visitors, and press come to our offices, we meld with a sharp, well-defined way of dressing that visually establishes our professionalism, our lack of hierarchy, our unity.

Our dress code is basic black, navy, gray, summer white, or khaki (with brown, dark green, or burgundy as well), and it can extend to pinstripes or checks. But as a badge of belonging, we wear our specially made BrainReserve pins every single day. Each year, we pick out another enamel color for the tiny ringed-planet pin, set with little twinkly stars. So far, some of the colors have been navy, white, red, gold, platinum, green, and, this year, gray.

On casual Fridays (no big meetings, no clients), although the dress code is dropped, most of our staffers stick to the same singular colors (maybe wearing black pants, a black sweater). My Director of New Business (and facilitator of all our books), "Make-It-Happen" Mary Kay Adams Moment, explained, "It's simply easier to look good that way."

But no matter what, the pins are *always* worn as a sign of our clanning. Peripheral proof of the BrainReserve brand, our constellation of the future.

be as unique as your fingerprint. That's why no one should take their old formula card to the next place. It needs to change all the time, depending on the month of the year, your skin tone, your age, your look."

• • •

The Fourth Truth also demands that *you* look at your female customer in a whole new light. A soft, glowing light that illuminates the corners of her world. Because this is where you want your product to appear—on the periphery, in the natural settings of her daily life. Not jumping up and down and waving a

FAITH POPCORN'S BRAINRESERVE
THE BRAND LOOK

SUIT COLOR SPECTRUM

Black	Burgundy	White ⎫ Only in
Navy	Dark Green	Khaki ⎭ Summer
Gray	Brown	

Prefer matching top and bottom.
Pinstripes and subtle (very subtle) plaids, fine.
Shirt/Shell: contrasting color accepted.
Avoid wild, loud, floral, and distracting prints.

HAIR
Well groomed.

NAILS
100% presentable.

LEGS & SHOES
Stockings with skirts.
Prefer to match outfit.
No sneakers, ever.

T.G.I.FRIDAYS
Corporate Casual.
Any color, any style.
No jeans or sweats.

CLIENT FRIDAYS
Full Brand Look, please.

NO GUM EVER

JEWELRY
BrainReserve Pin,
Cuff links, or Pendant
are always a must.

flag to capture her wholehearted attention, but showing up unexpectedly, helpfully. In her real world.

Peripheral marketing is like one of those famous pointillist paintings by George Seurat—remember Broadway's "Sunday in the Park With George?" If you get close to the canvas, all you see are thousands of tiny dots of color. But when you stand back, your eye creates a unified, powerful image.

Keep that image in mind. Some of the components or tactics of Peripheral marketing may seem small when looked at closely, or individually. But stand back, let your sight take in the entire scene, and what emerges is a whole brand picture.

Creating a Peripheral Vision for your brand requires discipline, patience, and a little faith (no pun intended). Peripheral marketing isn't quantifiable, so you may feel insecure leaving the familiarity of media staples: the number tracking found in effective Reach and the instant recognition of Gross Rating Points (GRP). In this new world, you can't always say one plus one equals two. It's scary. But that shouldn't be a surprise. When I say EVE-olution is an entirely new way of seeing the marketplace, I mean it.

If marketing to a woman's Peripheral Vision is somewhat frighteningly new and difficult, then how should you accomplish it? It seems to me that you need to surround your female consumer with messages. Messages that are blipped out in a variety of formats, creating a range of powerful associations. Circling her globe.

In the past, a company (the Client) radiated its energy toward its Agency, in an effort to win the Consumer. Now is the time to shift alliances. You need to put your female consumer at the epicenter of your marketing universe (rather than letting your advertising occupy that coveted space).

Consider some unusual approaches: If you can find places for your brand to pop up where she least expects it, ironically, it will make a deeper impression than if you bludgeon her with those old hammer-over-the-head ads. That's what coveted brands as diverse as Ben & Jerry's, Banana Republic, Krispy Kreme, and eBay did from the very beginning. Each of these started out without tons of traditional advertising, relying instead on the power of oh-so-tantalizing word-of-mouth. These companies let a positive image do the talking. Ben & Jerry's with its do-goodism, ethical standards, and outrageous ice cream flavors/taste. Banana Repub-

D-I-F-F-E-R-E-N-C-E-S

Every so often, I read or hear some oddball story where women hear all sorts of sounds that men can't. The Bristol Hum, for example. Sounds like the name of a barbershop quartet's harmony, I know, but for dozens of women in Bristol, England, over the last thirty years, there's been nothing melodious or funny about it. The low buzz they hear all around town gives them headaches and keeps them up at night. The humming has been attributed at various times to gas pipelines, radio waves, and auto traffic, but the definitive source hasn't been identified yet.

What everyone *does* know is that the menfolk don't hear the irritating hum. Which shouldn't seem strange to us, because women have been tested out to be more sensitive to lower and higher sound frequencies and nuisance noises in general (hint to appliance manufacturers: That's why refrigerators, washing machines, vacuum cleaners, blenders, etc., need to run even more quietly).

Women are also more tuned in to touch, smell, tone of voice, and facial expressions. Scientists say women read body language and size up a situation faster than men. Understanding this, shouldn't women be used to the max in such predominantly male arenas as hostage/peace negotiations? (A resounding vote of confidence for Madeline Albright?) In board rooms? Courtrooms? Settling high-powered salary wrangles? At the poker tables?

Similar experiments have shown that women have a heightened awareness of pain (experiencing it, tolerating it without being cry-baby-ish about it). Yes, yes, we know that's why women are the chosen ones in the species to endure labor and childbirth.

lic with its young, gung-ho biz looks. Krispy Kreme doughnuts with hordes of evangelical gorgers. And eBay, as the answer to a collector-junkie's prayers.

Always keep in mind one of the prevalent habits that women have. One that women have engrained in our very nature. Consistent behavior (some may call it compulsive). We are forever scanning and clipping, ripping, tearing articles from anything we read. An informative blurb about the best doctor, real estate agent, caterer, dog trainer, nursery school, Tex/Mex joint (who needs the Yellow Pages?). Women follow up on the mere mention of a new IPO stock or name of a massage therapist we've been given at the gym or in an on-line chat room. If a neighbor arranges a soap basket in a clever way, we'll make a mental note and eventually copy it for our own homes. We notice the hairbrushes being used by our hair stylist and the wiper fluid used at our gas station. All of these tiny points of contact with a brand add up to an overall impression. That's the reason to make sure your message is laser-sharp, on every point, every time. It can make the difference in whether a product will soar or ultimately stagger.

Men are more pragmatic. After an evening out, a husband may casually comment to his wife on one specific bit of information he picked up ("Gee, Dan mentioned his company will probably be merged into Acme in Chicago."). A woman, on the other hand, will come up with a more intuitive read on the very same remark. More likely, the wife picked up on some fleeting emotional signal and ran with it. "Did you notice the look on Susan's face because she realizes that the merger means another move? Losing the local contacts for her mail-order business. New schools. Away from friends. Quitting the garden club. Packing up. House-hunting again. A nursing home for her Mom."

All this heightened awareness, reinforcing life's subtleties, applies equally to people, companies, and to brands. Because

New Faces, Strong Personalities

Two large companies, formerly male-pitched, are making a Peripheral impression by putting the faces of top women with their corporate names.

Third-generation (they call it "G3") Gina Gallo, at 32, has replaced the 90-year-old patriarch, Ernest, as spokesperson for the world's largest winery. E & J Gallo, started in 1933, now sells a monumental 64 million cases a year, and has successfully tranformed its image from a cheaper mass-produced product to a premium award-winner.

Gina, one of the grand-kids, is a chip off the old wine barrel, a crack wine taster. Besides her daily work at the Sonoma, CA, winery and being photographed for print and TV ads, Gina takes the time every afternoon to personally answer every e-mail sent to the address on the wine labels. That's an EVEolved use of an executive's time.

The other woman who has an industry (and the world) buzzing is Carly Fiorina, chief executive of Hewlett-Packard (HP), a company with 83,000 workers and sales figures of $42 billion last year. Her presence has been introduced here in frequent TV spots, showing Carly in full color vs. the black-and-white of young misters Hewlett and Packard who invented their first printer in a garage.

In *Forbes* magazine, Fiorina referred to HP's history by saying, "We talk about 'The Rules of the Garage'. . . the rules were that bureaucracy and politics are ridiculous. Work quickly. Invent something significant. Keep the tools open, that's the start of teamwork."

Fiorina brings in EVEolved practices to the hard-tech company: focusing on customers, not products. Seeing the larger picture. Visiting the company sites around the globe, and asking questions and looking for feedback. Again from *Forbes*, she apparently shouts out in a video, "Send me the 'The 10 Stupidest Things We Do!' I'll read it!" She listens to and reads all voice mails and e-mails, too.

Carly is in Control.

More than that, Carly is in Communication.

women pick up cues everywhere they look, even unexpected placement becomes meaningful and memorable. A message that is communicated contextually may have greater relevance and stay with you longer. This is similar to the application in education. The difference between facts that a teacher drills into you—and ones that you discover yourself in the scope of larger issues.

An art gallery owner recently told me, for example, that a surprising number of women, when looking at the current show, stop and ask particulars about the lighting. They're seeking tips on how to better light one of their paintings in their home or how to spotlight a particular sculpture on their patio. Interest doesn't stop there—women chat on, probing about products and angles and lightbulbs for improved lighting all over their homes and offices.

This more or less describes an ideal Peripheral opportunity for a lighting manufacturer to reach a potential customer at a moment where aesthetics count more than cost. Why wouldn't a smart seller of lightworks want to team up with nearby galleries, lending state-of-the-art fixtures to light the current shows and stacking up branded brochures on lighting techniques at the reception desks? In this time-greedy, time-speedy world, this one-stop strategy is perfect EVEolution.

Think about any possible place your brand or logo could surface. Ask yourself if these Peripheral messages are consistent with your overall marketing message. Because the area swept in her Peripheral Vision is exactly what your female consumer is responding to every day.

But don't think for a moment that you're going to have to abandon all the familiar terrain—Peripheral marketing creates a road map on which many of the usual marketing tactics are good detours. Licensing, co-branding, co-promotion, event marketing, cause marketing, sampling, and product placement are all useful tools that help forge the greater Peripheral picture. You just have to be experimental with the non-traditional tactics, as well.

The power of Peripheral marketing should be enough to

wean you from the heroin of Reach and Frequency numbers (call it prime-time media rehab).

And besides, consider that it doesn't really matter to your female consumer how much you paid for that commercial (surrounded by ten other commercials) that interrupts her favorite program, be it *Judging Amy, ER*, or *Family Law*. She's probably too busy paying bills during the break, anyway. (EVEolutionary aside: Did you realize that women write 80% of all checks?)

Attract a woman's Peripheral attention and she'll constantly recognize and be aware of your brand (like watching the slow bubbles of a lava lamp). There are a thousand ways to accomplish this, but here are some thought-starters:

Just around the FutureCorner . . .

- Why couldn't a clever manufacturer like Procter & Gamble work out a special deal with the Post Office called "Stampvertising," to build on the wildly popular commemorative stamp business? Subsidized by P&G, the Post Office could offer consumers up to 5¢ off any First-Class stamp that bears a Warhol-esque rendering of a Tide box or other targeted products. Mailing this stamp would become a Peripheral tool both for the sender as well as for anyone who receives it.

- Each day, millions of women spend an aggregate total of millions of hours in their cars. And each day, tens of thousands of trucks cross America with nothing in particular decorating their long, flat, rectangular sides. Doesn't this seem like a waste of a Peripheral marketing opportunity? Why don't marketers buy the use of these trucks for the opportunity of doing something good, such as cause-related marketing? For example, Microsoft could mount a child-literacy campaign; GE could encourage a cleanup of the roadsides; Coke could post basic family nutritional needs. These holy crusades could mean a hefty revenue stream for the trucking industry;

in turn, they could donate a substantial portion of their profits back to the advertised cause.

- The supermarket is still a female-dominated shopping world. Although it's crammed full of a mishmash of branded messages (on carts, receipts, end-aisles), there's still some Peripheral space left. Consider the parking lot as the largest and last uncharted territory. Brands such as Cheerios and Snapple could introduce "parking spot" marketing. Large product renderings, interpreted by

Opportunity Knox

Knox Gelatine, such a simple household product, originally started in 1890 to "gel" a dessert, was steadily purchased by women over the next fifty years as a "trade secret" for stronger nails. James Knox, the grandson of the founder, brought the "secret" public with Knox for Nails. Eventually, Cutex, too, chimed in with its Nail Strengthener with Knox Gelatine.

When Nabisco strategically acquired Knox from Unilever in 1994, they believed that the brand could have a more successful future, even beyond healthier nails. They, of course, were right.

Knox's popularity surged when physicians started touting collagen—the key ingredient in Knox Gelatine—as a treatment for certain kinds of arthritis. That's when Knox asked BrainReserve to partner with them in exploring the folklore of collagen and finding the best way to communicate it to consumers.

Collagen is a protein whose name comes from the Greek "kolla," for glue. And that's what the grains of Knox were supposedly doing—gluing the body together.

Anecdotal evidence spread. People were busily telling miraculous stories of how taking such a humble basic as gelatine was helping lessen their arthritis pain. Boxes of Knox began disappearing from supermarket shelves.

continued . . .

As we conducted our TrendProbes, we found out a concrete reason why women were putting their trust in this tried-and-true brand. A number of them pointed out that they were more at ease drinking a familiar liquid than they were swallowing pills or capsules.

However, there's always been one major glitch to gelatine. To make it, the crystals must be completely dissolved or it will turn lumpy. Nabisco solved this age-old problem with a technological innovation. The result was packaged as a health product: Knox Nutrajoint, an easier-to-use, ready-to-dissolve gelatine supplement.

In 1991, in *The Popcorn Report*, we termed this future combining of therapeutic food and drugs for a higher level of well-being, "foodaceuticals." Anywhere, anytime, the healing benefits of anti-arthritis gelatine, readily on hand for a cup of joint java . . . or tendon tea. Perhaps prevention and cure, in one sprinkle.

well-known artists, could be painted in each parking spot, say in the first two rows. This would be far more exciting than ugly blacktop. And what could be a better example of Peripheral marketing than a six-year-old saying, "No, Mom, we didn't park in Sugar Pops, we parked in Cap'n Crunch."

- Nursery schools, doctors' offices, clinics, hospitals. All have in common the rising threat of infections due to sloppy handwashing (in fact, *The New York Times* ran a shock-saga saying that 20,000 people die per year as a direct result of hospital-acquired infections and that "hands are the most dangerous thing in the hospital"). Why doesn't the maker of an antibacterial soap print its message on hangtags for the doorknobs for all these high-risk places?

- Nuances. Why don't interior designers and architects or the makers of paint, fabrics, and wallpaper get to sign their interiors, the way an artist does? A signature subtly embossed at the bottom of a wall offers a great opportunity for Peripheral branding (and talk about surrounding your customer . . .).

Nothing has mastered the ingenuity of placing brands in subliminal, Peripheral situations better than the Internet. Today, a woman types the health problem "bladder infection" into a search engine, and "Ocean Spray Cranberry" pops up. This can be deemed helpful now, but eventually may be resented as offensively intrusive.

Why haven't marketers yet used this technology to explain their Corporate Soul? To let the consumer know what your company believes in before she buys what you sell. The Internet would be a place to inspire trust. You could gently put out messages about your ethics/causes, your stance on child labor in Third-World countries, your recycling programs, or your handling of any anti-environmental waste.

Think of the opportunities to EVEolve. Apologize (also very Eighth Truth: Everything Matters) and take responsibility for any mistakes you've made (recalls and all). Tout what good things you have done. If a woman looks into "breast cancer," a magazine such as *Harper's Bazaar* could send a message about the Race for the Cure (dates of upcoming races, maybe even a runner's application), its support of research, along with links to sites offering information about the disease and caregiving resources. But not—underscore *not*—a link lickety-split to the Hearst corporate Web site. Believe me, the lack of the smack-of-commercialism will be appreciated.

With malls under such pressure from catalogs and e-commerce, why doesn't a smart landlord offer something called the Sampling Store? We know how valuable sampling can be as an expression of Peripheral marketing. And we also know how expensive and time-consuming it is for marketers to place their products into consumer's hands. Virtually impossible in the virtual world. The Sampling Store would collect freebies from a broad spectrum of manufacturers, including software and technology providers. When you enter the store, you might be asked to scan in your driver's license, only to track that each customer gets one sample of whatever she/he hankers for, once a day. Triple winning: Marketers would have their products smack-dab within a woman's range of vision. Women would get to try out something new without extra cost, a boon for themselves and their families. And the mall operators would have a successful new source of revenue and traffic.

Labels are another completely under-leveraged Peripheral opportunity. Imagine OshKosh overalls for toddlers with a secondary inner label offering some sort of reminder message to mothers: stain removal tips or even immunization or height/weight charts. Or the latest Fisher-Price developmental toy could come with play-date guidelines. Or those inflatable water wings with swimming safety rules.

A perfect example of Peripheral Vision marketing is the use of ribbons as a social statement. One color for every cause. Discounting the older phenomenon of "Tie a yellow ribbon round the old oak tree" (to bring the boys home), the first most visible, wearable one was red to stop the scourge of AIDS.

Blazoning the AIDS ribbon started big at the televised 1992 Tony Awards ceremony in New York City, when actor Jeremy Irons pinned a red ribbon on his lapel and faced millions in the viewing audience. It hit a nerve, because from that day on, the practice spread far and wide. The AIDS cause gained stature and clout, as the bright ribbon became the must-have fashion accessory for everyone from Barbara Bush to Madonna.

Although the show of support wasn't gender-specific, mainly women and gay men were leading the long-term effort to keep the disease in the forefront of awareness. It followed that a group of women slowly began to co-opt this Peripheral strategy to alert the public to another critical cause; this one, closer to their own hearts (literally). The pastel pink breast-cancer awareness ribbon, originally delivered by Avon representatives, has even made it onto postage stamps. Anyone who doubts the power of Peripheral marketing should ask themselves: Could a $100 million ad campaign have done as much for the cause of breast cancer as a little pink ribbon?

Yes, "breast cancer" is a lofty, intense, consuming cause, but what we are reminding you is: Every passionate marketer should see her or his brand as a "cause." Whether you're part of a large company with trainloads of marketing dollars or merely a small start-up that struggles to pay the receptionist, there's a lesson to be learned here for you.

Who is currently profiting from a Peripheral approach?

"Intel Inside" was a Peripheral branding strategy before it became an advertising slogan. With practically every piece of quality hardware boasting "Intel Inside," the Peripheral rub-off was marketing magic for both Intel and the hardware manufacturers. I always thought of this as subliminally female, womb-like, revering the inner mystery, the embryo. I'll leave the Freudian implications to you.

Meanwhile, Intel does other things besides resting "inside" on its laurels: It's produced a microscope, along with Mattel, that can plug physical specimens directly into virtual space on a PC. Maybe for an at-home Pap smear test that you could send on to a lab or distant specialist? Very cool.

Hotels and restaurants that cater to those notice-every-detail women customers are signing up such detail-oriented designers as Giorgio Armani and Dolce & Gabbana to create the staff uniforms. Everyone benefits. With the staff running around in fashion-signature clothes, the designers get their name out to remind potential buyers, "Look for me; see what I can do for you." The hotel guests/restaurant-goers are surrounded by well-dressed personnel and the hotel basks in the halo effect of a high-end couture association.

Sharpen Your Vision

Okay, we've established that opportunities to market to a woman's Peripheral Vision can be found everywhere. But in the matter of the enhanced CD, you may need to adjust your own Peripheral Vision goggles to get a clear bead on the action. In my seminar, I'm always telling people that they should listen to what their kids listen to, to find out what message is being beamed out to future consumers. To make my point, let's look at what the Wu-Tang Clan, a super-successful rap group, is offering.

Put the Clan's enhanced CD in your computer's CD-ROM drive and you're off on an interactive audio and video tour of the Wu Mansion, where you can meet the rappers themselves. As you navigate through various rooms, you can access clickable or "hot" items related to a specific band member—like the biographical info that contains the real names of Clan rappers U-God and Inspectah Deck. The disk also shows you how to access the Clan's Web sites.

What I see when I enter the Wu Mansion is an incredible Peripheral opportunity. Why isn't some woman-wise marketer placing products aimed at the Clan's young female followers inside the group's virtual world? A great opportunity for jeans, fragrances, temporary tattoos, blue nail polish.

In the proof-of-predictions department, I've heard from J. P. Haenen telling me about a recent "real-life" Dutch sitcom called *Big Brother* (*BB*), with its own Web site (big-brother.nl) that gave details about the regular people who were the performers. Haenen e-mailed me, "One interesting thing is that you were able to *buy the set* of the *sitcom!* This is one of the predictions you once told us at a lecture in Holland—and it has come true."

This concept sometimes extends beyond clothes. Todd Oldham, one of the hottest designers around, recently completed a Moroccan-inspired makeover of The Hotel (formerly the Tiffany Hotel) in Miami. Oldham put his stamp on everything from the chandeliers in the restaurant to the airbrushed tiles adorning the bathroom walls. Some EVEolutionary advice for the hotel, Todd, and all designers: Take advantage of your Peripheral visibility by making it easy for women to buy what we see when we see it.

Some that do: The W Hotels put catalogs in rooms, and sell everything from comfy feather bedding to cognac-leather waste baskets. The Maidstone Arms in East Hampton, NY, will let you buy almost any of the antiques in the rooms (just ask). And Post Ranch Inn, Big Sur, CA, has a catalog that's more hippie-California-y: sea kelp shampoos, hemp cloths, pine needle teapots, and eucalyptus chairs.

Another brand built on the Peripheral premise is Starbucks. It transformed a simple cup of coffee into one of the most valuable brands in the world—and along the way, won the hearts of coffee-drinking women everywhere (approximately 60% of Starbucks' customers are female).

Oddly enough, Howard Schultz, who acquired Starbucks in 1987, swears that he never set out to build such a rarefied, pervasive brand. "Then one day," he recalls, "I started getting calls asking me, 'Can you come and tell us how you built a national brand in only five years?' It was unusual, people told me, for a brand to burst onto the national consciousness as quickly as Starbucks had. When I looked back, I realized we had fashioned a brand in a way no business-school textbook could ever have prescribed."

Schultz spent little on advertising—not because he didn't believe in it, but because he couldn't afford it. "Instead," Schultz says, "we concentrated on creating value and customer service. . . . Our success proves you can build a national brand without 30-second sound bites. . . . It proves that the best way to build a brand is one customer at a time."

And in another unconventional move, Starbucks started line-extending well before it would have been advised in any packaged-goods wisdom. These line-extensions created multiple Peripheral impressions for the brand. Imagine the eye-contact impact in one supermarket—besides their coffee bags, to see a dozen containers of Espresso Swirl, Java Toffee Ice Cream in frozen foods, a stack of six-packs of Frappuccino in the soft-drink aisle, and rows of single bottles filling the cold case. What started as a flutter of coffee-colored snowflakes had turned into a blizzard. It all adds up.

What Starbucks' success also proves is the value of showing up in a female consumer's Peripheral Vision.

You may not kowtow to the theory that Starbucks offers the greatest coffee in the world. But what no one can dispute is that it offers something of select value to the woman customer—a clean, cheerful, wonderful-smelling environment where she can relax in comfort and safety. Where she can linger with a magazine and nobody will push her to drink up and move on. Where she can catch up with old friends and meet new ones. (Not to mention, the cookies to keep kids happy when in tow.) Where the ladies' room will be well-stocked and sanitary (a real plus, by the way, for the female customer).

Starbucks' Peripheral sales include the CDs of the music she's sipping by (they actually bought their own music company); reliable appliances to make Starbucks-blend coffee and tea at home or in the office; terrific mugs for gifts; educational pamphlets on the growing and brewing of coffee and tea; and other subtle magnets that draw users over and over again.

The sunny aura of good feeling that surrounds the Starbucks stores has given wings to the branded coffee itself. Starbucks products can be bought through a mail-order catalog or on-line (plus you can sign up for automatic replenishment). And you can taste the brew perking in grocery stores, restaurants, airlines, and hotels.

But perhaps the biggest Peripheral coup for Starbucks was its alliance with Barnes & Noble bookstores. Next biggest: Joining up with Oprah's Book Club to sell her personal selections in their Starbucks cafés. By appealing to the female customer in an entirely different and extremely attractive context—stress-free, with books to browse through—Starbucks has extended its reach beyond the storefront café.

In little more than a decade, Starbucks has blanketed this country with stores, becoming a $1.7 billion-dollar enterprise built on a fresh (Peripheral) Vision of how to sell coffee to all, but especially to their female customers.

Another noteworthy Peripheral Visionary is M.A.C. Cosmetics. Frank Toskan founded M.A.C. in his kitchen in 1985. To market his line, Toskan and his partner made a rational decision to eschew traditional advertising and try something new. In a bold move, they hired the hippest of makeup artists to work with their products, hoping to spread the word to their customers, many of them models. The founders offered these pros a 40% discount and then extended the tempting discount to models and actresses.

Soon, celebrities everywhere were singing M.A.C.'s praises on talk shows and in fashion magazines (where M.A.C. could never afford to buy actual time or space). Furthermore, it became known that all the proceeds from their most popular Viva Glam lipstick's sales were being donated to AIDS charities. Against the tough odds in the cosmetic world, M.A.C. rapidly became a $200 million global company, eventually selling a large stake in its business to Estée Lauder, which is wisely leaving the marketing to the original partners.

Case Study: A.1. Steak Sauce

Peripheral Vision was also the main ingredient in A.1. Steak Sauce's recent recipe for success.

In the mid-1990s, America's collective palate suddenly grew hotter. The influx of immigrants from Latin America and Asia were introducing zippy new tastes—and we were all biting. With little warning, the bland and the boring white bread, macaroni, and rice pudding were out; the adventure of sourdough, pad thai, and dense caramel flan were in. Supermarket shelves were stocked with new labels, and many old favorites were gathering dust. The condiment market was exploding. Salsa was outselling chips; there were a thousand and one variations of mustard; dark bottles of teriyaki, barbecue, and mesquite sauces. Ketchup, once the undisputed king of condiments, was losing ground. So, too, were steak sauces. Every conceivable flavor spike was sitting there, crowing, "Buy me and spice up your family's meals!"

A.1., the venerable sauce, around since 1914, was caught between a perceived old-fashioned rock and the hard fact of changing tastes. Yet A.1.'s ingredients were right—if they were ready. On one hand, Americans were embracing novel culinary experiences. On the other, steakhouses were the fastest growing restaurant segment, up to 73% in the past five years. A.1. wanted to be along for the ride.

BrainReserve was hired to lend its expertise and help A.1.

On the Fringe

A few of the odd places brand names are showing up:

- High styles from Giorgio Armani's A/X line are pictured on the labels of Jones Sodas. A white tee on a Blue Bubble Gum beverage. A black one for Fufu Berry.

- Lift off, Pizza Hut. A 30-foot logo will be emblazoned across a Russian rocket. The Peripheral Vision marketing value? It will be filmed as it soars, for future TV spots.

- Those free postcards. Movie stars and trendy products and funky local spots catch your eye as you exit your gym, Kinko's, coffee shop, or music store. Max Racks is a clever way to advertise without spending big media dollars. From Absolut to Chanel to Warner Lambert to Esprit. You get a double hit: The person who sends the card and the one who gets it (56% are mailed). The rest are collected for their hip images.

broaden its market share. We set to work putting A.1. under our usual multi-lensed microscope—in this case including interviews with A.1. management; 27 BrainJams; TrendTreks to butchers, specialty shops, and restaurants, ranging from fast-food emporiums to the country's best steakhouses; one-on-one TalentBank interviews with some of the world's top gourmets, including caterers, chefs, restaurant owners, food-page editors, and grocery buyers; and CreativeThink sessions with some of these same gustatory geniuses.

After adding it all up, we advised the Fourth Truth of EVEolution: Market to Her Peripheral Vision and She Will See You in a Whole New Light.

Why did we think this EVEolutionary tactic would work? Selling more steak sauce to women? I mean, what could be more masculine than steak? A thick juicy hunk of red meat grilled over a roaring fire is one of the all-time, all-American male icons. Right up there with the Super Bowl, a fishing pole, and a couple of beers. We believed that A.1. should continue its love affair with the male market, but it also should expand its marketing push to women and families. After all, men might cook the steak, but it's women who buy them—*and* the condiments to enhance them. The strategy was to keep A.1. on the grill (male) but also move it onto the all-season, everyday dining table (female).

With a market-leading brand, there's no need to introduce the consumer to the product, no need for all that splash and dash. You're trying to show up where she doesn't expect you, to insinuate yourself a little more deeply into her life. Marketing to her Peripheral Vision, via numerous channels of communication, is the way to do this.

It didn't take us long to figure out the steakhouse phenomenon: It was clearly a manifestation of the Pleasure Revenge Trend. The Trend that says we're fed up with self-deprivation and long to be semi-destructive. We're tired of working hard, watching what we eat, suffering through stints on the treadmill, being goody-goodies. It's payback time in the pursuit of pleasure. And what could be more devilish Pleasure Revenge than a double martini, a sizzling prime sirloin marbled to perfection, a Mount Olympus of onion rings, a slab of creamy, dreamy cheesecake, finessed by a crystal snifter of cognac and a Cuban cigar?

Unfortunately, all the cavorting and carnivoring of Pleasure Revenge did little for our client. Although a resounding 95% of steakhouses stock A.1., in truth, the bottles only made it to the tables less than 50% of the time. Furthermore, none of this madness for cow converted into the needed supermarket sales.

Our question was, of course: How can we establish a link between the steakhouse experience (more male) and the use of A.1. at home (more female)? And that's where a second BrainReserve Trend came into play: Cocooning. Remember: Women are tucked into their cozy nests as never before. Safe and secure, insulated against the harsh realities of the outside world. Passing a sublime time with their in-home businesses, sophisticated entertainment systems, Jacuzzi baths, and unlimited cell-hours. Being mouse potatoes (today's version of a couch potato—staring at the computer screen, not the TV); surfing and shopping on the Internet. I mean, who needs to leave the house? Especially when it's so *unpredictable*, even frightening, out there.

Cocooning vs. Pleasure Revenge, Pleasure Revenge vs. Cocooning. Were these two Trends always mutually exclusive? Contradictory? Not necessarily. Not when we merged them together for an even stronger Trend-positioning for A.1. that read as follows: "Bring Home the Sizzle of the Steakhouse Experience."

What is this statement really saying? Enjoy a Pleasure Revenge Experience at Home. Or: Have Your Cocoon and Eat in It, Too. It's an experience-centric way of branding, one that doesn't directly promote A.1.'s many benefits or compare it to other sauces.

Next problem to solve: How do we connect the Steakhouse Experience with the A.1. brand in ways that will appeal to women's Peripheral Vision?

The first thing Kate Newlin, President, BrainReserve Consulting, accomplished: She helped A.1. form strategic alliances with famous steakhouses (The Palm restaurants across America and Ben Benson's), whose marinade/grilling recipes using A.1. were then put on the bottle label. Steakhouse chefs are not your everyday backyard barbecuers. They're expert chefs with expert secrets. By putting their professional tricks-of-the-trade on the labels, A.1. was opening Peripheral pages: Showing that steaks can be prepared in many different and exciting ways. In cuisine-based ways that will appeal to women. It's also a way for the brand to have value in a context that isn't advertising-driven. Although to solidify the connection, the company also featured the steakhouses in its commercials.

Kate Newlin also devised a unique way to sample A.1. in all its glory. Delta Airlines agreed to our plan of offering its passengers a delicious Omaha steak dinner, made with A.1., with a bonus of their recipes. (This unique union won the Onboard Services Award and The Mercury Award.) We were raising the quality of an airline meal to that of a steakhouse. For the women passengers, it was a way to see A.1. in a higher setting (!) and for the men, hopefully, a reason to request that A.1. be brought home.

Or for more Peripheral Visibility, we suggested that the A.1. logo could be branded on steakhouses' doggie-bags (more women than men take their leftovers home for a sandwich the next day). And to top off the line, why not A.1. marinade bags and recipe cards. Single-pour bottles to stimulate trial-use and impulse buys. An alliance with a fast-food restaurant—making a small-sized steak sandwich for kids. A cooking show on the Food Channel. So that just about everywhere a female consumer turns, the A.1. sign will be flashing—right smack dab in her Peripheral Vision.

Best Cuts

Peripheral Vision in the steak department? The market of choice for years in East Hampton has been Dreesen's. We order our Thanksgiving turkeys from there (owner Rudi DeSanti will give you the best advice on timing and temperature or even stuff and cook it for you). Lys and I stop in there at least once a week to pick up their special roast chickens (for our kids; more so for Lys's little dog, Tulip, and mine, Miyake). Now, Rudi has teamed up with a classic: His well-marbled steaks can be ordered through the well-regarded Brooks Brothers catalog.

A small town shop that sells great meat.

A traditional clothing store with a name you can trust.

That's Peripheral marketing at its best.

A.1.—seen in a whole new light. The light of marketing success.

• • •

Peripheral marketing works in mysterious ways. It's definitely the most psychologically complex form of marketing. It's about catching the corner of a woman's eye and capturing her heart and mind. It is really about finding that small window of opportunity that, when opened, can lead to a profoundly loyal customer.

But before you earn that loyalty, as with every other EVEolutionary Truth, you must get to know your customer. Ask yourself:

- Is my brand female-friendly?
- Am I being too direct, too confrontational?
- When was the last time I personally contacted my female consumer and asked for her feedback?

Fascinating challenge, isn't it? It means looking at marketing with a whole new eye—through *your own Peripheral Vision*.

Like all muscles, your all-encompassing eye strengthens with use. Start to record what you see, when you see it—and learn something every day.

Don't try to master Peripheral Vision marketing alone or just with people you work with. Instead of advertising, you need to try free-associating. Go up to a woman who's buying your product and ask questions . . . about everything. Go beyond the obvious: shopping and buying patterns. Find out how she feels about downsizing, gene-splicing, global-warming, fat-free foods, Web-siting, pesticide-spraying, school-busing, champagne-pricing, hair-coloring, discount-brokers, shuttle-flights. Figure out a way to get inside her head and her heart—until you can actually view the world through her eyes.

The Fourth Truth of EVEolution is an extraordinary marketing tool; it's one that takes some real time and real thought. Be subtle, be clever, be consistent.

Peripheral marketing.

It takes Vision.

It takes EVEolution.

Chapter 5

The Fifth Truth of EVEolution:

Walk, Run, Go to Her,

Secure Her Loyalty Forever

In the beginning, there was home delivery. But that was when women stayed home. Waiting for those home deliveries. Everything, short of opportunity, knocked on her door. The doctor, the milkman, the knife sharpener, the perm person, the Good Humor man—all called the family dog by name.

Then, the Brady Bunch world changed. Women took off their aprons and entered the workforce en masse. Many opted to build a career first, delaying marriage and children. No one was home when Electrolux, the Avon Lady, and the Fuller Brush man came to call. So they stopped calling.

It wasn't long before working women—especially those with families—confronted the obvious: Working 8-to-6 outside the home didn't mean a lighter load after six o'clock. And becoming breadwinners didn't mean women were excused from shopping for bread (and sheets, tulip bulbs, and bikes). Women continued to shoulder the primary load of running the household. Even if husbands offered to help, women were still the overseers when it came to having dinner magically materialize, keeping up with social friends, scheduling the orthodontist, calling the phone repairman. How many times was a woman tempted to say something sarcastic to her hubby, like: "Make yourself at home. Clean the kitchen."

Today, women are caught in the rinse cycle of daily life. Swooshing and rushing from breakfast counter to the ATM to the dry cleaners to work to the supermarket to home. The time crunch has become a time crush. What little spare time we have is spent shopping for essentials. And the shopping experience, for anyone in a hurry, has been on a steady downward spiral of clumsy inefficiency.

That's because most marketers continue to operate under the *Field of Dreams* slogan: If I build it, they will come. And until now women have come—because they have had no choice.

EVEolution is changing all that.

The notion that women consumers are magnetically drawn to your product is over. The idea that women consumers need your product more than you need them is Neanderthal thinking. The new marketing Truth is to figure out all the ways to "get to her, go to her." The watchword is: Convenience. Selling to a woman at home . . . or wherever she may roam.

Smart companies have begun to realize that a minute saved is a sale earned. And that if you can go to a woman where she happens to be—in her home (early, late, on weekends), at work, at her children's school, on-line, at the local café, at the gym, in her car, while traveling, wherever—and make her life easier, you will win a faithful customer.

Or, as the Fifth Truth of EVEolution states, Walk, Run, Go to Her, Secure Her Loyalty Forever.

Study your female consumer's interaction with your brand: Not only what your brand offers, but in terms of how, where, when it's offered. One good clue would be to track her life, spend a day in her clogs, Keds, Tod's, Dolce & Gabbanas. By the end of this experience, you might plead "contemporary insanity," but it's important to understand just where her meltdown points are.

How hard is it for her to get to you? Must she navigate through endless automated voice mail systems? Does she have to face road rage on highways and byways? Does she have to take a lot of time away from her family, her friends, her workout, her work?

By going through this exercise, you'll be able to recognize and respond to exactly how to make your brand more integral to her life.

But how to EVEolutionize your thinking?

The first change would be to figure out a way to recross her threshold. This is more than being "retro"—hoping to find "the little woman" at home again. Women are returning, not as home-makers, but as home-workers. Disgusted. Tired of fighting the glass ceiling.

Even after these years of concerted effort, the statistics aren't encouraging. In the Fortune 500, 85% of the companies do not have a woman in the top five positions. In mid-level "line" jobs, 93% of the jobs belong to men. In over 340 of the major companies, only 1.3% have women of color anywhere near the top. And those women in high places are still not in direct line for getting to CEO. Instead, high-titled women are tucked away in the touchy-feely jobs: Human Resources, Advertising, and Public Relations.

For women who opt to remain on the corporate payroll, as we've mentioned, telecommuting has become one viable work choice. Another option is to figure out the most convenient way of keeping a salary and having a home life: flex-time, part-time, and work-at-home time. But with corporate downsizings, we really have been nudged into a nation of freelancers and consultants. Women by the tens of thousands have started their own businesses, right on the "kitchen table." (I always get a mental picture of those "tables" or "basements" where legends began: Estée Lauder stirring her makeup formulas in tubs and testing on friends/family; and Mrs. Bigelow, blending little bits of orange rind and spices into premium tea leaves to make the first batches of Constant Comment.)

Home Again

Thus, Go to Her home selling becomes a strategic imperative once again. Marketers have to rethink their tactics and figure out how to get things, from vacuum cleaners to encyclopedias to cosmetics to household products, directly into a woman's home. Don't reckon on just copying the way it was done in the past. Fundamentals have changed.

We now have a *Clockwork Orange* fear factor of any stranger at the door. We peer out of peepholes, alarm on, locks locked, Mace in hand, and shout "Go away" to anyone who dares approach without warning. Compare this with Willard Scott's interview of a 100-year-old woman on *The Today Show* who recalled the Depression days when "hoboes" came a'knocking. "They were always welcomed in, to share a meal, a piece of pie," she explained. That was before gated communities and sophisticated security systems.

If you're working, there's also an annoyance level of being interrupted. Who needs a doorbell ringing, right in the middle of an important phone call or concentrated thought? Yet, the Go to

Her Truth works. Look at the success of Amway, with over eight million "distributors" in 1996 and $20.84 billion in U.S. sales. Look at Nu Skin with well over $800 million in 1999.

This EVEolving Truth will grow if you tune in to the major change: Go to her home, not as a *solicitation*, but as a *service*.

A good example of service comes from one of the rental car outfits. A company called Enterprise has built its reputation and its business on being the one to bring your car to you. Instead of making you fill out forms at some rental office or counter, then having you search the lanes of some desolate lot, Enterprise drops off the car right in your driveway. The highest in convenience, plus offering a safety factor, greatly appreciated by women drivers.

Remember running to the Post Office to buy a roll of stamps, and stamping your feet in a line longer than the Snake River? Since the postal system found out that women send the majority of the non-commercial mail in the States, it started offering stress-reducing shortcuts: Selling stamps by mail, at corner stores, in vans stationed on city street corners, at ATMs, and, the latest, on the Net. But I suggest going even further in the service area—with pre-scheduled home-delivery via the mailcarrier right into every mailbox (and you leave a check). That would really be Go to Her thinking.

In 1991, a well-known department store chain hired Brain-Reserve. Their CEO wanted to know the Future of Shopping.

For this daunting project, we started off by visiting most of his stores and also some of his competition; interviewed experts and consumers; held proprietary BrainJams; analyzed his business strategy; and examined the state of retailing in general.

Our conclusion: The shopping experience for women had become un-welcoming, un-inspired, and un-fun.

When we sat down with the CEO to discuss BrainReserve's picture of the future landscape, I had to give him my harsh prediction. Our FutureScape conclusion: In twenty years, many of

You Call This Fun?

It's been a long-touted rule of marketing: That women enjoy going to the supermarket. "Shopping," the president of a major grocery chain once told me, "is a social experience for women."

And recently, the #2 person at a very large food company actually said, "I agree with you about home delivery, but don't women need to get out of the house once in awhile? And don't they enjoy meeting each other at the supermarket?" I questioned him back, "Did you ever ask a real live woman if that's true?" He couldn't say that he had.

Sure, a trip to the supermarket is fun, if you do it as an outing every now and then. But it's not a lark in the park if you have two whining kids under the age of four, buckled into a wobbly cart, with their hands grabbing at every Twizzler bag and Froot Loops box. Nor is it the greatest for a female executive who has a nano-second before leaving on a business trip. Nor for a much older woman who can't maneuver very well and needs only a few things in manageable sizes for single use.

Shopping a social experience?

Maybe for a masochist.

When women want to get out, here's what gets them going. Movies. Lunches. Sports. Concerts. Book clubs. A fast coffee.

Not the supermarket.

today's large malls would become modern-day ghost towns. (Being ever optimistic, I could imagine them being turned into assisted living facilities for the increasing number of elderly.)

He looked at me like I must be crazy. Undaunted, I went on to say that the "ladies-who-love-to-shop" tradition would eventually go the way of tethered phones.

It seemed to me that most time-consuming trips to the mall would be replaced by something far more enticing: Virtual Shopping.

Not good news for department stores.

That's how some of our toughest assignments break out.

Clients come in for a future checkup and the first-take looks bleak. We then launch into the fix-it stage: Developing a strategic prescription based on a fit with at least four of BrainReserve's seventeen societal Trends. This marketing repositioning will prime the brand or business solidly for the future. A necessity today to get ready for tomorrow.

As we explained to our department store client in his FutureScape report, the world is at the embryonic stages of a massive change in the retail industry.

A shift in marketing gravity—from the retailer ("I'm over here, and these are my hours") to the female consumer ("I'll tell you where and when I need things")—is taking place.

Technology will make this shift complete and irreversible.

Before long, you'll be able to tap your touch-sensitive television screen while watching a favorite show—say *Ally McBeal*—and stop the action. If you like the suit that Ally is wearing, you can just point to it and fill in an order for the size and color you want. This coming technology might also allow Ally to respond as a Virtual Shopping pal: "You want my suit in navy blue? But you already have so much navy in your closet. Why not try it in gray? Okay, it should be there in two days. By the way, it's a great suit for travel because it doesn't show wrinkles. And since you're going to that meeting on Friday in Chicago, you might want to look at the briefcase Ling will be carrying in the next scene. I know you're looking for one. Bye for now."

At last, a shopping solution that will be fun and fast. The perfect answer to women's search for "Ease, please!"

In an interview with Bernadette Tracy, the President of NetSmart-Research, a company that surveys Web usage, I asked, "Why are women the fastest-growing population on-line?"

She gave me the top two answers: "88% of women say that they go on-line because it's an overall time-saver; and 90% cited the convenience of 24-hour shopping."

Charlene Begley, a busy mom and executive at GE, told me

about her experience with eToys.com. Thinking that the Barbie Jeep she had ordered for her daughter's birthday hadn't arrived (it had, but her husband hid it in a closet and forgot to mention it), Charlene called eToys in a panic. Even though the eToys Customer Rep was certain the Jeep had been both shipped and received, she immediately sent off a second one to Charlene's home.

Now that's Going to Her. And Going to Her again.

"It was so easy and eToys.com service was excellent," added Begley. A lifesaver, in more ways than one. End result: Charlene Begley swears that she won't ever walk into another bricks-and-mortar toy store again.

But, of course, you can't just start up any new dot-com and convince yourself that you've virtually captured the women's market. There's still homework: You have to find out your female consumer's specific needs, figure out her quirks, and then Go to Her with an ergonomically-perfect fit.

Going to Her means that you will be there whenever and wherever she can find time to find you. And that you fulfill your promises.

- That means that if, at 11 P.M., she needs to send a last-second (that's all it takes) birthday card halfway across the world to her Dad who's vacationing in Venice, she can type in bluemountain.com and instantly send a personalized e-mail of a flapping bat or a jumping Palomino or a chorus line singing "For He's a Jolly Good Fellow."
- That means that if she wants to browse on her laptop and compare product offerings before purchase, she can do her homework on dealtime.com or brandwise.com. A perfect use of time while waiting and waiting at the doctor's office (a place and profession that definitely needs EVEolutionizing).
- That means that if she desperately needs a moment to relax while waiting for a teleconference to begin, she can seek some solace in meditation. With no time to

trek to Tibet, she can either sit lotus-legged in front of her home altar . . . or calmly visit up to 535 sites with such soothing names as spiritweb.org; quietmountain.com; globalmeditations.com; tm.com.

- That means that if she's frazzled beyond belief, she can turn to a bring-home site like urbanfetch.com that tackles its job doggedly (like a Jack Russell holding onto a bone). She can request whatever she needs from them—say, a new printer with paper, ink cartridges, a package of Hostess Twinkies, and small garbage bags— for delivery within an hour. Speed is the essence of this site—and indeed, of life today.

We all know that on-line shopping isn't perfection yet. It can be overwhelming with a virtual Vesuvius of unlimited choice. When will there be an organized on-line Yellow Pages? I have scribbled scraps of paper everywhere of names taken off 30-second commercials or out of magazines. Engines and portals. Ever-flowing sites for products and more products. Links and more links. Personal Web pages and more pages. User names and passwords. And in our opinion, too many options equals a Sign-Off.

But just you wait. The Internet is still in its infancy. At this point in time, clever ideas have outpaced most delivery systems. Certain on-line orders—such as video rentals or offbeat foods for supermarket delivery—are only time-savers if you happen to live in the heart of a major city.

So where does a Go to Her marketer begin? Still and always, by closely examining where and when a product fits into a woman's daily life. Or doesn't.

Just around the FutureCorner . . .

- What if General Motors previewed its cars and arranged test drives where women work? At their supermarket parking lot? At their kids' schools? At the beach (a perfect backdrop for convertible sales). Women would rather give up an hour on the fly than spend a weekend car shopping (something men generally enjoy far more than we do).

Even e-mails will Go to Her. Watch for cars with voice recognition systems so she can connect from the road. (Road sage?) Check the condition of her stocks, her lovelife, and what's on sale on-line. She can even leave a scan order, "I'm looking for a white leather jacket that Elvis wore," and a request to see her three-year-old, post-nap, at the daycare center. A multiple-level existence happening while stuck in traffic in her Expedition.

- Wouldn't Oxford Health Plans, Inc., become more profitable and warm up its image by making a real effort to improve the relationships between wives and husbands? Oxford could provide roving marital therapists who would counsel couples at home. What better way to understand a relationship than to see the interaction "live," checking out its dynamics *in situ,* seeing the sources of conflict first hand? A Go to Her "Marriage Manager." Less stress, fewer claims.

- Why shouldn't BabyGap have a BabyVan that pulls up in front of the pediatrician's office or a KidsVan that lines up next to the car poolers at grade schools?

- What if travel agents followed the example set by smart summer camps? A friend of mine said of the three camps she was considering for her child, only one sent a head counselor to her home. The camp person brought along a video the campers themselves had made and spent extra time telling her how the camp would fit her daughter's special interest in horseback riding. Even showing a photo of the speckled horse her daughter would probably be assigned to ride.

Just imagine if a travel agent would go to a woman's office or home or local Starbucks, bringing brochures and videos of vacation destinations? Pre-edited for preferences. No husband-hunting locations for the happily wed; no hot spots for sun-haters; no no-pet hotels for Westie lovers. Rather than panicking about being replaced by on-line booking, travel agents could feel secure about their future.

- Wouldn't it be wonderful if the local ExxonMobil made house/office calls with small (safe) tanker trucks? No more having to drive to the station just to wait in line to pump gas. Or have the car inspected, oil changed, hoses checked, windshield wipers replaced. All fixed, without going anywhere.

- One of the most untapped Go to Her arenas is house cleaners. What an opportunity for a trusted, national, branded cleaning service. What a good strategic fit for P&G from a cleaning products perspective and great fodder for really believable how-to TV commercials. Or how about combining cleaning with caring-for? Here's my teensy prayer: For someone to not only dust my Levolor blinds, but also to replace the cord, if needed. Maybe an outfit such as Sears could step in and own the "harder side," home maintenance.

- What if Sony offered a built-in "media record" so that Moms could keep track of what the kids are watching in real time? The recorded information could be sent directly to wherever she is via e-mail, voice mail on her cell phone, her Palm Pilot, or even her watch. This concept could be built into computers, too. It's time-consuming to program in access-restrictions (and for junior keyboard-whizzes, what can be blocked, can be unblocked), so why not have an internal check?

- Why doesn't someone combine the miles-away outlet store model with the neighborhood yard sale? Calvin Klein or Mikasa or Nike could take their overstocks, discontinued models, and late-season merchandise and sell everything out of a school parking lot over the weekend. Long-distance shopping goes local. And, of course, following EVEolution, give a percentage of the profits back to the school.

- What if Louis "The King of Color" Licari and Home Shopping Network got together to offer a customized hair-coloring system that any woman could apply at home? Or if Licari arranged for hair stylists, manicurists, masseusses, and tarot readers to go to an office or home to create a mini-day spa for female co-workers or a few friends? There is already a small company, Jacqua Girls Inc., started by three sisters (in their garage), that fills large metal cans with at-home pampering products. One of these, the Beauty Parlor Night Kit ($35), offers a convenient reason for a "girls get-together."

- And if anyone out there remembers Bookmobiles, wouldn't it be great to have bookstores-on-wheels back? Instant gratification for bedtime reading (aloud or to yourself).

Practicing the Go to Her Truth takes creativity and flexibility. Concentrate on where else you could find your female consumer. What about all those in-between times when she is on the way to somewhere else?

- Look at the malling of airports. This phenomenon has allowed retailers from Au Bon Pain to Bath and Body Works to the new DKNY in JFK to leverage those aimless hours of pre- or between-flight waiting. The dramatic rise in the shopping possibilities in airports perfectly mirrors the dramatic rise in the numbers of female business travelers. Coincidence? Not.

- Gyms are turning up in supermarkets and Internet service is turning up in gyms. Cardioexpress, a mini-fitness center, has opened a branch in a Kroger supermarket in

Georgia. By Going to Her at the supermarket, Cardio-express is attracting women who thought they couldn't possibly squeeze in a workout. And Kroger is attracting more female consumers who now wouldn't shop anywhere else—because while they're on the treadmill, a Kroger employee will do their shopping for them. Now that's the Fifth Truth in action.

Since women's two biggest reasons to give up their exercise regimen are boredom and lack of time, gyms across the country are installing Netpulse touch-screen computers so they can check e-mail while they work out. That's multi-tasking—an EVEolutionary time-saver.

- I can see a future in which America gets kiosked. Major brands and service providers will open temporary or permanent outposts, in places where women hang out. The weekend soccer field might have a sports-gear kiosk set up throughout the fall season. The day spa will have a vitamin kiosk where we can stock up for our whole family's needs. Toddler takeout at the playground (Twista-rella string-cheese sticks? Snack-size yogurts? Turkey dogs?). Microsoft software at the movies. Ben & Jerry pops at ATMs.

But convenience is only one chord. The Go to Her Truth also carries a highly valued and increasingly hard-to-come-by benefit—privacy.

When I was a teenager, our local pharmacist would wrap sanitary napkin boxes in brown paper to protect the privacy of his female customers ("No one should know your business," he would say).

Although today's female consumer might be less concerned with modesty than women of earlier generations, does she really want the rest of the world looking over her shoulder when she's buying Trojans, e.p.t., KY, ExLax, or Depends?

For that reason, the Web is a privacy haven (barring hackers). It's the perfect place for women to purchase the most intimate products, but also to find answers to "embarrassing" questions and to chat with others on personal issues.

In the privacy of the Web, a woman's comfort level rises, providing an opportunity for marketers to form an intimate bond with her. The more questions she asks and the more information you provide, the more her trust will grow. And the more she'll buy from you.

This strategy could be particularly effective in those areas where women historically feel on unequal footing with men. It's an ideal place to have her ask "dumb" (meaning: Never Before Explained) questions. On topics many women have heard mentioned, but have never thoroughly, patiently discussed. Such as, in the stock market: "What does shorting the market mean?" Or in estate planning: "What exactly is a Charitable Remainder Trust?" Or auto repair: "How long does a battery last?" Or house purchases, major home repairs, and legal problems. You get the point.

Case Study: Streamline.com

Coupled with the Internet, there's another enormous category of opportunity opening up for Go to Her marketers. You'll be seeing an imperceptible shift in selling to female consumers that's tilting toward direct-delivery services.

Nearly a decade ago, I predicted in *The Popcorn Report* that "Home delivery will become, not an extra service, but a way of life. One truck delivering to a hundred customers will be a much more efficient use of resources than a hundred customers driving to stores. There will be holding tanks in your house for milk, soda, mineral water (all refrigerated), and bins for laundry soap and dog kibble, for example, all delivered like home heating oil." Today, I believe that 90% of all purchases will be direct-to-consumer by 2010.

That is exactly what Streamline.com, a grocery home-delivery company (and BrainReserve client) decided to do.

Currently, there are several models, including WebVan and Pinkdot, that are grappling with this issue of getting goods into the home. All stem from a common need—the need to circumvent the archaic shopping process. The issue is such a large one that I believe there will be room for many players. And Streamline (what we call the company internally) will be a major one.

My friend Tim DeMello conceived of his revolutionary concept in 1993. While taking a year off to spend more time with his family, he was amazed and dismayed to see how many hours per week were spent on mundane chores.

DeMello identified a need and came up with a powerful EVEolutionary concept that builds on the Go to Her Truth in two ways: by home delivery and customization. After reading those pages in *The Popcorn Report* that prophesied the end of super-

On the Road Again . . . and Again

Here, there. Everywhere.

Mothers with school-age children make 20% more car trips than the average woman and 21% more than the average man.

On a typical day, mothers make more than five trips, adding 29 miles to the odometer. Single mothers spend an average 75 minutes behind the wheel, compared to 66 minutes for married mothers.

The majority of working mothers (61%) make at least one stop on the way home, and 30% make two or more stops.

Half of a woman's car trips are dedicated to errands and chauffeuring, compared to 41% of men's.

No wonder Go to Her is a go.

The Speed of Life

Unilever Chairman Niall Fitzgerald predicts that 15% of all groceries will be purchased on-line within the next ten years.

I disagree. I say the number will be closer to 75%. After all, the ball is rolling faster these days. While it took radio 38 years to get into 50 million homes, television needed only 13 years, cable TV accomplished it in ten, and the Web did it in five.

The half-life of change is accelerating. And EVEolving.

markets as a distribution channel, Tim DeMello called me to say, "You predicted my business!" And he became a client. A client with a mission.

When DeMello asked his customers what they wanted, they answered: More time for their families, for themselves, and for helping out in the community. His mission was to give the American family back one full day a week.

Here's how it works. Streamline, now an Internet-based, direct-to-consumer delivery service in the suburbs of Boston and Washington, DC, has no retail outlets, just a 100,000-square-foot warehouse where it stores the products it sells. At the start, Streamline will come to your house and scan the bar codes on all products, mainly in your kitchen and bathroom, creating a customized shopping list that can be added to at any time. Customers can then place their weekly order over the Internet.

Streamline strives to make women's lives time-efficient for only $30 a month. Groceries were only the beginning of this big vision. Dry cleaning, postage stamps, prepared meals? "You got it." The new Julia Roberts video? "No problem." Nail polish, batteries, flowers? "When do you want them?" Insurance, auto sales, computer rental? "Coming next."

Streamline installs boxes with freezers, refrigerators and

storage shelves in your garage or basement. To give its delivery people secure access, Streamline installs a keypad lock system for entry when no one is home.

Customers love Streamline's automatic-replenishment service. The days of running out of basic household supplies are over. By tracking usage rates, Streamline remembers that you're going to need a few rolls of Charmin, a loaf of Pepperidge Farm 7-Grain bread, or TRAC II's—even if you forget. An intriguing aspect of direct-to-consumer sales is the way it now helps build sales of designated brands—by limiting exposure to the competition.

Jumping Off the Brandwagon

If in tomorrow's world a company that delivers directly to consumers doesn't receive its shipment of, say, disposable diapers from a factory, the reps would have to contact all of their customers who depend on this necessity.

The imaginary scenario would be like this:

"You're kidding," says the young mother, a grocery-delivery customer. "I use this service so I don't have to store those bulky boxes. I count on you to keep me supplied each week."

"I know, and I'm really sorry about this," the rep answers. "But I'll tell you what I'll do. We have our own brand of disposables. I'll give you three weeks of diapers—at no charge. If you like them, I'll keep sending them."

"Well, okay," she says, relieved. "I'll give them a try."

The point?

The Go to Her Truth is about to usher in a different kind of loyalty. The consumer will become comfortable with—and reliant on—her personal relationship with the service provider. Not logos, not advertising. Brands beware.

"The younger female consumer, especially, has seen through the supermarket manipulation," explains DeMello. "She says, 'Let me get this straight. They want me to come to their store, hike all the way to the back to get a staple, such as milk, hoping that I'll impulse-buy a bunch of costly items I don't need?' She sees through this and she's insulted."

Once you start thinking the Go to Her Truth, there's no end to the services you can offer. DeMello noticed, for instance, that women were driving around with bags of old clothes in the backs of their cars because they didn't have time to get to charity drop-off centers. Now Streamline offers seasonal pickup, to benefit chosen local charities.

Since its inception, Streamline has focused on customer relations. "The further away the consumer moves from a physical store," DeMello says, "the more credibility must exist." Establishing trust becomes priority Number One.

A Friend of the Family

Tim DeMello gets up close and personal. He has built $50 into his budget for each household so that on special occasions, Streamline.com sends surprises like balloons on a child's birthday or a bouquet for Valentine's Day.

When was the last time you got a present from your supermarket?

DeMello has found that female customers who initially said, "I wouldn't let anyone pick out my produce, fish, or bread," change their minds after about a month of Streamline's efficient service and quality offerings.

Reinforcing this trust is Streamline's guarantee to replace a too-ripe banana (or any other unsatisfactory item) without question.

Just how strong is the bond that DeMello has built? One indicator: Meat and produce are Streamline's top-selling grocery categories.

Another indicator of the personal bond DeMello has with his customers: At year's end, the "thank you" e-mails flood in. Here's one such love note: "Thank you for making my home more conducive to happiness. For making 1999 a better year. For giving me more time with my children."

Want to know what the Go to Her Truth is giving back to Streamline and Tim DeMello? An average customer buys over $4,000 worth of products and services per year with a retention rate exceeding 90%. And a remarkable referral rate—every 1,000 customers refer 600 new ones.

By acting on sound EVEolutionary premises, Streamline is operating on strong financials for a company that's well under ten years old. It has major investors who are backing its ability to

A New Definition for Webster's

Is there any surer sign of success for a brand than for its name to enter the lexicon?

"Mom, have we Streamlined this week?" is often heard around the house of a Tim DeMello customer.

The word "shopping" has changed to "Streamlining." Women who have come to depend on this company are refusing to move anywhere other than to another "Streamline neighborhood."

Smart real estate brokers have taken notice. In addition to a good school district and other attributes, they're advertising a house as being Streamline-able, to help close the deal.

What would it take to make your brand part of our everyday language?

grow: The future-oriented Dan Nordstrom of Nordstrom; Saul Steinberg of Reliance Insurance Co.; and GE Capital Services. Streamline.com went public in June 1999.

As far as DeMello's concerned, his home-delivery philosophy isn't merely a clever marketing model. If you ask Tim DeMello if he's in the "grocery business," he'll answer, "No, the lifestyle solutions business." If you ask me, he's in the Go to Her business.

It's a must-do as we move into the Third Millennium.

• • •

To fully seize this Go to Her Truth, you have to not only go to her head, but go to her heart. Are you ready to employ these EVEolutionary lessons?

Ask yourself:

- Where is she? What's the best way to reach her?
- What tasks can I do for her?
- How do I give my customer ten minutes back to spend as she wishes?

No single Truth in this book is EVEolving with the rapidity of this one.

Get ready.

Get set.

Go! (to Her.)

Chapter 6

The Sixth Truth of EVEolution:

This Generation of Women Consumers Will Lead You to the Next

Brand names are hardly the first thing we think of when we leaf through our childhood memories. But picture specific occasions and, we bet you, some specific brand name will pop up.

"Splish, splash, I'm taking a bath." With a bar of Ivory soap and Johnson's Baby Shampoo.

"Ouch, I fell off my bike and scraped my knee." Out came the Band-Aids and Neosporin.

"Yoohoo, I'm home from school." On the counter was Skippy peanut butter, Oreo cookies, or Wise potato chips.

Certain brands evoke the ooh's and aah's of nostalgia. We

tend to hold on to the things we loved during our childhood and adolescence, whether we're recalling Dr. Seuss books, Raleigh bikes, Pez dispensers, Barbies and Kens, faded Levi's, or new Bass Weejun loafers.

It's an essential reality of marketing: So many brands are overlaid with warm fuzziness, reminding us of our Home Sweet Home and our do-right Mom. It may be as corny as Kansas in August, but to most of us, it's as normal as blueberry pie.

Carl Jung described the mother-child relationship as "certainly the deepest and most profound one we know." Apply this to EVEolution and you've hit upon the Sixth Truth: This close connection creates a pass-along dynamic between mothers and their children that is practically invincible.

In her book *Cherishing Our Daughters*, Dr. Evelyn Bassoff, a well-known expert on parent-child relationships, describes the phenomenon well. "Mother is the child's most trusted 'interpreter,' the one who defines the child's inner and outer worlds by telling her what to approach in the world, what to avoid, whom to like, whom to dislike; she gives words to name the things around her and feelings within her . . ."

If "mother" is the primary filter of all things in life, it seems obvious that a woman's buying habits would be greatly influenced by what her mother bought. And obvious that most of our tastes would be indelibly etched into our behavior patterns, by the time, say, we're applying for our driver's license. So while there's no iron-clad guarantee that a Nivea user will beget a Nivea user, the odds are stacked in favor that a young woman buying her first face cream will automatically lock on that familiar blue-and-white label.

Think I'm overstating the case? Look at some comments I've collected on my own Web site survey:

"My mother is picky about her products, so they must be the best if she has used them all these years. So now I'm using the same dishwashing soap, laundry detergent and cooking oil as she does . . ."

"My mother is a smart woman and I trust her . . . so it makes it easy to trust the brands she chose."

"Jergens Lotion. The very scent of the product reminds me of her and I use it still."

"Revereware pots. They were a reference from my mother—who was my 'expert' on things around the home."

Whether the reason is trust, habit, or remembrance, each and every one of the brands our mothers used exerts a powerful sway over us.

Lest we forget the men in our lives, why not tap into iron-clad memories of the father-daughter relationship? Like, "My Dad always drove a Lincoln," or "He always drank Bacardi Rum and Coke on a hot summer's night." There is a way to let these reminders spill over into today's female buyers.

But for reasons that escape me, few mainstream marketers seem to be aware of how vital this dynamic is to their brands and their businesses.

I've consulted with hundreds of companies over the years and yet, not one of them has a so-called Generational Specialist in any reporting-to-the-CEO, able-to-spend-significant-dollars position. In fact, not one has even ever mentioned the need to hire one.

And I've read thousands of marketing and media plans and yet, not one of them has had anything resembling the topic of "Next Generation" as a specific budget line. It goes beyond being a murky area; it's totally ignored. And therein lies the EVEolution egg.

I've suspected for years that the mother-child bond forms the basis of a business opportunity of staggering proportions.

In fact, I stumbled onto the power of the mother-daughter connection early in my career. Back when I was a young advertising Creative Director at Smith/Greenland, one of my copywriters, Rick Johnson, wrote a headline for the kitchen pots-and-pans maker, Farberware, that simply stated, "Ask Your Mother." That one ad won us awards and won me a promotion, but more important, it won Farberware a whole new generation of customers.

The generational reminder struck a universal chord with women. It made the connection between them and the brand of cookware that their mothers used morning, noon, and night in the golden glow of their kitchens. Farberware became the trusted, credible resource for family meals. All this imagery in a three-word reference to a fundamental reality, "If you don't know, ASK YOUR MOTHER," for when it comes to reliable brand names, Mother Knows Best.

And to reinforce this tie, Farberware is making branded cookware products for little kids' play kitchens.

So why don't more marketers build structured marketing programs around the idea of selling to succeeding generations? Why don't more marketers strive to build brands that can be passed down from generation to generation? Why don't more marketers create their own roadmap for Brand-Me-Down success?

Or as the Sixth Truth of EVEolution states it: This Generation of Female Consumers Will Lead You to the Next.

Follow this Truth and you will never again have to embark on a "new user" search. Follow this Truth and you will have an endless, rolling supply of already-loyal new users—the children of current-generation users.

How does a brand set itself up for Brand-Me-Down success?

Let's take a look at Disney. That company has created a successful Brand-Me-Down segment by perpetuating an existing dynamic: Mothers want to hand-down the same movies that they watched in their childhood. Bambi, Dumbo, Sleeping Beauty, Cinderella, and Snow White are still as cherished today as a half-century ago (I wonder if Pokémon will be around in 50 years?). And Disney cleverly times the releases of its classics on a once-a-generation basis, so that mothers can look for and look forward to special viewings with their children. This careful doling-out of its properties creates an on-going tradition, meaningful for both mother and child, making memories that last.

Actually, there's something inherent in kids' toys and books, too, that inspires loyalty and longevity. With so many other areas

Our Children, Ourselves

A national survey by Youth Monitor, an arm of the polling firm, Yankelovich, has found that the younger generation is deeply affected by the experiences of their parents. Increasingly so.

For example, the study reported that the majority of teenagers today express a desire "to work for myself." This is a direct result of hearing parents, relatives, or neighbors express their anxieties about job security in the face of nonstop layoffs, early retirement plans, or massive downsizing.

According to this survey, many children are feeling "trickle-down stress." Girls are experiencing it more than boys, apparently because girls are more nervous about the challenge of balancing family and career—an emotional tug-of-war they had observed in their own homes.

The survey uncovered a marked increase in the number of children who didn't trust advertisements, whether on radio, television, or in a magazine. They are ultra-sensitive to being "sold" to and are cynical about any kind of traditional advertising. If it seems as if it's more about conning them out of cash, they simply don't buy it.

This new generation remains fickle and elusive. If brand skepticism and buyer's stress are the mood of youth today, marketers need to try a different approach, or that will be the legacy of tomorrow's shoppers. My suggestion? Deflect the negative start by replaying a familiar authority: Let One Generation of Women Consumers Lead You to the Next.

of "cutting edge" consumerism, it's reassuring to find that in this new millennium, "the more things change," the more these things don't. For every fad start-up, the Number One book to croon to your baby at bedtime is still *Goodnight Moon* and sleds are still Flexible Flyers and yo-yos are still Duncans and crayons are still Crayolas (although "Flesh" has gone the way of . . . all flesh). The list of longtime childrens' favorites goes on: Slinky, jacks, jump ropes, Monopoly, Clue, jigsaw puzzles, and Mr. Potato Head. And by the way, there is a Mrs. Potato Head (see her in *Toy Story 2*), but so far not a Ms., Jr., or Baby Potato Head (Spud-nik?).

Schools are also a step ahead of the EVEolutionary curve when it comes to the Sixth Truth. At the simplest level, educa-

The EVEolvution of a School

It's almost as if they foresaw this book. The private Hayground School in Bridgehampton, NY, was started three years ago, based on many of the very same foundations as our EVEolvutionary Truths. It's a model of female thinking. No hierarchy. Multi-tasking. Collaboration. Process, not product. A journey of learning.

It's where Lys's daughter, Skye Qi, at 4½, is technically in kindergarten, but her class of 16 has first and second graders as well. The slightly older kids help teach the younger ones the alphabet and reading, thereby reinforcing their own skills. There is no principal at Hayground; parents, teachers, educators, students, and interested members of the community all participate in the running of the red-barned school (this educational philosophy is being spread to other institutions).

Each year, a traveling theater troupe, Shakespeare & Company, comes for three weeks of intensive work on one play. Making puppets, banners, visualizations of lines from *Hamlet* or *Macbeth*. So instead of studying the basic children's books, *Where's Spot?* or *Run, Spot, Run,* little Skye was exploring every nuance and cranny of some pretty heavy characters. And coming home spouting, "Out, out, damned *spot!*"

tional institutions start to engender Brand-Me-Down loyalty by offering standard baby T-shirts with "Class of 2018," and granting a favored-status admissions edge to alumni children. (The downside of this happens when you went to New York's Public School 63—as I did, and then try to get your child into a few well-known private schools—as I did—the admissions directors look you in the eye and say, "Sorry, siblings only.") Many colleges today are holding reunions and fundraisers geared specifically toward women—where children are not only welcome, but are catered to with kid-geared food and special play areas. This friendly approach guarantees the next generation's allegiance.

In the food arena, there's one cereal brand that's cleverly pulling the generational heartstrings. A recent commercial for Chex cereals flashed back (in grainy, flickering home-movie style) to a 7-year-old girl being shown by her mother how to mix up a batch of that crunchy nibble so beloved by guests, Chex Party Mix. Switch to smooth color photography: The little girl has grown up, ready to have a holiday family gathering on her own. The tagline: "Now it's my turn to be Mom."

Many of the clothing designers have turned on the genera-

Family Talk

Look at the newest EVEolution attempt by AT&T: Connecting a family (up to five) with unlimited local wireless calls between members. A painless incentive to ring up and say "Hey, kids, dinner's ready," "Please pick me up at the train station," or "Where did you hide the key?" A sure draw for today's cellular-pop teens (picture: nose-rings with Call Waiting) who are not used to, not comfortable with phones on cords.

Even AT&T's hook-up number is user-friendly: 1-888-Our Family.

AT&T is laying down a bedrock of family loyalty. And passing that solid kind of attachment down to the next generation.

tional searchlights. Beyond being a logical line extension, the strategic goal of making a kids' line is: lock in loyalty early. Become a part of the family. Once at ease in a look, the consumer will be hooked.

The Gap, Inc., originally filled the need of this nation's young adults who were looking for an easy, casual way of dressing. Now, the retail giant has moved on to a family plan. The first GapKids opened in 1986, followed by BabyGap in 1996; and together these spin-offs have become a destination stop for tried-and-true children's clothing. Besides the confidence in quality, it's the rapid turnover in styles/colors that pulls in the same customer one or two times per week. To check out what's new, to see what's on sale, to get a pair of socks to match the sweater. The addiction makes it a spectacular success.

And the Gap is hardly alone in making pint-sized fashions. Ralph Lauren, DKNY, Liz Claiborne with Liz Kids, Talbot's, Guess?, and my favorite Dutch designers, The People of the Labyrinths—all are making a big push to woo and shoe children—and their parents. But aren't some of the style leaders missing the little boat? Gucci, Prada, Hermés, Issey Miyake?

The number of businesses catering to multiple generations "has definitely been on the increase," points out Scott Krugman of the National Retail Federation, a trade association based in Washington, DC. Think continuity. Which means that department stores should adopt this marketing idea: A Bloomingdale's woman will raise a Bloomingdale's girl who will grow up and give birth to another Bloomingdale's child. Maybe department stores could get on the Brand-Me-Down bandwagon by organizing by category instead of by age group—putting all coats together, all sweaters, all shoes—so that Moms and their daughters can really shop together. The same floors, the same fitting rooms, the same cash registers.

One store is already ahead of the curve. When I talked to Bill Nordstrom of Nordstrom, he told me that one of the main

Kids with Clout

Shake out those piggy banks. Lower the screen of your ATMs. These days, children with bucks are being heard as well as seen. And paid attention to as well. (We call them SKIPPY's: School Kids with Income and Purchasing Power.)

When professor James U. McNeal of Texas A&M University began to study the children's market thirty years ago, he says, "You weren't a consumer worth considering unless you were at least twelve years old."

Today, his research shows that children under the age of twelve are in control of (or have a say in) about $500 billion of consumer purchasing. That's a lot of Beanie Babies. Or Nintendos. Or whatever else catches the fancy of a kid with cash.

reasons they keep the children's shoe department so well-stocked is not because it is such a money-maker (it's not), but because of continuity. Nordstrom wants to be the generational provider, "from first shoe to middle to last."

Some companies are bluebloods in Brand-Me-Down quality. Perhaps none more so than the best known name in luxe: Tiffany & Co.

Tiffany has been masterful at making its brand a member of the family, a symbol of security, of moving from one lifestage to another, and from one generation to the next.

With its instantly recognizable robin's egg–blue box, Tiffany has retained an image of class and customization for well over a hundred years. It has held on to the coveted title of "The Place" to look at, to try on, and sometimes to hand over your credit card for sparkly diamond engagement rings (even long-term bachelor Jerry Seinfeld whisked his bride there for her Big Rock).

Yet, besides selling diamonds in the thousands, Tiffany cleverly has made their store accessible to all, by selling a sterling line of affordable silver items. In a series of smart Brand-Me-Down moves, they offer signature baby spoons, rattles, and picture frames, as well as numbered, monogrammed key chains. Surprisingly, for all its snob appeal, it's not snooty. Tiffany has trained its staff well, maintaining a firm policy of never making anyone feel uncomfortable when strolling into their stores.

Tiffany has also been adept at developing sub-brands (Paloma Picasso, Elsa Peretti) with golden names and quality workmanship (work-woman-ship?) that will endure. This balance of tradition and newness, of continuance and relevance, is an element that makes its way often into Brand-Me-Down success.

One afterthought: Since everybody, at one time or another, loses a pin, a bracelet, an earring, wouldn't it be a terrific loyalty-catcher if Tiffany (and other jewelry sellers) would give a break on replacement costs? Charging less each time (you may have guessed that I've lost quite a few things), if you've kept the receipt.

This "heirloom" concept, long a successful element of marketing high-end goods, is being reinvented now by marketers at the mass level.

Prime example: Martha Stewart. She is the living, breathing embodiment of Brand-Me-Down-ness. Martha works on so many levels—TV/radio/magazine/Web/retail (hey, no wonder she's a billionaire)—and anything with Martha's stamp sells, and sells big. She gives her audience an insight into the Holy Grail of Taste, showing anyone tuning in to her wavelength how to create instant heirlooms, form instant traditions.

Maybe it's pure jealousy, but it's become part of our pop-culture to poke good-natured fun at Martha's unbelievable perfection-isms, do-it-yourself-isms. The latest jibe is a make-believe, must-do-before-Christmas list for Martha:

- Organize spice racks, not alphabetically, but by Latin names and genus.
- Replace air in minivan tires with Glade holiday scents in case tires are shot out at mall.

- Align carpets to adjust for curvature of Earth.
- Lay Faberge egg.

But nobody can take away the fact that Martha Stewart delivers. She generates more and more products through her Kmart line (branded sheets/towels and can't-keep-in-stock garden furniture) and shopping on-line (newly made Majolica, giant cookie cutters) that copy the nostalgic quality of the classics—at a more reasonable price.

Those who grasp this Truth—who seek-and-find continuity though the generations for their brand or service—can turn their product into an "heirloom" to be passed on.

Mercedes Benz Manhattan has put an upper-crust and generational spin on their new Saturn-like selling strategy. Their newspaper ad features a grown daughter with her mother and announces, "If her mother didn't negotiate for her SL, neither should yours." Introducing a plan called NFP (Negotiation Free Process), the Mercedes dealership explains that the female buyer doesn't have to "dicker, haggle, negotiate or involve yourself in any other gauche behavior to get our best price." That is good. But then the next sentence, quite condescending, falls down into Old Think: "So you can spend more time choosing the color scheme you want." As if that's all that women are interested in.

Moving from the well-to-do to the do-it-well, Home Depot, Inc., is also adept at being a family brand, at passing the hammer from one generation to the next.

The phenomenally successful chain has free classes for kids—where they learn to build anything from wooden gaming boards to simple birdhouses. It's sound strategy. While Mom is off studying the racks of paint chips, her little Ms. Muffet is concentrating on completing her project with special Home Depot junior-sized tools. By the time Ms. Muffet gets ready to paint her first apartment, won't she remember where she first learned about Spackle and high-gloss, Phillips screwdrivers, and carpentry nails years before? We think so.

In this age of school shootings and sex-saturated media, mothers are zealously seeking wholesome role models for their children. With all the fallen idols, it's hard to pinpoint someone who represents good clean fun. Especially for girls.

The primary place to find that needle-in-the-healthy-haystack is in sports. Talk about role models—every one of the unstoppable Women's World Cup-winning soccer team had all of America in thrall. In one exuberant moment, Brandi Chastain did

Little Ones Are Big Business

Ask any kid any question, and she/he will spew forth an answer. Or venture a good guess. At a certain age, all kids are smarty-pants. So, some major corporations have decided to funnel that know-it-all attitude into a fresh perspective for brainstorming sessions. And in the process, make more brand connections early on.

Companies like Xerox and Compaq are tapping young minds (ages 7–18) to experiment with new interactive video games...or to get the scuttlebutt on more general topics, like the future definition of "work."

And what brands do you think these kids will remember fondly as they grow up?

Not only do kids have open minds (they're naturally EVEolved), but they also have oddball imaginations. Knowing this, an iconoclastic company called Autodesk gathers groups of kids and lets them tinker together, creating such things as an electronic model of a racecar.

These kids are weaned on television commercials. They're brand-conscious. Environmentally-aware. Ethical. Upstanding. My god-daughter, Skye Qi Marigold, when she was *three*, would lecture me in the car, "Popster (her pet name for me), please put your seat belt on."

But in marketing to this generation, things we take for granted as "common knowledge" can fly right by them. There's an e-mail list making its rounds that supposedly gives the mind-set of 18-year-olds:

continued . . .

- Their lifetime has always included AIDS. Safe sex.
- The Soviet Union broke up when they were ten. They don't know about the Cold War. Never had a drill at school to prepare for a nuclear attack.
- They've always had answering machines, beepers, VCRs, cable, remote controls, CDs.
- Popcorn has always been cooked in the microwave.
- The expression "You sound like a broken record" means nothing. Neither does "Roll down the window," or "Dial so-and-so," and about-to-be obsolete, "The line is busy."
- McDonald's never came in Styrofoam containers.
- They don't have a clue how to put in a typewriter ribbon.
- Never heard: "Where's the beef?" "Walk a mile for a Camel." "Don't squeeze the Charmin."
- The wreck of the *Titanic* was found on the ocean floor? Didn't know it was ever missing.

How do *you* reach these children? By reaching out. By listening and learning to talk their language.

more for sheer hurrahs and sports bras than anyone in women's sports had ever done. In the week after the championship match, there wasn't a soccer ball to be found in the stores. It seemed as if every patch of green grass held a newly-formed girls' soccer team.

Women's basketball, too, has dribbled and bounced its way into our hearts. Val Ackerman, President of the WNBA (Women's National Basketball Association), which only started in 1996, sends out the message that the WNBA and its players are committed to being outstanding examples. Watching a fast game of basketball can teach girls so many good things. Focus, independence, teamwork, sportswomanship, fitness, and how to think on your feet.

The WNBA, because it was so recently built around

Sign Up the Kids

The IGA, a large grocery chain, is reaching out to families with an in-store club called IGA Hometown Kids—so far, in about 20% of their markets. The areas are large and colorful, and there's a well-stocked "fun bucket." Kid members are issued I-Belong club cards, which qualify them for free toys, coloring books, stickers, and pencils—with an IGA logo. Other benefits are offered by the individual stores, such as a discount at Six Flags, a free afternoon at a local bowling alley, or a ride in a hot-air balloon.

"The primary thing the store wants to do is reach young families with kids," says Mark Harsha, Advertising Director for the IGA Fleming in Oklahoma City, OK. Video cameras are set up so that when Mom is shopping, she can see that her child is playing safely and sweetly.

Clubs for kids aren't rocket science. But they create experiences that seal the generational bond and create the brand legacy.

Is there a "Kids' Club" equivalent for your business?

women and girls, has made the games into bonding events. Who wouldn't catch the excitement as tall, lanky heroines, Sheryl Swoopes or Teresa Weatherspoon, race up and down the court, competing for the final winning points? (There seem to be more sister-acts in women's sports than in men's. In basketball, there are twins, Kelly and Coco Miller; sisters, Deanna and Felicia Jackson. And tennis aces, Venus and Serena Williams.) It's electric—and certainly has electrified girls and Moms—for not surprisingly, about three-quarters of the fans at WNBA games are female.

At the first All-Star game at New York's Madison Square Garden in July 1999, the sell-out crowd of 18,650 fans was treated to fast-action—plus such group-pleasers as dance steps and autograph signing by the giant-sized female athletes (literally, women to be looked up to). And hundreds of children took part in the on-court festivities. "Fun" was the name of the game that night, especially for the young fans.

Val Ackerman and the league have intentionally reached out to the younger set. Since a ten-year-old girl can't go to a game alone, there's an EVEolutionary opening when Mom (or Dad) buys the tickets for the upcoming game. It's a marketing opportunity to win over a different generation of female fans and present new Brand-Me-Up situations.

Fair-priced tickets are another tactic the WNBA is using to attract families. The games provide something affordable for working mothers to do with their daughters, other than go shopping at the mall. Ackerman points out that "you can bring four people for only $50, instead of the $300 that a men's pro-sports event would cost." That is smart EVEolutionary planning to entice kids and their friends, the ticket-buyers of the future.

The excitement the WNBA generates among younger fans is showing up strong in the demographics. The high-octane involvement with every player attracts a 72% in-arena female audience, compared to a 37% women-share for the NBA. Statistics like these should jing-a-ling a bell with marketers and advertisers to jump on the EVEolutionary brandwagon.

To measure Ackerman's success in building an audience for the WNBA, consider this: It took the NBA a full 29 seasons to average 10,000 fans a game. It took Ackerman and the WNBA two.

Ackerman shares a personal anecdote that puts the power of EVEolution into perspective. She recalls that out of the blue, her six-year-old daughter piped up with, "Why can't they call the WNBA the NBA and the NBA the MNBA?"

Once you accept the potential and power of the mother-daughter bond, you need to ask: How can my brand become a part of this connection?

Just around the FutureCorner . . .

- If girls do not perform as well as boys in math and science, the reason has to be in the way these subjects are taught. As they say, it's a self-fulfilling prophecy: Since girls are not expected to do as well, they don't get the attention, and so they don't shine in the classroom.

  Imagine if a company such as American Express or Merck, for example, made a major push to change things: concentrating on girls and math/science. This could be promoted through a Web site or special software. Girl-sensitivity-trained teachers could be sent into the schools. The participating companies could create mentoring networks with successful women in math/science intensive careers. The sponsor would establish such a good relationship and reputation with mothers and daughters, enough to create a generation of loyal customers.

  The former Westinghouse competition is now the Intel Science Talent Search. One semi-finalist, 17-year-old East Hampton High School student, Stephanie Talmage, has discovered a new compound in the sumac berries behind the school. Her compound kills the bacteria that causes staph infections and may lead to cancer research. Good work.

- What if American Airlines found a way to turn the value of a mother's frequent flyer miles into a college tuition fund that accrued interest? At high school graduation, the kid would then receive a tuition voucher from the airline. Wouldn't that help any child understand math?

- Computers will help erase the old-think science/math disparity between boys and girls. MamaMedia, a kid's Web hang-out, was founded by Dr. Idit Harel (now CEO), based on her educational ideas of "promoting playful learning" and "technological fluency." So far, there are over one million members, opening up new ways for kids to create and share their games and projects. These 12-and-under kids will interact on the Internet instantly. Fast and furiously—girls will be up to speed.

This wonderful, wacky Web site came to our attention when Mary E. Sculley, Director of Advertising and Sponsorship Sales, sent g.g. and Skye Qi some wonderful wacky e-cards. Sculley feels this job isn't "selling," but "a chance to give back." "Computers are the great equalizers," she added, "erasing all the old dividing lines—how much education or money you have; whether your personality is outgoing or quiet; or female-male power."

We have one other pique, that if corrected, could subtly raise a girl's self-esteem on the computer: How come all the voices, even, "You've Got Mail," are male? Why not a female voice? A child's voice sometimes?

- What if a local bank with a credit-card affiliation (VISA?) offered junior classes on financial matters, such as credit, debit, savings, checking? Facts tailored to teach children about financial responsibility and how to build a credit history. Whose card do you think the next generation would sign up for?

- There are 13 million single mothers across the country and they're the fastest growing segment. Yet, if I asked you to name a marketer that has targeted the needs of those single Moms, you probably couldn't think of one. What an opportunity for a major marketer to support and bond with this neglected group. There are many levels of practical and emotional support needed, including financial services, childcare, educational assistance, and more. Where could this help come from? A phone company, utility company, or even a health insurer. The one who lends a hand could become part of the family: A brand for life.

Many companies are catching on to the EVEolutionary Truth that they can create a Hand-Me-Down brand by increasing their product's value and meaning to the mother.

Still, grasping the truth and acting on it are two separate issues. Too many companies are squandering opportunities to build and solidify their brands' status as a tradition to be passed from one generation to the next.

They need to tie up to the apron strings of EVEolution.

Case Study: KitchenAid

Although we've chosen to use KitchenAid as the case study for the Generational Truth, you're probably Truth-savvy enough by now to realize that SnackWell's (in the Connecting chapter) could quite as readily have been used here as well as vice versa. This proves one simple point: A real EVEolutionary is often supported by two or more Truths.

KitchenAid, a company in business for over 75 years, was confident that their good name was often passed from mother to daughter. But they sensed that they could do more with their generational potential and, in 1996, came to BrainReserve to build a plan for a Brand-Me-Down future. Many of the recommendations BrainReserve made have been incorporated into new KitchenAid plans.

BrainReserve began the assignment by looking at the heart and soul of the matter: The kitchen. It doesn't matter whether a woman works or not, whether she's a serious cook or a take-out junkie; for most, today's kitchen is mission-control, the center of the household-universe. Look at the messages/photos magneted to the fridge. Count how many home businesses are started around the table. And note how many computers are replacing the small TVs on the kitchen counter.

Thoughts of the kitchen strike many emotional nerves. A stove isn't just a metal box that heats—it's a modern-day hearth, creating warmth in more ways than one. A mixer doesn't just blend ingredients—after making the Sunday mashed potatoes or holiday cookies, it's a creator of memories. So therefore, kitchen appliances are infused with more meaning, going beyond being mere workhorses (strong, reliable).

KitchenAid, realizing the new emphasis, needed to reposition itself. BrainReserve started by staring at the name and all that it implied. We repeated it like a mantra: "Kitchen aid; kitchen aid." Help in the kitchen.

This simple idea was expended into "My KitchenAid is my kitchen aide," a powerful platform on which to base the new strategy. You'll see this platform reflected in many of the new things KitchenAid is implementing.

In the future, the brand will become the passionate expert and approachable mentor in the kitchen. According to Josh Gitlin, KitchenAid's head of Opportunity Creating Investments, "It will inspire and enable home enthusiasts to express their personal style while delivering professional results." The team at KitchenAid is now creating a new intergenerational life for the brand, focused on establishing the "kitchen aide" notion as a kind of emotional connection that product alone can't make.

We continued on our fact-finding (and feel-finding) quest by asking women about their first contact with the brand. Many talked about seeing the name on their mother's mixer and dishwasher when they were first making cake batter and cleaning up. Leading us to conclude that the Brand-Me-Down truth is the one to be applied. Loyalty comes from early exposure to a product— the earlier, the better.

Driving the Future

If you were a woman with a child in tow, where would you spend time shopping for a car? In a sleek, glass-and-steel environment or one offering safe amusements for the wee one? AutoNation USA, a chain of car dealerships, has wised up to the EVEolutionary power of family selling.

Its showrooms are chockablock with friendly play centers where kids can actively climb little plastic mountains, ride around in miniature cars and trucks. (Are they branded AutoNation? They should be.) Or the children can simply get engrossed in watching television, or becoming junior Picassos with crayons and coloring books.

Besides making the car-shopping experience fun-and-games for the youngest members of the family, the play center also frees up any teenage siblings from baby-chasing duty. Now teens can concentrate on helping Mom pick out the sharpest car (even if it's not Jigglypuff pink). All the while, the whole family is developing an AutoNation allegiance.

Being involved with the car buying process is especially important in the adolescent years because that's precisely the time when kids start picturing themselves behind the wheel.

I think there's room for an EVEolved dealership to become even more involved. How about offering help on getting one's driver's license by providing examples of sample written exams or expert tips on passing the road test? How about extending this idea to starting AutoNation Driving Schools? If a teen learns on a certain car, what will they be likely to covet, to buy?

As toy companies know, children constantly test the real world through play, honing their mimicry of adulthood. We concluded that tying KitchenAid to positive experiences of mastering culinary skills would create deep bonds to the brand. In our BrainJams, we worked on that question of how KitchenAid could further reinforce itself as a Hand-Me-Down brand. One option for the company would be to create toy replicas of its appliances.

We imagined millions of Janes (and even Jacks) working with their mini-KitchenAids alongside their Moms. We also suggested that the toy appliances be donated to daycare centers, nursery schools, hospitals; as well as sold in toy stores, catalogs, special vending machines, and, of course, on the Internet.

How could KitchenAid link in with older kids? We saw its role as replacing the old Home Economics model. We suggested sponsorship of young-chefs clubs through cooking schools across the country. Moving further up the generational ladder, we proposed that KitchenAid develop cooking classes and clubs for college grads and newlyweds.

Then there is the company's Web site. KitchenAid is fast becoming a resource center with all manner of on-line how-to's, such as the perfect time/temperature to cook a rib roast or how long eggs stay fresh in the refrigerator. And the site has a design center that consumers can use to ask questions and get advice on how to go about remodeling their kitchens. Perhaps getting a future chance to put in the dimensions of their rooms, and consult with top kitchen designers for expert opinions.

Wouldn't it be great to have the ability to order new appliances or upgrades, dealing directly with KitchenAid representatives on-line, in addition to their dedicated, "pre-buy" phone line? The bonus is: You get to avoid the horrific experience of the appliance store, second only to car showrooms in its abuse to women.

Another idea: We think appliances should be available for lease, much like a car. Think of how many more people could then afford a KitchenAid kitchen, new or refurbished. The real power of a Hand-Me-Down brand will come when a single person or young couple can easily outfit their kitchen and then upgrade their appliances every 5-10 years, especially if upgrades and even buy-backs are handled on the Web. Later on, even empty-nesters could take advantage of this, selling back their used KitchenAid appliances to buy more space-efficient models for their one-bedroom condos.

A generational theme also showed up in our suggestions for:

1. Changing the appearance of more of the products to look like their award-winning classic standing mixer, a retro '50s line. Think: the new Volkswagen.

2. Addressing future health concerns. One of our recommendations was that KitchenAid incorporate technology capable of measuring the nutritional value of meals. While the bar-code-scanner refrigerator now exists, wouldn't it be terrific to find out if the dinner you planned filled your personal requirements for daily vitamins and minerals? Wouldn't it be great if your refrigerator "ordered" your whole week's groceries with your family's health and wellness in mind—and requested them home-delivered? Or if your microwave came with a probe to read post-zapped bacterial levels?

What this KitchenAid case proves is this: You need to see where all your intergenerational strengths and weaknesses are. You can then develop a strategy that focuses on the bonds that exist through all the stages of life. Childhood, college, first apartment, career, early years of marriage, parenthood, second career, retirement. The key is to look along the branches of a woman's family tree for marketing opportunities.

• • •

Ask yourself, how can my brand be repositioned to:

• Become part of her family tradition and folklore?
• Remain equally relevant to all generations, past and future?
• Provide lasting value to this generation and the next?

That's marketing to family.

That's marketing to life.

Chapter 7

The Seventh Truth of EVEolution:

Co-Parenting Is the Best Way

to Raise a Brand

E VE, mother of us all in creation. (Or was it Lucy, the 3.2 mil-
lion-year-old skeleton found in Africa, DNA'd to be Mom
One?) Whomever, it's women who are the natural nurturers.
Birthing, loving, feeding, teaching rights from wrongs, showing
off their young to the world.

Whether it's a child, a puppy, a cockatiel, or a brand,
women protect their own.

Ancient sexual stereotypes portray women as the more nurturing of the two sexes. But like many stereotypes, this one's
based on fact: Women make better "mothers." As authors Jeanne

and Don Elium state in their book, *Raising a Daughter*, "from antiquity, the feminine has been called the 'Vessel of Life,' 'Life-giver,' 'Great Mother,' the 'Cosmic Egg.' At some point in a woman's life—no matter her race, social class, education, religious creed, marital status, career choice, political affiliation, and so on—she will face the question of whether to have a child. To be female is to carry this biological urge." I don't know too many women who would describe themselves as a "Cosmic Egg," but I certainly know a lot of women whose nature is to nurture.

Well-known anthropologist Helen Fisher explains the biological and cultural reasons why in her book, *The First Sex*, "Nature has made mothers; feminine nurturing is driven by a host of chemical compounds ubiquitous among mammals." Fisher cites the increased levels of estrogens during birth that trigger motherly behavior in all female mammals, as well as brain chemicals and specific genes seen only in females that drive maternal instinct. Mothering simply comes naturally to women, Fisher concludes. No surprise.

Dr. Christiane Northrup states in her book, *Women's Bodies, Women's Wisdom,* that in aboriginal cultures "all of the mother's sisters—the child's aunts—are considered the child's mothers. . . . If you ask an aboriginal child who her mother is, she will point not only to her biological mother but to her aunts as well. The child always has a place in the group."

Any book that deals with women and what's important to them needs to address the role that is so basic to so many women. Being "Mom" is still, after all, the role of millions of women on the planet today. And that number doesn't include those who parent beyond children: What about parenting pets, parents, employees, a career, an idea? Women nurture all of these, even if it's only a plant on a windowsill.

So why don't marketers recognize that women have different drives and parenting is part of our basic make-up, and leverage that part of us? That's what I'm suggesting—that women would want to join a brand that they themselves help bring into the world. I believe that marketers must invite their female consumers into the delivery room to be a co-parent at the birth of the brand. And then encourage these female consumers to stay around and help raise the brand to a healthy maturity.

That's why developing a Co-Parenting approach to marketing is an EVEolutionary imperative. Because without an emotional attachment to your brand, it's too easy for a woman to dump your brand. Walk out on you for good. Partner with your female consumer to nurture your brand, and you are tapping into one of the most powerful forces in human nature. By letting her see only "your vision" of the brand, you'll never get her deep commitment.

What do I mean by Co-Parenting? I mean develop complete honesty in your relationship with her, and allow her access to every corner of your brand. I mean always give her public credit for her contributions, and never fail her or embarrass her by failing her friends. I mean establish consumer visitation rights, which requires more than an 800-number and a standard-issue Web site. I mean actively solicit her criticism and suggestions for change. I mean welcome her thinking on absolutely everything, large and small—and then seriously consider her ideas (no form letters, no black hole in the consumer complaint department, no legal paranoia about listening to unsolicited ideas). I mean offer consistency in your dialogue.

You can't turn deaf when your Co-Parent asks you to take action—whether it's changing the fliptop on your bottlecap or the software on your Web site. You have to believe—genuinely—that if her suggestions take you into territory that is uncomfortable, expensive, or difficult, that's okay. It's an EVEolving experience. Giving you, the marketer, the chance to gain the deepest loyalty you can imagine: a marketing mother-love, unconditional and unassailable.

Co-Parenting requires that you listen to your female consumers as closely as you do your Board-of-Directors (whether it's only a business partner or sounding board)—even more closely. Your "board" gets to vote on decisions critical to the future of your brand; your consumers are stakeholders who vote with their dollars. Board members can even be replaceable; consumers usually aren't. And the best way to make a female consumer a Co-Parent is to integrate her into your product development and marketing processes. This means taking input and feeding it back in a continuous loop.

It's an ongoing process that works something like this:

- The female consumer offers her idea and the marketer listens.
- The company internalizes the idea and consults with the consumer to refine it.
- The company implements the new concept and ultimately shows the consumer (and the world) what it has done with her idea.

It's a marketplace dialogue, with each thought building on another until something successful happens. Something that could not happen without the full participation and agreement of both parties. Something that would be less wonderful without the benefit of two attentive parents.

Don't confuse Co-Parenting with market research. It's not simply reacting to consumer input from focus groups and one-on-one interviews. Or conducting reader surveys and fielding advertising tracking. Or circulating customer mail and tabulating business reply cards. These are tools, often mistaken for ends in themselves (like, "I've just lived through another round of mall intercepts in Peoria. Now I can go home and forget the whole experience"). This is not it. Not.

There is very little room for an exchange in any of these old techniques. And generally their only output is a black binder that sits on a shelf with a lot of other black binders. Far too many marketers think they've done their job once they've read a stack of qualified and quantified research results.

Out of Focus

Building on the strange-but-true insight that women are more likely to "tell all" to several million people on a TV talk show than in the privacy of a focus group, Mary Lou Quinlen started "Just Ask A Woman." Quinlen was formerly CEO of N.W. Ayer, a large advertising agency in New York. She saw an obvious need for better research techniques when it came to getting input from women. As she stated in the September 1999 issue of that EVE-olved magazine, *Fast Company* (built on the premise of listen-ing/working together): "If you want to design products that are relevant to women, you've got to understand how your women customers think—and if you want to understand how they think, you've got to engage them in compelling conversation."

The problem with focus groups, argues Quinlen, is that they are more like police interrogations than discussions: "Because focus groups are designed to be analytical, they treat participants as if they are lab rats. What we're trying to do is to put women in a relaxed situation so that they can communicate openly." She is currently creating a cable TV show, produced by Jen Levine (our ex-TalentBank director), to get women to reveal their true opinions.

Co-Parenting is not just about being listened to—it's about being heard, really heard. Anybody can gather consumer input—and in today's research-driven world, everyone but the marketing brain-dead is. In fact, for years marketers have talked about "understanding and meeting the needs of consumers." This idea is so familiar, it's become a marketing cliche. This just isn't enough. Because a one-way marketing monologue (or a two-way, one-time conversation) doesn't work for women today. You need a longer and larger dialogue—one that creates a dynamic, ever-EVEolving relationship.

The difference is that Co-Parented brands share every aspect of brand responsibility. They relinquish control, rather than imposing it. And that is really hard for marketers who have been told that they are the "brand steward" or the "brand leader." Even the ubiquitous title "Brand Manager" has an element of "I'm in control here; I'm managing my consumers." But you have to learn to let go. Like all good parents.

There are some Early EVEolutionaries among us. After all, the PTA has been allowing mothers and teachers to Co-Parent the school experience for decades, and there is evidence to prove that schools with stronger PTAs are stronger schools.

M&M's conducted a highly visible Co-Parenting demonstration when it asked its devotees to help pick the new candy color: Blue. Just imagine the uproar if the marketers had picked blue all by themselves? And put little blue M&M's in the candy packet without preparing the public? People would hate it as much as the initial surprise introduction of New Coke.

o.b. tampons changed the rules of its category by going first to a practicing woman gynecologist, among others, to Co-Parent in the radical new design of its brand. That doctor, Judith Esser, M.D., also came on board (contining the nurturing) as spokesperson in the early years.

Look at other successfully Co-Parented brands:

Stew Leonard's, a warm and cuddly supermarket mini-chain in suburban Connecticut and New York, has built enormous loyalty among its customers by making them Co-Parents of its three stores. Stew Leonard built his empire by following his Three Rules of Marketing:

Rule 1: The customer is always right.

Rule 2: The customer is always right.

Rule 3: Reread Rule #1.

Stew Leonard bills his business as the world's biggest dairy, reflecting its beginning in his grandfather's barn in Norwalk, CT (co-author Lys's hometown, where "Stewie" coincidentally dated Lys's *au pair* long ago). The emphasis is on fresh, fresh, fresh—dairy products, fruits and vegetables, baked goods, and a full line of fine meats and fish. These days he claims $150 million in annual sales, and his Web site offers nationwide delivery, in-store specials, "fun facts," and career opportunities. Involving the customers has been part of Stew Leonard's marketing by-laws since the first store opened in 1969.

"Our mission is to create happy customers," Stew Leonard's announces, and to keep people smiling, the supermarkets double as entertainment centers. Employees dressed as cows and chickens stroll the aisles, chatting with customers and their kids. Overhead, mechanized figures that look like milk cartons, chickens, and butter sticks dance, sing, and play original ditties. All of which makes it easy for mothers to persuade their kids that it's time to go to the grocery store.

Stew Leonard and his top managers regularly run in-store feedback sessions. These aren't focus groups; they're honest consumer dialogues, interactions with customers that have a sense of immediacy because they are conducted in a glass booth in the middle of the store.

Shoppers can actually see that their opinions are being listened to. The mostly female participants are paid to talk about the store's shortcomings. "What do you like about the competition that you don't like about us?" is the most frequently asked question.

Cleverly, the store provides a daycare center that serves ice cream to keep kids busy, so their Moms can offer concrete suggestions for everything from the restrooms to the cashiers, from product improvement to recycling to store layout. Nothing is out of bounds.

Not only is this input more valuable than the age-old suggestion box, it makes customers feel that they have a stake in the place. They feel they are having a real impact on their shopping experience. As one Stew Leonard's shopper puts it, "You bet this is the kind of place I like to shop. It should be. I helped make it this way!"

• • •

And then there're the *Zagat Survey Restaurant Guides*. These books are the ultimate Co-Parented brand—with their contents culled from the responses of its all-volunteer reviewers. *Zagat's* would not exist if it weren't for its 100,000-plus Co-Parents.

Contrast that with the old way of doing a good-food guide: Can you think of a more paternalistic, anti-EVEolutionary model than the usual restaurant review and how we read it? "Tell me, mighty soothsayer of culinary wisdom, where should I eat and what should I order, and I'll follow your opinion like a good little girl."

Zagat's had a better idea. Now selling well over one million copies annually, they are the restaurant "red book" of choice, and now cover hotels, spas, some food markets as well, in more than 40 U.S. and foreign cities. (Chew on that, Michelin!) The guides were started as a hobby by New York lawyer, Tim Zagat, and his wife, Nina, in 1978. They say what motivates their "reporters" is the satisfaction of having their opinions matter. "Let's say 100 people say a restaurant is 'crowded' and 'noisy,'" Tim says. "We print that and all 100 of them say, 'They've quoted me, they've heard me.' There's a real sense of participation. What we've done is really touched on interactivity. It's a two-way street."

P.S.: Women outnumber men in *Zagat's* voting 3-to-1. Proof-positive that a Co-Parented brand is what attracts women.

• • •

Ford's "Windstar Moms." Not everybody at Ford Motor Co. was wild about this twist on Co-Parenting: Enlisting the expertise of a total of 50 female engineers for the 1999 redesign of the

Windstar Minivan. The breakdown was well-founded: Thirty had children; ten were pregnant; ten, no kids. Some un-EVEolved souls thought that celebrating the "Soccer Mom" would be a contradiction with Ford's cultivated image as a cutting-edge company.

Not true. Ford, to its credit, recognized that Moms are the biggest users of its minivans, so who better to tell the company what the car needed?

And since the ideas of these women were incorporated in the redesign, both Ford's sales and market share for Windstar have increased.

Some of the family-oriented innovations drawing raves:

- A low-wattage "baby mode" dome light that doesn't glare in an infant's eyes when a door opens.
- Guards to keep bits of food from slipping into crevices.
- Bins with space for folded diapers as well as CDs.
- And a switch that keeps the driver's side door from locking if the driver has to jump out suddenly (to tend to crying or quarreling children) while the key is still in the ignition.

Since the project's success, respect for Ford's female engineers has grown. And Ford followed another rule of Co-Parenting—make sure your co-parents get credit—by featuring the women engineers in ads for the Windstar.

One executive said the project proved that "we could put a woman in charge of a vehicle line and not go to hell-in-a-handbasket." Nice attitude, but probably strong praise in the steely world of Detroit. And the engineer/Moms feel their choice to combine career-with-family has been validated. Seat engineer Gretchen Zobel told *USA Today*: "I'm proud to be a Mom, and I'm proud to make a contribution."

More Co-Parenting to come: Ford's Women's Auto Center on iVillage.com has an area called "Design Your Dream Car." All ideas, good and bad, are fed from this site back into the development area. In fact, at the Specialty Equipment Marketers Association meeting, Ford unveiled a prototype car that included many customized features submitted from the Dream Car site. A woman's dreams can become reality.

Stew Leonard's, *Zagat's,* and Windstar have shown that Co-Parenting works. But in the wired world, the concept can reach an entirely new level of execution. The Internet is the perfect place to co-author and co-develop a brand. Instantaneous information means that all things can be known by the consumer, and all things can have input from the consumer. Manufacturers and customers can now dialogue back and forth through every stage of development, in an ongoing feedback chain. Frequently and fast.

Everything about a brand can now be "voted" on.

I'm talking about the ultimate in democratization—brands that everybody (from kids to seniors) can have a hand in shaping and that anybody can improve on to the best of their desire and ability.

And it's happening . . .

Oxygen.com, is an on-line network for women, that its Chairman and co-founder, Geraldine Laybourne—the woman who built Nickelodeon—calls "a new kind of relationship between women and the media that serves us." And it's all about Co-Parenting.

Its many Web pages and chatrooms (as well as its sister cable TV channel) cover everything from raising a family and cooking dinner to job-hunting and building an investment portfolio. Its search engine, Ask O2, is user-friendly, with impressive range and sophistication. Its television advertising is pure EVE-olution, showing a multi-tasking woman reading over a guy's shoulder while hugging him (he is doing nothing but hugging back). And the tagline is: "Another great reason to be a woman." And Oxygen.com's emphasis throughout is on helping its users tailor the network to suit their needs.

"Welcome to Oxygen. We're thrilled you're here," is the

opening line. "We hope you'll join us in building a gutsy new women's network. . . . Tell us what you want and we'll work on creating it." Or as Laybourne herself puts it, "The essence of what we're doing is about the users. It's their network. Our marketing campaign is a bus that goes across America asking women to participate in the creation of Oxygen. The whole company is set up to listen to them." That's real EVEolution.

Deja.com has taken the *Zagat* model into cyberspace, compiling more than 500,000 consumer opinions on about 12,000 products and services in its Deja Ratings. Each item can be rated only once by each user who fills out a detailed survey form. After checking out a product's ratings, a visitor can click to an e-commerce site to make a purchase.

In addition, Deja.com, which is dedicated to empowering consumer decision-making, offers access to more than 40,000 discussion forums. It's the *Consumer Reports* of the Internet space. Thinking of which, why can't you order from *Consumer Reports*? "Oh, that's the best washing machine, I'll take it." A gap?

All this is particularly helpful to female small-business owners. If you're nervous about whether you're on the right track or not, but don't have the resources to conduct full-scale focus groups, you can check out your instincts on the Web. There's one site that lets you create a survey to customize your questions and helps you edit your survey so that you can get some zingy feedback. Called Zoomerang.com, it provides the templates for basic business questions and steers you in the right direction. Best, it's free.

And then there's Priceline.com. We were wondering about what the concept will eventually do to the categories it's interacting with. If you let a consumer tell you how much she is willing to pay for a Delta flight from New York to Chicago; how much for a room at the Four Seasons in L.A.; how much for a box of Tide or a can of Progresso split pea soup, won't providers and manufacurers have to look long and hard at their pricing structure? After they've heard the loud voices of their consumers?

They should, if they want to live by the Co-Parenting Truth.

Oxygen.com, Deja.com, and Priceline.com are only the beginning of virtual Co-Parenting. Soon, customization technology will enable each consumer to birth her own brainchild brand, that perfect "segmentation of one" that has eluded marketers for so long.

Brands can also Co-Parent with other brands. Amazon.com has an Associates Program that links up site-to-site and gives its current associates referral fees. Each one fosters the other's strengths. Food companies are now joining up to sell together, such as what Pepsi-Cola, Ore-Ida, Tyson, and Hot Pockets did for Super Bowl XXXIV. But why not go further than cross-promoting existing products? Why shouldn't different companies work together to develop truly compatible new ones? For instance, why doesn't McDonald's sell its delicious thin French fries (closest to the fab Dutch street food) frozen? And Hellman's could make their own interpretation of mayo-like Dutch frite sauce. Co-coupon both and you've got Co-Parenting.

Just around the FutureCorner in the virtual world . . .

- Web sites will be used extensively by companies for polling their consumers and asking them to vote on the various aspects of a product. Clairol can put forth a question like, "Should we substitute rosemary and sunflowers for marigold and thyme in our Herbal Essences shampoo?" And tabulate the answers. The virtual survey will replace the focus group as the research tool of choice.
- Companies won't have a single Web page and a single 800-number. Co-Parents will have special access to an ongoing interactive one that will differ from the page available to those who have only bought the product once and just want to register a complaint.

And in the physical world . . .

- A liquor store will be Co-Parented and run by women.

Everybody's an Expert—For Real

Anita Borg is a Co-Parenting pioneer. As creator and head of the Institute for Women and Technology (IWT) in Palo Alto, CA, she leads workshops on the future of technology and feeds back the results to every top player in the field (Hewlett-Packard, Xerox, Sun Microsystems, Compaq, to name a few).

But Borg is unique among technology consultants: All of her participants are women, and all are what the technology industry calls "users." As she says to her workshop participants—who range from high schoolers to celebrated computer scientists—"You are all experts. This is not a focus group. Each of us is an expert in her own experience." Then she takes all the input and lets the major companies know what these women want, hope for, look for, and would buy. Co-Parenting can happen before buying a woman's next computer and its programs.

Borg's long-term goal is to change the face of technology—to one with slightly more feminine features. As she says, "How can it be that 'technology changes everything' when a majority of the population has little or no say in how technology evolves? What if only thirty-year-old women developed technology—all of it—and that technology was geared mainly for thirteen-year-old girls? Technology would be out of whack, out of balance. But that's the world we live in: Men hold the power and boys drive the market."

Not for long. Maybe we need somebody new in the driver's seat.

Such a store will be vastly different from those we are forced to navigate today. For instance, all the Merlots (from every country), with descriptions of each, will be displayed together (the Sephora cosmetic model) and individually rated. There will be writing pads next to each wine (going well beyond "white with fish, red with red meat") where women can write what they served it with, along with menus and suggestions for entertaining and serving. Wouldn't it be great if you were planning a leg-of-lamb dinner and you read, "This was the best, fullest flavor wine when I served it with my Turkish-style grilled lambchop recipe. Inexpensive, too. And by the way, here's the recipe."

The store will dedicate one corner to a cholesterol-screening center—where you can check and get an instant read on whether that one-glass-a-day of wine or alcohol is helping modify your cholesterol. And helping your heart.

Wouldn't it be fun if the customers could really get their hands on a bottle or two—and make personal changes. Be able to customize wine labels in celebration of a birth, promotion, new house, or quiet dinner for two. And certainly this store will have a registry to keep track of its customers' birthdays, anniversaries, and holiday habits. In this Co-Parenting store, there will be Internet access to let customers put in take-out orders from local restaurants to go along with their drink selections (like China Fun's Crystal Shrimp Dumplings with Moët & Chandon).

The store's own Web site will have a fast-delivery service; a constantly changing array of wine-linked features; chat rooms for customers to exchange tips and experiences; and a continuing dialogue with customers on how the whole enterprise could be improved.

- A chain restaurant Co-Parented and run by women will sell wholesome food that both kids and mothers enjoy eating. The atmosphere will offer more than the hard seats and harsh lighting designed to move customers in and out of today's fast-food joints.

This chain will offer edu-tainment for children—interactive video games that actually teach kids something, PC stations equipped with Encarta, and desks available for homework. There will be a staffed childcare section, where Mom can leave the kids and enjoy a quiet meal with pals. Classes for kids will be offered after school, on topics ranging from cooking and nutrition to table manners and early job training.

This restaurant will develop its menu in collaboration with its customers, who will also approve its layout and furniture, consult on new diet trends, and serve up a steady flow of ideas. And the restaurant will offer home delivery, links to baby-sitting services, and shuttle service to and from home for teens too young to have their licenses. Watch out, Chuck E. Cheese. Such a restaurant chain will eat your wedge of the market.

- A housewares store Co-Parented by women. A female customer will no longer have to stand red-faced at the counter, stammering descriptions of the switch that needs to be fixed while a guy behind the counter smiles patronizingly and shrugs his shoulders. No more narrow aisles with large items that fall over when she touches them. No more VFW-hall atmosphere.

  Instead, the store will make women feel comfortable. It will have a computerized catalog of widgets for quick, easy searching and identification—and when a customer finds what she's looking for, she can click on "how to" install it. The salespeople, mostly women, will empathize with her problems and want to help her solve them.

  Tools will be displayed with short videos illustrating their use. The paint and wallpaper section will have a collection of videos suggesting decorating ideas—and also the latest home-decorating magazines, with comfortable chairs, a reading lamp, and coffee.

  The store will be open before and after regular work hours, and it will offer videos and free classes in woodworking, painting, minor electrical repairs, and the like. Above all, it will listen to its customers. It will ask them what they want, discuss their answers, and then respond.

And women will drive 50 miles from home to visit it.

Case Study: GE Financial Assurance (GEFA)

So who understands the Co-Parenting Truth? GEFA, GE's family of insurance and investment companies.

When BrainReserve went to GEFA, we proposed that they develop a proprietary strategy for winning the long-term loyalty of women business owners. We took this idea to them because of their broad distribution and product capabilities, as well as their ability to focus on a market.

GEFA agreed that the opportunity was compelling and, as a result, became one of the first financial services businesses to change its model to meet the needs of women in business. The strategy for GEFA was based on and developed through a painstaking application of the Seventh Truth: Co-Parenting Is the Best Way to Raise a Brand.

Look at the fundamentals that we brought to the table. Remember: Women in the United States are starting businesses at twice the rate of men. And women now own close to 40% of all small businesses. Yet this market is under-valued, under-served and under-marketed to by financial services companies. The insurance industry, for example, should be focused on and scrambling to change the fact that fewer than 10% of women-owned companies with fewer than 25 employees offer disability insurance.

That's because the typical female-owned business tends to be a small, service-oriented, kitchen-table-run enterprise. And most insurance companies are structured to accommodate companies with sales resembling the GDP of a small country. GEFA knew that something radical was required if they were to fully service this "foreign" market.

In the assignment's initial phases, we conducted BrainJams and TrendProbes and interviewed experts, consumers, and management. We realized that this market required a company to think big about a small business customer's interconnected financial needs: borrowing, investing, and managing, as well as insurance, wealth transfer, and business continuance. The case for EVEolution was clear.

After many interviews all over the country, we discovered that women business owners felt they lacked one of the critical advantages men have always had: mentorship. Someone to turn to, someone to ask advice of, someone with a wealth of experience. And most emphatically, a single simple solution. The "here's my product, make your business fit it" approach was just not going to work. A perfect place for Co-Parenting.

The delivery system GEFA developed was relationship-based, designed to provide objective advice and information to women. GEFA hired "Relationship Managers" who are paid a base salary in order to alleviate any concern that their financial recommendations might be biased. Relationship Managers help their customers understand the scope of their financial needs, and offer options and resources to enable those clients to fill the gaps. The Relationship Managers also serve as concierges to GE's many other arms, putting together customers with resources to help them grow their businesses.

GEFA has also originated an innovative approach to conducting educational seminars. These are not the usual thinly-veiled vehicles for selling term life and mutual funds. GEFA's seminars create an ongoing net of support for women business owners, providing a forum for these women to develop exactly the right mix of financial products for their individual situations.

The Power of Words and Numbers

The American Dialect Society (ADS) has been specifying a "Word of the Year" since 1900, representing "Who we are and what the language is." Some examples from the past: 1938 was "teenager"; 1952, "Ms"; and 1984, "yuppie." Now the ADS has designated the word of this past millennium: SHE. Apparently, it based its choice on the fact that this pronoun dates back to 1000 A.D. among English-speaking peoples.

We respectfully disagree and believe instead that the SHE millennium has just arrived. In our lexicon, Millennium 2000 will most definitely be the Millennium of the Woman. Why? Because every year of the last thousand years started with the number 1: a male number. Solitary. Penile. Hierarchical. Authoritative. Direct. These next ten centuries, however, will begin with the number 2: a female number. Relationship-oriented. Curvy. Connected. Lateral. Sharing.

Promoting women doesn't mean putting men down. In the ideal world, 2001, 2002, 2003, and on, will mean partnerships. A balance of power. An EVEolution.

Throughout the sessions, women business owners trade experiences, stories, and frustrations, along with business cards. Together, they develop new ways of solving problems based on their diverse perspectives.

What's in it for GEFA? Beyond the obvious goodwill generated by underwriting a productive and business-building day, GEFA becomes a part of a woman's tapestry of trusted advisors, helping her grow (a.k.a., Co-Parent) her business. And let's face it, the bigger her company grows, the more valuable she is as a client. GEFA's involvement is no longer about selling a product—it's about developing the right kind of relationship—a relationship that a woman helps develop herself.

• • •

How can you tap the power of Co-Parenting? Ask yourself:

- What would my brand or company be like, if it were run by a woman? (We always use this question in our TrendProbes and invariably, the answers come back as, "cleaner, more honest, more humane, more in touch, more intelligent." What do these qualities mean specifically when you apply them to your business?)
- If my brand were my child, how would I like to raise it?
- How could I get my partner and my family (both actual and extended) to help me?

The real magic of Co-Parenting is the magic of numbers: Two (or two million) heads and hearts are more powerful than one. I certainly put this truth into practice—several thousand women (and many men, too) birthed this book with me.

But Co-Parenting is a hard truth to accept. It means welcoming help, which companies often find difficult to do. They're not set up for it and it's hard to share the credit. You have to give up some control, and have the will and courage to let your brand be influenced by many parents.

But it's worth it. Once you have allowed women into your brand, they're invested for life.

Chapter 8

The Eighth Truth of EVEolution:

Everything Matters—

You Can't Hide Behind Your Logo

Never try to deceive a woman. She has X-ray vision. Eventually, she'll see right through you.

You *might* get away with it once. But it'll never work twice. Remember Shakespeare's warning, "Hell hath no fury like a woman scorned." Once she's on to you, you've lost a customer forever.

Which is a long time.

If you think a famous logo, clever ads, a Fortune 500 ranking, even that the expertise of your sales reps will protect you— think again. When it comes to marketing to women, there's nowhere to run, nowhere to hide.

Women do business with people they trust. Trust happens when you're open about your actions and act with a conscience. Therefore, responsibility is no longer just a good public relations idea. It's a necessity for doing business.

If your company is accustomed to business-by-spin, you'll have to either reform now or find another line of work. It's that simple.

Your new EVEolutionary goal: A reputation—built and maintained over the long term—for honesty, integrity, ethical behavior, community give-back, and a maniacal attention to detail.

While men and women alike are both tuning in more closely to a company's ethics and practices, women especially care about the details. It's genetic. As Mary Pipher says in *Reviving Ophelia*, "Endlessly girls discuss the smallest details of conversations and events—who wore what, who said what, did he smile at her, did she look mad when I did that? The surface is endlessly combed for information about the depths."

The Personal Is Political

Few people know more about what motivates women at the ballot box than Celinda Lake of Lake, Snell and Perry, a Washington, DC–based political consultancy specializing in the female voter.

When I asked Celinda to talk about the differences between how women and men vote, her answer was right out of the Everything Matters script: "Women want to know more about the personal background of the candidate. They also want to know about the values that led to the political position a candidate has taken."

"The personal is political for women," Lake added. "Men, on the other hand, are likely to say, 'Just tell me your top three policies.'"

Consumer analogue alert: Get out and get the dollar-vote by letting your brand's background be a hide-nothing statement of honesty and integrity.

A few months ago, the son of a friend of mine came home from college and announced he'd met the girl of his dreams.

His father asked, "What's her name? What's her major? What does her father do?" And, because he couldn't help himself, "Is she a looker?"

His mother (my friend), on the other hand, annoyed her son by asking seemingly irrelevant questions. "How many siblings does she have? Is she the youngest, middle, or oldest child? Does she have any pets? Where was she born? Where were her parents and her grandparents (on both sides) from? Does she believe in God?" And, because she couldn't help herself, "What size does she wear?"

Why does this sound familiar? Because it's happened to you. I'll bet if you thought about it, you could come up with dozens of examples of how women evaluate people, events, even institutions, in a way that's completely different from men. Because women tend to view everything as related in some way, they need all the details to connect the pieces.

You could write off this female behavior as "nosy," "prying," or "who really cares?"

Or you could seriously consider the way in which this gender difference, this affinity for detail affects the way women view your brand. (Here's a tip: Only one of these ways of thinking will be a positive influence on your business.)

If you decide to dismiss women's holistic thinking, consider this: Suppose you've convinced your female consumers to bond with your product without giving them the full story. Suppose their relationship with your company or institution stops at product performance, and doesn't go all the way to Corporate Soul.

Now suppose something goes wrong with the product. Suppose an unavoidable defect is discovered, a recall is mandated, tampering occurs, or a consumer is just plain disappointed. Where does she turn for information, help, comfort, or some kind of restitution?

Certainly not to you. Who are you? No one she's ever had a relationship with before.

I'll tell you where she turns. To your competition.

The Five Ps Of Marketing

Women are driving a new millennial marketing model. Getting women to join your brand is not only about the traditional four "Ps" of marketing (sorry, MBAs). Product, Pricing, Promotion, and Place are not enough. *Today you need to add a fifth "P" to the marketing mix: Policy.*

Because things you would never have thought to focus on ten years ago *matter*. Issues that are normally banished to obscure corners of corporate communication *matter*. The things that management do *matter*. The things that the companies you do business with *matter*.

In other words: *Everything Matters.*

Because marketing to women today isn't just about value. It's about values.

What I'm suggesting is an EVEolved marketing model that women will respond to. Products that follow this model will rely less on standard marketing tools like commercials (the hype means nothing) and point-of-purchase materials (it's what's inside the package that matters). And the "badge value" of these products will come not from whether they were expensive, or exotic, or cool. The new "badge value" will be based on values like conscience, responsibility, openness.

Think of this new model as the *transparent brand*.

Transparency means inviting your female consumer to see all the way through your brand to the company behind it—back to its origins, its roots, its founder. Transparency means there is no room for inconsistency of mission, strategy, execution, and communication. Transparency means no secrets.

I was talking about this with Gail Evans, CNN Executive

Vice President, who added her own take on the subject: "Women care about integrity, but not in the sense of not telling a lie; more in the sense of understanding everything about a person or a product, including fallibilities. They want everything out there."

What are the "everythings" that women want to know? What is transparency made of? Beyond the quality of the products and services that you deliver, the components include:

- The personal ethics of your owners and managers.
- How you treat all your employees.
- How you treat women and minority employees.
- The number of women and minorities who hold corporate offices.
- How much money top executives make.
- What kind of perks top executives receive.
- The salary gap between the highest paid man and woman.
- How much money your CEO gives to political campaigns. And to which candidates.
- Who you give charitable donations to and how much.
- Your environmental record.
- The origin of the materials you source and how you source them.
- Your distribution policies (for instance, not opening locations in tough inner-city neighborhoods).
- The policies of your outside resources, like your bank and law firm.
- Whether you give reporters and consumers on-demand access to inspect your factories and offices.

The good news is, you don't have to rely on your product alone to create a joinable brand. Every other business component offers your company an opportunity to show your female consumers that this is, in fact, the kind of company she can live with.

This might sound like a dangerous amount of exposure.

Lifting the Corporate Veil

If Procter & Gamble didn't invent the "brand-as-hero" philosophy, it sure perfected it. With great success, of course. However, only the "star" products stand in the spotlight, never the backstage parent.

We're suggesting that it's time for P&G to step forward and show off the company behind the products. Start a campaign of corporate advertising. How many people outside P&G's corporate walls know, for instance, that the company runs a program asking the junior women to talk with the senior men to give male managers insight into the female perspective? Now that's an EVEolutionary idea.

Or that the company produces videos describing how top women executives balance home and work lives, to help younger women find their way? Or that female job satisfaction at P&G has risen 25% in the past five years?

This is great work. These programs would surely win applause from women consumers—if they knew about them.

If I were sitting next to P&G's CEO, Durk Jager, on a plane tomorrow, I'd tell him this: Given the fact that most of P&G's consumers are female, rethink your products-only strategy. Share your good works with your women consumers who really do care. You'll find that Everything Does Matter.

Who doesn't cringe at the thought of the klieg lights of public scrutiny shining on his or her every move? But in the end, the fact that Everything Matters actually turns out to be a very healthy (read: good for your business) thing.

Because if every company, every brand, every board member, and every brand manager believed that they had to be prepared to explain everything about their brand, believe me, their businesses would be better off for it.

If you think your female consumer doesn't look past the surface to read the fine (or even the not-so-fine) print, you might be surprised to learn that she's got a few questions for you. And be prepared. Women are likely to have noticed things about your brand that may raise some awkward questions.

"Why are your 800-number phone reps so rude?"

"How come Jay Leno was making fun of you last week?"

"How can you permit discriminatory practices by your franchisees?"

"What's up with that sex scandal concerning one of your division presidents?"

None of this is her business, you say? Well, she's made it her business. And if she doesn't like what she sees, it'll be bad for your business.

The Internet has taken access to a whole new level. Female consumers will be using it more and more to find out minutiae about a company. And to trade information with other consumers in a way that no corporate public relations program can control. So you'd better have a clean act. And shout about it. By creating a complete ethical biography in virtual space, a company is giving the female consumer what she feels she's entitled to know. Added benefit: If you get your ethical ingredients list cleaned up, she'll not only buy your brand, she'll buy your stock.

Howard Schultz, CEO of Starbucks, put it succinctly: "If people believe they share values with a company, they will stay loyal."

Just around the FutureCorner is a dramatically different world for marketers and consumers alike. Imagine . . .

- If Arm & Hammer laundry detergent promised that, for every box of soap powder a woman buys, the parent company, Church and Dwight, will make a contribution to a college fund for the customer's children or to a retirement fund (or favorite charity). The savings fund would mature in X-number of years, at which point the loyal consumer would receive a hefty check from the company. What incentive to stay loyal, what an inspiration for company and customer alike.

- If there were such a Web site as Boardmem.com, where stockholders and customers can interact during the actual Board-of-Directors' meetings. Certainly beats those impossible-to-read proxy statements. Or what if there existed Factorycam.com, where we can actually watch the way products are made around the world. Wouldn't it be reassuring to see that the sweatshirts or pairs of running shoes or plastic computer toys (and who knows what else) were being made by a grown-up, and not a skinny pre-teen. Or maybe this issue of child

Formula for Product Success

Don't be surprised if a woman demands that you include an "ethical ingredients" list on every product and service you offer. She wants an X-ray of your corporate practices *before* she buys.

You may already be telling her through well-placed and well-documented public relations programs about how you don't do anything to punch through the ozone layer or stagnate a pond. And that you grant generous paternity as well as maternity leaves. And that you believe in helping out shelters for battered women—with money and man/woman-hours.

As we've said, she's really interested in knowing all these details, and more, much more: Do your CEO or other executives belong to any of those still basically "segregated" or "male-only" clubs that accept a few token members to get around the law? Do you offer creative solutions to assist your employees in balancing their work and life demands?

It takes more than a tiny mention in a company newsletter or business magazine. Organic food marketers have tried to do the right thing—and they tell us so. We want full disclosure about no chemicals on the plants or in the soil. We want reassurance that no strange "natural"

continued . . .

pesticides are used either, or certainly that the tomatoes were not tampered with to be bigger, brighter red, firmer, and fleshier. Good news: Frito-Lay has announced that they would not be using any genetically-engineered corn in their products.

Brands like Annie's Homegrown Mac n' Cheese and Stonyfield Farm Yogurts print their statements right on their packages, detailing their commitments to causes such as scholarships and efforts to save this planet. Of course, the best example of a company with a conscience is Ben & Jerry's Ice Cream, which gives a percentage of profits to good causes and states its ethics on its cartons. Saying, "We oppose Recombinant Bovine Growth Hormone. The family farmers who supply our milk and cream pledge not to treat their cows with rBGH." And, "Bleaching paper with chlorine releases dioxins, substances the EPA identifies as some of the most toxic ever created. This new brown-on-the-inside 'eco-pint' is part of our plan to do less harm to the planet." Now that the owners are selling the company, they've put a condition on the sale: That the purchasers pledge to continue the good works.

So why can't more mainstream marketers let their policies be known at point-of-purchase?

Women want to know.

labor should be addressed head on, right now. A photo of the workers at the factory where the products are made, and a few facts about working conditions could be put right on the tag or box.

• How about an EverythingMatters.com—a new Web site that monitors companies and their businesses, from many points of view. Because what is highest priority to you isn't necessarily Numero Uno to someone else, this site will analyze and assess companies from different perspectives. Ratings could be grouped into categories, or you should be able to punch in any one of your affil-

A Breath of Fresh Air?

Women, especially, would love Honda's sponsorship of the Broderick Cup—the Heisman Trophy of women's collegiate athletics.

Never heard of it? That's because Honda hasn't talked about it.

According to Paul Sellers, National Advertising Manager of American Honda, "We support the programs we do because we feel it is our responsibility as a guest in this country who is striving for citizenship, not because it's a public relations opportunity. We've been its [the Broderick Cup] sole sponsor for the past eleven years."

Memo to Mr. Sellers: Start airing your clean laundry in public!

iations, from the Girl Scouts to AARP, to see how a company measures up to the specified group's mission statement.

- Wall Street should start a system to value stocks on an "EM" (Everything Matters) index, in addition to the traditional P/E (Price/Earnings) ratio.

- Corporate Ethicist should become the hot new profession. Prizes and grants could be established (à la Nobel, Pulitzer, Ford Foundation) to reward individuals and businesses that have outstanding ethical records. Maybe businesses could be issued a renewable Ethics License, along with a Consumer Rating System, compiled from a company's ethical record, with up-to-date data collected over the Internet.

- If the experience of the tobacco industry (did you see that movie *The Insider*?) spills over into the liquor business—then any products that could be addictive are potential targets for big-time lawyers with big-time profits in their sights. This may well be the critical moment to win the allegiance of female consumers before drinking becomes as stigmatized as smoking. (Since people have to step outside to light up, will we also have to sneak out to sip a beer?) The media spotlight has focused on the tragic alcohol abuse at the college level recently, which results in young women being the victims of rape or car crashes. What if Seagram's took the lead in helping college officials combat this serious problem?

A Drink-O-Meter could be developed to instantly measure a student's body mass and corresponding alcohol tolerance level. Significant incentives could be offered to fraternities, sororities, clubs, and other social and living groups in order to get a pledge against binge drinking. And why doesn't the beverage industry get behind the development of a foolproof breath analyzer that locks a car's ignition if the driver's alcohol level is excessive? Rather than waiting for car manufacturers to develop the device, the alcohol people should be the ones that step out in front and say, "Don't misuse our products"—and mean it.

Ditto for any other products that contribute in any way to the shortening of life, directly or not. What about high-fat foods? Next?

- Consumers will demand to benefit from the consolidated buying power of the companies they support. For example, if Ford gets a special discount from HP because of the volume of equipment it buys (even for the employees' homes), then a woman who buys a Ford Explorer should benefit from the same consideration. When Everything Matters, companies should extend themselves in every direction for their female customers.

- Time Matters. Women prefer a live person instead of a disembodied voice-mail response, but who doesn't? (The trick is, when they tell you, "Hit #1 if you have a touchtone phone," ignore it. An operator will usually get on the line.) Who has time to listen to MovieFone with its high-decibel male voice and endless requests to push this, push that, hold for this, that. And if you make one mistake, what to do? Start all over again?

It should be that the longer a woman spends on a phone line waiting for information, the more she should save on her next purchase. Today's technology could deliver this—for example, if you call Dell, you would punch in your customer ID number, and for every minute you wait, you get dollars off the next Dell accessory you purchase.

At BrainReserve, under the umbrella of the Trend, 99 Lives, we talk about the incredible importance of being service-oriented. But look at what happened to me one day in December. I went into a shop on Madison Avenue in New York City called Portantina (blocks from my house) and bought a beautiful (and expensive) Christmas present of Venetian glasses. Since I was rushing between meetings, I inquired whether these fragile glasses could be wrapped. The person helping me grumbled, "It will take a long time." So I said, "Okay, but then would you deliver them to my always-open office?" She replied, "If there wasn't a time frame, I could do it." I said, "May I speak to the owner about this?" She replied, "I *am* the owner."

My question: How does that store expect to build a loyal customer base?

Doesn't she know that women like service? Need service? Demand service? Or they don't go back.

There are endless stories about companies who need some EVEolutionary conscience-raising. Like:

Dayton Hudson (now Target). Any definition of Chicago has to include—along with the Cubs, the Sears Tower, and that mean wind off the lake—the Marshall Field's department store. And any definition of Marshall Field's has to include its famous candy, the smooth but bitingly refreshing Frango mint. (One bit of useless information: The candy was first sold in 1929 as the Franco Mint, but its name was changed in 1939 when Franco became dictator of Spain.)

Suddenly in March 1999, Dayton Hudson, Marshall Field's owner since 1990, announced that the store's on-premise candy kitchen would be closed. Boom, that was it. Generations of families with delicious memories of the aroma of freshly-made mints could do nothing but rage. At the *Chicago Tribune*, the story was front page news, and one columnist suggested that the leaders of Dayton Hudson had suffered a "brain melt."

The way Dayton Hudson handled the closing fed the fury. The Frango employees—some with 20 years on the job—were tossed out without warning. Many were black, Latino, and Asian women. The next day, some started a picket line in front of the store. Now, this is the same Dayton Hudson that replaced the store's signature green shopping bag. Public protest brought back the bag—but not the workers.

In its own defense, Dayton Hudson claimed it tried hard to preserve many of Marshall Field's traditions. But *talk* wasn't enough for the store's women customers.

• • •

For years, we've been bombarded with commercials touting Dial-10-10 for cheaper long-distance services, offered by "upstart" companies, like Lucky Dog (AT&T).

Sure, you can save money—if you study all the fine print. The details differ from company to company, but here's the reality: Despite those promises of 10 cents a minute, some 10-10 plans charge considerably more if you call during the week at certain specified times/days. If you're a real yakker and your calls last 20 minutes or more, a 10-10 plan may be a good deal. But if your calls are short, you'll end up paying a minimum fee.

But I think the 10-10 providers are about to face the EVE-olutionary music. First of all, instead of creating cool, hip aliases, certain big guys should just try to offer more EVEolved options. Same goes for other industries, such as a division of Miller Brewery coming out with Red Dog beer. (What is with all these hounds?)

You can't hide behind a phony logo. EVEolution won't let you.

• • •

But other companies do get it. They make Everything Matter.

We read in *BrandWeek* about a survey that showed that women are more likely today to buy a holiday gift from stores or companies that do good deeds (up 27% from 1997).

For instance, Lands' End donated $50,000 worth of clothing to the Grace Children's Foundation and arranged to ship the goods (courtesy of United Airlines) to children in Chinese orphanages. And Target hosts a sweepstakes where customers can win $2,000 for themselves and $2,000 for their favorite school—every single day. Sears, too, has given $1 million to Gilda's Club and during the holidays, donates something to that charity from every purchase made with a Sears card. That Matters.

Remember we said that if something goes wrong, if a customer is disappointed, something should be done? Paul Clayton, President of Burger King North America took out a full-page ad to apologize to his customers, entitled: "Why I am not the most popular parent in America." He explained to thousands of disappointed kids and their Moms that demand for Pokémon toys and trading cards far exceeded supplies. Clayton ended his published letter by thanking customers for their loyalty and saying "Sorry." That's a royal attitude, Burger King.

Whole Foods Markets, Inc., based in Austin, TX, also "gets it." The world's largest chain of natural-foods supermarkets, it has sales of more than $500 million a year and profits that are twice the industry average. At Whole Foods' biggest revenue producer, the Bread & Circus store in Cambridge, MA, things Matter. Example: When an order for a special birthday cake was misplaced, a replacement was quickly baked, decorated, and then rushed to the customer's home. The logic is: "If we screw up someone's birthday, they'll tell all their friends at dinner. But if we screw it up and fix it, they'll tell all their friends that, too."

Whole Foods sells healthy foods that have been produced in environment-friendly ways. They don't have an organic "section"—the whole place is filled with organic products. And they're zealous about recycling.

These things Matter to women.

Some other examples of Whole Foods' EVEolutionary approach include: Its nickel-per-bag rebate for customers who use cloth totes; taking the customers on tours of farms where their produce is grown; giving 5% of after-tax profits to environmental nonprofits—more than 1,500 of them at last count (you'll find them all listed on the Whole Foods Web site (wholefoods. com.); and urging their employees to volunteer thousands of hours toward local clean-up projects.

When it comes to open communication, Whole Foods is off the chart. Workers are regularly updated on store and company sales and profit margins, and on the salaries and bonuses paid every individual—top to bottom—at every store.

According to John P. Mackey, who was a founder of the company in 1980 and now serves as Chairman/CEO, the open-salary policy sparks disagreements. Workers want to know why so-and-so is being paid more than they are. His response: "If you accomplish what this person has accomplished, I'll pay you that, too."

No one enjoys such conversations, but they can have huge benefits. Mackey puts it this way: "If you're trying to create a high-trust organization, an organization where people are all-for-one and one-for-all, you can't have secrets."

Whole Foods actually cedes to team members the right to

hire-and-fire. Store managers can recommend an applicant, but the hiring doesn't become official until approved by two-thirds of the team members after a 30-day trial period. When they turn down the manager's choice, Mackey says, they are "taking ownership of their team."

One dismayed candidate who didn't make the cut came to his manager—and heard the plain truth: "Three people on the team had to talk to you about having your hands in your pockets and leaning against counters in front of customers."

Whole Foods employees have high standards.

High enough to match those of their women customers.

Enough said.

Another Everything Matters business: Brightpoint, Inc. This company, a leading provider of services for the global wireless communications industry, started a program named "Call to Protect." This project centers on re-programming old, out-dated cell phones to dial only 911. The phones are distributed to women who are at high risk of being battered or abused, so that they can call for instant help. Based on this, Brightpoint should start branding its name (like Intel): a welcome addition to the EVEolutionary world.

Who else lives and breathes the concept that absolutely Everything Matters? Who was seemingly born to champion the Eighth EVEolutionary Truth?

Clue: It's a division of General Motors.

I know what you're thinking. "Oh, God, not another Saturn case history!"

Entire forests have been cut down to make paper for the articles and chapters in marketing books praising this four-wheeled phenomenon.

There couldn't possibly be anything left to say about Saturn's successful launch or its unique marketing strategy.

Well, maybe just one more thing.

In all the dissection of the Saturn marketing model, nobody has pointed out what, to me, is the most important factor in its success. *Women love Saturn.*

Maybe it's because I've been obsessing on this subject for the last few years, but it seems pretty obvious that the way Saturn behaves—both as a brand and as a company—is perfectly designed to attract women.

And this in an industry that does a really good job of ignoring and offending women. I can't resist relaying horrifying stories from two turn-of-this-century meetings I had with the Marketing Directors of two huge car companies (one American, one Japanese). Both acknowledged strong sales to women, yet after hearing me explain the Truths of EVEolution, the director of the American outfit said in front of a conference room filled with women reporters: "Advocacy groups. I'm sick of advocacy groups: Hispanics, blacks, women, gays. They all buy my cars anyway."

The second guy, an American director of the Japanese company, wasn't so John Rocker-ish, merely dismissing the particular needs of women buyers: "Look, we don't thread our marketing through a needle that way." Some big needle—50% of the market.

Conversely, Saturn is such a highly EVEolved company, I've been tempted to cite it as an example for each one of the Truths.

But it's the Everything Matters Truth that Saturn has really mastered. It goes a long way in explaining how the brand has utterly captivated the female car buyer. To start with, let me start with its chief, Cynthia Trudell, President. In a *U.S. News & World Report* article, Trudell was quoted as saying, "If I have to get involved in the heavy-duty, top-down decision making, something is wrong." It went on, "For her, managing means working on relationships and understanding 'interdependency.'" That's pure EVEolution.

Take the Saturn theme line: "A different kind of company. A different kind of car." When is the last time you heard a car—

or any brand—lead with a focus on the company *behind* the star product? That's a transparent brand.

From the very beginning, Saturn urged the car buyer to look beyond the hardware to the behavior of the company and the buying experience—something women are naturally inclined to do anyway.

The transparent brand is beautifully symbolized right there in the Saturn showroom. What's that cross-sectioned, cutaway car doing on the main floor? It's screaming, "Hey, as long as you're kicking the tires, go ahead and look at everything, from the engine to how the polymer door panels work."

Then there's the experience of buying a Saturn. From the beginning, the brand revealed its EVEolutionary leanings with a no-haggle policy, the famous "no-dicker sticker." (Meanwhile, the rest of Detroit is still arguing over fake imagery, nuts and bolts and price and miles-per-gallon. Yawn.)

Here's an example of a piece of corporate behavior that's so powerful, it almost defines the brand. With this one small step, Saturn broke ranks with an industry that had institutionalized the awful buying experience—especially awful for women. In fact, research shows that a woman typically pays 28% more than a man pays for the same car.

The more you look at the Saturn strategy, the more you see the Everything Matters scaffolding supporting all that the company says and does.

Ironically, even Saturn wasn't prepared for the female consumer's response. Apparently neither was its ad agency.

Steve Morrissey, account director at Publicis & Hal Riney, admits: "We were really surprised. I mean, I knew we were resonating well with women, but when I first saw the breakdown of the gender statistics, I thought, 'Holy cow! Nobody has done that.' "

Saturn's got it all: A transparent brand, a consistently articulated mission, integrity from product to retail floor to Corporate

Soul. This EVEolutionary Truth could have told them: Women would fall in love.

Then there's the case of the marketer who was bad, but made good. Nike has done a great job of learning from their sneakers-made-in-sweatshops crisis. Maria Eitel, a Nike VP who reports to Chairman Phil Knight, formed a group called the Corporate Responsibility Division in 1998. At Nike, good ethics has become good business—or, as Maria says, "I like to say that I don't run the Feel Good Division; I run a piece of this business."

There is nothing gratuitous or unnecessary about the programs Nike has put in place—from education opportunities for factory workers in Vietnam—to a commitment to eliminating pollutant-causing PVCs in their products—to a recycling program that sells shredded sneakers as footing for horseback riding rings. Maria knows that "having a strong record on corporate responsibility issues is an essential piece of connecting with the consumer, especially women, teachers, coaches, and parents who are much more activist on a lot of these issues." Good for you, Maria. Better for you, Nike.

One other thing: Nike has learned that women like to express their opinions. Now they can do it right on their Nikes. Consumers can choose their own colors and add an 8-character name or slogan to customize their running or cross-training shoes for just $10 more.

Shouldn't other major clothing manufacturers see the truth in this Truth? How about Levi's, Tommy Hilfiger, or Guess? letting consumers customize their jeans with their names or beliefs?

Any marketer of any brand in any industry can learn something from these EVEolved marketers. And from the Everything Matters principle.

As we discovered when we took on the challenge to re-reign the *Queen Mary*.

Case Study: *The Queen Mary*

In the saturated sea of Southern California entertainment options, the great ship was adrift. Since 1967, when the city of Long Beach, CA, bought the *Queen Mary* from the Cunard Line, the ship had been operating as a day-tripper attraction, hotel, and small-convention center. Under the city's ownership the grande dame had been floundering.

In 1993, Joseph F. Prevratil leased the *Queen Mary* for 66 years. He had already begun a major facelift on the ship and its surroundings when he came to BrainReserve for advice in 1998. What he was looking for: Guidance for positioning the *Queen Mary* for a future of growth. Along with Joe's core business team and his consultant, Norris Bernstein, we set out to learn what matters about the *Queen Mary*. We collectively discovered one overarching message: *Everything* Matters.

In the age of EVEolution, women are still the ones to make the family vacation plans, set up business events, and arrange every outing from their children's class getaway to the senior citizens' spring fling. Building the *Queen Mary* brand meant attracting women-share by paying attention to detail. Every detail.

We knew, without question, that every element of the onboard experience had to be under control. Nothing could be left to chance—if the *Queen Mary* wanted to impress her female visitors.

By consulting with our TalentBank experts, and conducting TrendTreks to other entertainment sites all over the United States and Europe, we learned that the *Queen Mary* had an invaluable equity to leverage—her fabulous history. It could drive every single aspect of the *Queen Mary* experience.

Here's her background: The ship, launched in 1935, set new standards for luxury in the four years she sailed between Southampton, England, and New York. Her world changed during World War II when the gallant *Queen*, painted a camouflage gray, ferried troops, weapons, and food across the Atlantic. Known as the "Gray Ghost," she was at the top of the Nazi High Command's hit list. At war's end, thousands of American soldiers made the voyage home on the *Queen*. It took almost a full year to return her to her former glory, but she once again became the yardstick against which all luxury liners were judged.

The lineage of the *Queen Mary* literally pulsed with passion. Not only was she steeped in the champagne and starlight of a bygone age, but her decks had witnessed the dreams, fears, and courage of young men sent to war. BrainReserve's summation: The *Queen Mary* captured a unique mix of nostalgia, romance, and heroism. This was the positioning against which we measured every recommendation.

We knew that we had to convincingly return both the passengers and the crew to the standards of that bygone era. It was a tricky charge: To make everyone feel part of the ship's resplendent history.

The target audience: Female.

The lesson: Do it right or don't do it.

The Truth: Make Everything Matter.

We advised that the *Queen Mary* create an experience that will go beyond everyday tourism. Visitors should feel enveloped by the past—to stroll the decks and enjoy the opulence—hearing a string quartet playing, dining like royalty, being pampered by service rarely seen these days.

It was imperative that all employees know the Ship's history so well that it belonged to them. They should be able to enthrall visitors with stories of the great personalities who sailed on the *Queen*—Winston Churchill, Fred Astaire, Lady Astor—or with tales of the Gray Ghost's perilous wartime crossings, evoking memories of doused lights, hushed conversations and unspoken fears of Nazi U-boats.

Then there was the question of the service itself. As befits a vessel whose mission is "First Class, Unsurpassed," the service needed to be upgraded to formal, yet friendly. We proposed borrowing a maxim from the stately Greenbriar Hotel in West Virginia: "We Are Ladies and Gentlemen Serving Ladies and Gentlemen."

Employees are also encouraged to talk to passengers and more importantly, listen to what they have to say. They are then expected to report back to management on ways to improve the ship's hospitality.

We suggested to the staff, in order to truly understand the mission of the *Queen Mary* (and management's commitment to it), that for a few nights they should become passengers themselves. Sleeping in a cabin on fine linen. Dining in the salon on sumptuous foods. Immersing themselves in the total passenger experience. What better way for employees to get a feel for the *Queen Mary*?

They would then know firsthand if any detail wasn't up to snuff—service, quality, authenticity.

We then turned our sights to finding new sources of growth and profit. First, we had an idea that would allow visitors to obtain what we call a "memory trace." The ship should open a museum shop on-board—selling everything from *Queen Mary* postcards, videos, and books on the history of ocean liners, to CDs of songs of the sea. No ticky-tacky tchotchkes.

The first impression the *Queen Mary* makes at dockside came under our scrutiny. Since the Long Beach waterfront surrounding the ship was nothing but a parking lot, it needed a plan of extensive development. The Cunard Line (again) and its owner, Carnival, have agreed to become strategic partners—making plans for the site to be the portal to the sea-faring world, docking its cruise ships right there in Long Beach instead of Los Angeles. Also in the works: Dick Clark's American Music Experience, themed restaurants, interesting retail shops, and an upscale, small landside hotel. What a difference.

We figured that "If God is in the details," the *Queen Mary* should have her very own bible. BrainReserve's Senior Consultant Tiffany Vasilchik worked closely together with the *Queen*'s BRIT (BrainReserve Integration Team), and that's how the "Image Bible" was created. This 24-page book recounts some of the legends and gives the guidelines for continuing her greatness. By setting a tone of missionary zeal for continuing the ship's exemplary style and tradition of quality, the Image Bible commands that everyone *must* do her or his part to ensure a superior passenger experience.

How? By accepting, as a sacred trust, the proposition that *Everything* Matters.

BrainReserve and the *Queen Mary* management team decided to recast the Image Bible as "The *Queen Mary* Compass." But this Compass isn't just another to-do list for employees. It promises "First Class, Unsurpassed" employment through training, career opportunities, and benefits. With the staff primed for peak performance, attention-to-detail became management's model. From the way the staff addresses its guests, wears its uniforms (designed by Stan Herman), erases the stains on the carpet, leaves the shampoo in the bathrooms, twirls the butter, sets the typeface on the menus, shines the brass rails, makes the glassware and china sparkle—Everything Matters.

The legend has been restored. And it is now an experience fit for a Queen. In every(Thing Matters) detail.

• • •

Women are demanding customers, and are becoming more so as the EVEolution marches on. From measures as lofty as values and morals, to those as prosaic as cleanliness and courtesy, Everything Matters to women.

To start you on your way to practicing the Everything Matters Truth, ask yourself:

- If my consumer knew every single detail about my brand, from the process to the product, would I still be selling as much of it?

- Am I doing as much as I personally can to better every aspect of my brand? Can I sleep at night?
- Does my brand have a soul? And can my consumer see right into it?
- Does she like what she sees?

When you come to realize the power of the transparent brand, you suddenly see that the opportunities for gaining her trust and keeping it are infinite.

Just remember: Everything Matters.

And Matters.

And Matters.

And Matters.

And Matters.

And Matters.

And Matters.

Chapter 9

A BrainReserve Future Case Study:

The Truths Can Set You Free:

Revlon, Reborn

U p till now, I've been writing this book as a kind of personal letter to my readers. But now I'd like to expand my audience just a bit. To include one more person: Ron Perelman. The reason I'm writing to Ron (along with you) is because he has taken one of the great global brands and hasn't managed it to its greatest potential. *Fortune* (2/21/2000) listed it #2 on its "America's Least Admired Companies" list. Total return for 1999 is –51.5%. A 1999 third-quarter loss of $165 million, compared to net earnings of $12.7 million in 1998; and in the midst of this raging bull market, Revlon's stock has been at a low of around $8 per share. No small accomplishment.

Revlon has lost its moorings, lost emotional contact with its consumers, lost touch with the way women feel, shop, and interact with the brands in their lives. As a result, Revlon has lost market share and money. Do you detect an echo here? Lost, lost, lost. The question is: Can the magic be found, found, found? Can Revlon be recharged, restored, remade as an EVEolutionary model?

The short answer is . . . yes. And what I'd like to do, in the rest of this brief chapter, is take you through an accelerated BrainReserve project. How would we EVEolutionize Revlon and undo the damage of the last ten years? Where would we start and what would we do if Ron Perelman hired us? Now some of you may be wondering why am I giving one of the richest men in America free advice. It's not Ron Perelman I'm trying to help— it's you. Because by seeing the EVEolutionary Truths applied to a real live business, you'll be able to better understand how to apply them to your company or your brand.

First, let's take a look at how Revlon became Revlon. It was started by three guys, it's true, but one of them was a marketing genius who had an intuitive understanding of women that was remarkable. Charles Revson built Revlon by practicing many of the EVEolutionary Truths in a way that came perfectly naturally to him. In Andrew Tobias's definitive biography, *Fire and Ice*, he writes that "If you were a bank president or an advertising hotshot or a potential supplier, you couldn't get him on the phone. But if you were a woman with a Revlon lipstick that smeared, you got through to him like that. 'The reason I talk to them,' he used to say of such consumer calls, 'is that they are the real boss.' "

A simple idea. A basic Truth. But how many male executives of companies that target women would get on the phone for a woman with a problem? None that I know.

Revson also practiced one of the Truths that I've written

about and that I believe in with all my heart and soul. Everything Matters was a philosophy that Revson lived by. As Tobias writes, "He set up a full-scale laboratory and sophisticated quality controls long before anyone else in the industry had them; he recalled batches of products long before . . . product recalls and 'consumerism' were invented."

And here's a wonderful example of putting consumers before profits. Tobias tells us that "After the successful launch of Sheer Radiance makeup base, Charles began to have second thoughts. 'It could be better,' he said. Right in the middle of a promotion he made them empty every bottle in the house, wash them all, and refill them with an improved formula. Sheer Radiance was out of stock for three months; Revlon lost a small fortune. But he didn't care. He thought the product was a little too frosty, and that it had to be a bit oilier so that women could have more time to put it on their faces."

That's the kind of loyalty to your customers that makes them loyal to you.

Revson also found an absolutely brilliant way of putting his products in the Peripheral Vision of his customers. He invented the idea of color promotions, creating themes for his products and building events and cultural buzz (back when bees were the only thing that buzzed) around them. Before Revlon, products were stuck in the bottle; Charles liberated them, and splattered them into our lives with joy and exuberance. In 1945, more than a half century ago, Revlon introduced "Fatal Apple" as "the most tempting color since Eve winked at Adam." Although the language is somewhat dated, the techniques are fully Peripheral and totally early EVEolutionary. Yes, there was advertising. But there was much more. As Andy Tobias writes, "department stores were furnished with window displays; the Revlon showroom was decorated to match . . . an elaborate press party featured not only Maurice the Mindreader, but also a snake and snake charmer . . . a hollow gold apple door prize from Cartier, a grove of miniature apple trees from the Washington State apple growers' association, and fashions from Forever Eve."

Revson understood the need to reach women through a series of contact points, a cascade of connections, a multitude of moments. Let me give you one more example that's a classic of Peripheral marketing. It's the Fire and Ice promotion from the fall of 1952. Revson surrounded women with his two-page ad that posed fifteen questions, asking "ARE YOU MADE FOR FIRE AND ICE?" Some of the questions were, "If tourist flights were running, would you take a trip to Mars?" "Do you sometimes feel that other women resent you?" "Do you think any man really understands you?"

Again, some of the questions are quaintly old-fashioned. But Revson was onto something huge—linking his product to the emotional lives of women. Elevating the dialogue. Identifying his products with feelings and desires that were difficult to express directly in the rigidity of the early Eisenhower years.

The notion chimed with women. Nine thousand window displays featured Fire and Ice. Tobias writes that "Fire and Ice beauty contests were conducted around the country. Disc jockeys and newspaper editors were sent questionnaires . . . Twenty-two hotels, from the Plaza in New York to the Cornhusker in Lincoln, Nebraska, were introduced to stage Fire and Ice preview parties . . . Dave Garroway gave the Fire and Ice quiz to one of his secretaries on *The Today Show*."

Just think. More money is spent today on cosmetics marketing than ever before. But when was the last time you can remember a brand or an idea capturing the country's imagination like that? I can't. And with the current Revlon management, it's not likely to happen at all—unless they toss out their current marketing plans and e-mail this chapter around the company.

Now, let's move to today. Unlike Revson, Ron Perelman's over-riding passion isn't the cosmetics business and each female consumer. Back in 1995, *Business Week* recognized this when it wrote about Perelman, "His vocation and avocation is collecting companies, and he is driven by desire to acquire and own them."

By ignoring the needs of real women while marketing to them, Revlon has been put at risk. If you've read any of the business press, you know the story.

Job cuts. Factory closings. Downgraded debt. Changeovers at the top—Revlon lost six-year-veteran Kathy Dwyer as President of Revlon Consumer Products, USA. No wonder *Women's Wear Daily* was blunt and brutal, saying that Revlon "lost credibility with both investors and retailers after twelve months of dismal financial results." And *Cosmetics International* keened, "Revlon appears to be coming apart at the seams." Even more amazingly, this collapse has taken place during America's incredible economic boom—when more women had more money to spend on more cosmetics than ever before.

What happened? A series of misjudgments, all growing out of a failure to understand EVEolution.

- Obviously, Revlon's marketing team didn't understand that women's identities were changing, that the days of building a brand merely by hiring the hottest models-of-the-moment were coming to an end. Brands like M.A.C. and Bobbie Brown appealed to more affluent women by presenting a more off-the-glamour-track story. Much to the delight of makeup artists and younger women, M.A.C. satirized the supermodel mold by gleefully hiring transvestite RuPaul and anti-fashion provocateur k.d. lang.

  Eventually, Revlon's nemesis, Estée Lauder, was wise enough to invest in M.A.C. and Bobbie Brown. That was smart and revealing about the Lauder Company's perspective on the future. Lauder knew enough to understand talent and fresh thinking whenever it blossomed—inside their company or outside it.

  Meanwhile, Revlon still had its overly mascaraed eyes firmly fixed on the rear-view mirror. How many Revlon ads ever featured a working woman or a Mom with kids? Or, that no-no of an older woman with laugh lines and life-defining wrinkles? Like Banana Republic did with silvery-haired Sigrid Rothe; or Donna Karan who shows craggy faced, 60-plus Benedetta Barzini; and Estée Lauder who pulled its featured model from the 1970s out of retirement, the 54-year-old Karen Graham. When would a Revlon message ever connect with the way women really live, think, and feel?

Hopefully, soon.

- The Revlon team must not understand that the old hard-edged glamour has been replaced by a softer sensibility. While the fashion industry was moving to the drama and subtlety of black-and-white photography, Revlon advertising stayed with aggressive four-color and seemed imprisoned in a time warp. I took a look at the current *Vogue* just before this book went to press, and guess what? There was a traditional Revlon ad, with all those perfect, unattainable women.

And there is Sephora, the aforementioned store from Paris that's been transplanted to American soil. Its premise will change the way women will view and choose cosmetics: Instead of being segregated by brand, all moisturizers are together, then all lipsticks, then all nail polishes—allowing women to see which item, rather than which trademark they prefer. Sephora features no women at all in their ad, just two beautiful, watercolor ink blots. Suggestive, emotional, inviting. What better crystallization of the differences: Of old imagery vs. the future.

- Revlon didn't understand the phenomenon that was elevating taste levels, bringing "class to the mass" in category after category. While brands like Calvin Klein and

Hold Everything and Starbucks and Ikea were attracting women with a jolt of style, under-the-radar sophistication, and cultural irony, Revlon is stuck in its old formula.

- Revlon didn't totally understand that innovation was just the beginning of a relationship with women—not the end. So its ColorStay lipstick, which was a breakthrough, never took the next step to become the brand that went beyond color-stay and literally "stayed" with women throughout their days, throughout their lives. Revlon "line-extended" it into new products, but never "life-extended" it.

- Revlon didn't really understand the Uber-Truth that women were looking for brands to *join, not just to buy.*

- And Revlon didn't understand that the public attention focused on Ronald Perelman's personal life (his public divorces, the custody tug-of-war and the lavish lifestyle)—tends to spread a toxic cloud over the brand. Women know too much about this one side of him, and they don't like what they know. (Although through mutual Hampton friends, I have heard he does have other nicer, funnier, private sides.)

So, having said all that, what's to be done? Can Revlon be saved? Or is it destined for the corporate archive, the once-great-brand garage sale? I believe it can be saved and made successful again, but only with a bold and radical re-direction. So hang on— it's going to be a fascinating EVEolutionary ride.

The first thing that Relvon has to do is stop thinking of itself as just being in the "cosmetics" business. It needs to change from a company that's only about selling the top layer of a woman's beauty to a company that celebrates the underlying beauty of being a woman.

That is a major paradigm shift.

What exactly does it mean when we say that Revlon needs to celebrate the underlying beauty of being a woman? It means that Revlon can, should, and *must* address the richness and totality of a woman's life:

The beauty of self-confidence
The beauty of motherhood
The beauty of being married
The beauty of being single
The beauty of aging
The beauty of learning
The beauty of remembering
The beauty of reconciliation
The beauty of coping
The beauty of friendship
The beauty of starting a business
The beauty of EVEolution

Think about the implications of this shift. Suddenly, Revlon is the emotional center of a woman's life. Suddenly, Revlon isn't just about cosmetic color on the outside, but about the colors of our lives on the inside. Just like Nike isn't about marketing to a woman's feet (it's about confidence, conquering), Revlon won't be about marketing to a woman's face.

It's a Revlon-olution!

A reborn, revved-up Revlon can reach women on all these dimensions by applying the EVEolutionary Truths to its current and future businesses. Let me take you through some applications of the Truths to see how they work.

Revlon can celebrate the beauty of being a woman through the *First Truth: Connecting Your Consumers to Each Other Connects Them to Your Brand*. It can bring women together around their needs, their life-stages, their goals. Why can't Revlon, with the equity that resides in its name, give the women's sites a run for their money, and create the place on the Web where women gather together and share their hopes and fears and dreams? And beauty tips.

Why can't Revlon sponsor a new kind of beauty pageant—focusing on beauty from within? Where a woman's artistic or architectural or archaeological interests are the basis for the competition rather than her face, her figure, and her ability to yodel and answer a few save-the-world questions.

And why can't Revlon become the facilitator of women's support groups (job-training/assertiveness-training/even weight management)? Going into the inner cities (all over the world) to help young girls (and boys) polish their images for the road to success. The brand that becomes known for helping people overcome their shortfalls becomes the brand that builds through the new millennium.

As in the *Second Truth: If You're Marketing to One of Her Lives, You're Missing All the Others*, Revlon should market to a woman's many lives, and by doing so, it will become a many-faceted brand. Throughout this book, I've talked about the ways in which a company or a brand can become the key that unlocks the many portals of a woman's life—with all its richness and complexities. Revlon, up until now, has limited its potential by constraining itself to what she carries in her bag or stocks in her bathroom.

Now think about the world that lies beyond and the possibilities are endless. Start with her workplace. Revlon is just about invisible on the job—whether she works in a dot-com, a Fortune 500 company, or at home. I remember that when I first started working in advertising, the coffee wagon was a fixture in downtown offices. The elevator would open, the cart would roll out, its bell would ring and a social situation was born. It wasn't as much about the coffee or the Danish, as the opportunity to take a mind-break and chitchat. What a terrific opportunity for Revlon to bring this tradition back with a Revlon wagon. One that would not just offer the best coffee and pastries, but could sell Revlon cosmetics, pantyhose, Slim•Fast®, and other things that work-focused women want but don't have the time to shop for during the day.

Another workplace opportunity is for Revlon to identify itself with women's health. I have long believed that company Intranets are an under-utilized communications pathway, and here's a way for it to really work harder for women—and their employers. Revlon, in partnership with other major employers, could take the responsibility of delivering women's health information on various topics, such as cancer or stress or lupus, through the installed Intranets.

Here's what it would look like. Say that you're a woman who works at Ford, and you need information about hip replacement for a parent, or asthma for a child, or you need to learn about calcium and bone loss for yourself. Before Revlon's innovation, you were at the mercy of the Internet, where there's tons of health information, but it takes tons and tons of time to find it. Instead, you log on to the Ford Intranet and click the icon that says "Revlon Health Link." You're brought to a site that aggregates the best health content on the Web—in one place. The latest information, insights from the best doctors, connects to the latest researchers. Access to caregivers and support groups.

Everyone wins. Ford is happy, because they're offering a major benefit that saves on sick days and strengthens loyalty. Employees are delighted. And Revlon becomes a more loved, trusted, and powerful brand.

One last Multiple-Lives thought: Have you spent much time at Kinkos? I have. More than 75% of the customers, in my experience, are women. Small business owners, college students, you name it. Why isn't Revlon marketing to the Multiple Lives of these women, with a special Revlon kiosk at the thousands of Kinkos locations across the country?

Revlon will celebrate the beauty of being a woman by Anticipating a woman's needs as she moves through the arc of her life. Just imagine the opportunities if Revlon adhered to the *Third Truth: If She Has to Ask, It's Too Late* and started to think of itself as a company dedicated to what she needs next?

Take financial services. I've talked a lot in this book about the opportunities here. Since 50% of all marriages end in divorce, I see a huge co-branding opportunity for Revlon and one of the large financial institutions. What about holding a seminar (real or virtual) for brides-to-be that would cover different areas a woman will need for her new life, from a beauty makeover to relationship management . . . and for the "half-nots," divorce insurance. All tools to love and protect women.

Revlon's and, say, PrimeAmerica's divorce insurance would go like this: If you're nervous or insecure, you take out a policy before you get married—women who are planning to have a large *family* could take out bigger policies; career women who will focus on making a large *salary* could take out smaller ones. Instead of your female friends buying you another toaster you don't need, they can contribute to the policy you "register" for in the traditional way. (If you think this is a negative approach to marriage, think about life insurance.) The Internet, once again, is the perfect place for this, with sites like weddings.com. What woman wouldn't broaden her thinking about Revlon instantly if they offered this product?

Revlon can celebrate the beauty of being a woman by following the *Fourth Truth: Market to Her Peripheral Vision and She Will See You in a Whole New Light*. After the Revlon-olution, the company will be everywhere a woman is. That includes mini-stores in downtown areas, in malls, and around airports. I'm talking 1,000 square feet and less—tiny outposts of branding, of experimental new products, of targeted visibility.

Women, as we've discussed, are the largest purchasers of greeting cards. Because women are more open and in touch with their feelings, Revlon, as the company that understands and inspires women, should help them communicate through either a paper or Web pathway. I see an innovative line of Revlon-branded greeting cards. (Actually, "greeting cards" is too trivial a name.) They would be more like Revlon Expressions, dealing on a far deeper and more meaningful level than ever before. Messages from women like Toni Morrison and Susan Sontag and Maya Angelou. Funny quips from women like Tracy Ullman and Whoopi Goldberg and Margaret Cho. (The latest Revlon colors, of course, would be communicated in some subtle way.)

What more perfect vehicle to flash-card the Revlon image?

When you think about the Peripheral Truth in its fullest sense, there are also some profound implications that emerge for Revlon's traditional marketing and advertising. Here's what I mean. Revlon has always spent most of its advertising dollars in popular women's magazines. They include the Condé Nast group (*Vogue, Glamour, Mademoiselle*), *Elle, Essence, Good Housekeeping, Ladies' Home Journal, Martha Stewart Living,* etc. Other than on some scattered magazine pages—plus their Academy Award extravaganza—can you think of many other places that you've noticed Revlon's messages? I can't, and that's a Peripheral oversight of major proportions.

Revlon needs to break out of the traditional beauty/fashion pages and put its advertising messages everywhere a woman is. Hot new mags like *2wice, eBay, Spin, Teen People, YM, Victoria, Jane, Cosmo Girl, Bust, Bitch, Honey, Flaunt,* Peripheral ones such as *Brill's Content.* Television messages on MTV and VH1 and Lifetime, for example. Taxicabs. Stickers on grocery bags, computer boxes, tampon applicators.

Finally, here are two last Peripheral thoughts: I can envision Revlon as being a really hot, really exciting publishing imprint. A smart publisher would want to create a nest of books targeted to women—from wise first novels to sensitive self-help solutions that help women ladder their lives to the next step—all with the feisty and newly meaningful Revlon name. These books could also be interactive on the Web. Or what about a helpful-hint newsletter. Or a "mag-a-log," like Abercrombie & Fitch's, which combines a magazine with a selling catalog. Or a Revlon music CD with the coolest music.

I can also see Revlon putting its name in front of women by creating licensing relationships with the world's best plant and flower growers. Imagine hybrid roses and geraniums named for Revlon's shade colors—what a romantic way to infuse a woman's life with beauty and optimism? Strategic alliance with 1-800-flowers.com? Home Depot's Gardening Centers? Or how about having the colors made into flowery sheets? Towels? Paint colors?

Revlon should celebrate the beauty of being a woman by supporting the *Fifth Truth: Walk, Run, Go to Her, Secure Her Loyalty Forever*. Revlon must stop thinking of itself as a brand limited to mass distribution in drugstores. How about mobile vans that don't just sell product, but offer videos, tapes, and DVDs on female-oriented subjects?

By the way, when I talk about "product," I don't just mean cosmetics. I see Revlon selling a line of self-defense products, including pepper sprays. Or how about Revlon entering the wide-open world of feminine products, such as lubricants for the post-menopausal market. (They could even sponsor Eve Ensler's *The Vagina Monologues*.) Or strategically link up with a pharmaceutical company to create an EVEolutionary birth control product. Since Revlon is global, this new method could build the brand by benefiting women all over the world.

How about taking on Avon in the world of at-home selling? Of course, it can't be done as a me-too concept. Revlon needs a fresh way to Go to Her where she lives. My suggestion: Give a *generous* portion of Revlon's door-to-door sales to ten charities, representing a spectrum of everything from AIDS to Alzheimer's Disease to hospices to literacy programs.

With this bold new model, the Revlon Representative

would spend as much time raising money for the charity as selling product. Conventional wisdom would have it that the more people spend on charity, the less they'll spend on your products. But once again, conventional wisdom is wrong. Women will feel better about themselves and feeling better leads to spending more. A phenomenal partnership of not-for-profit and profit. Lots of profit.

Of course, the Web is the newest and most perfect form of Going to Her. It's almost criminal that P&G beat Revlon to the punch with reflect.com, a Web site that offers personalized beauty products. Now, Revlon needs to make up for lost time. Its name is a huge advantage while "reflect" is new and means nothing to women . . . yet. Hmmm . . . something to reflect upon.

Customized cosmetics, ironically, would be the ultimate realization of the vision of Charles Revson and his just-about-obsessive customer focus.

By studying the *Sixth Truth: This Generation of Women Consumers Will Lead You to the Next*, Revlon can create its customers of the future, today. How do young girls learn about cosmetics? From their mothers, of course. Few brands have the opportunity that Revlon does to embed themselves deep in the consumer consciousness of young girls—just as they are identifying with concepts of womanhood, just as the insoluble mother/daughter bonds are being cemented.

But where is Revlon in this matriarchal matrix? Nowhere. How can Revlon become a Brand-Me-Down? One obvious way is to market cosmetics for girls. But this is a tricky area, a slippery slope, because many Moms aren't too thrilled when their daughters start wearing makeup at a tender young age.

A solution could be for Revlon to take the lead in educating young girls (and Moms) about "wearing makeup responsibly," much in the way Seagram's has taken steps in educating young people about drinking. The idea is that wearing makeup is part of becoming a woman, and Revlon will help you understand when to do it, and how to do it. Wearing makeup is about feeling beautiful as a woman, not about making yourself more attractive to men—what a terrific message at any age. What a way to make Moms feel better about Revlon—and to create a special relationship with young girls that will sustain their loyalty for years to come.

This is a wonderful, female-friendly position that no cosmetics company is taking. Revlon should be the one to do it.

Another way that Revlon can become a Brand-Me-Down is to connect mothers and daughters in a way that is totally unexpected—and totally necessary. Revlon could be that company devoted to helping young girls succeed in math and science—those subjects we talked about where, according to the statistics—boys perform better.

I see a future where Revlon becomes identified with girls' education. That means special homework sections on the Revlon Web site. It means Revlon-sponsored tutoring at places like Sylvan Learning Centers. It means awards to talented teachers who have helped girls achieve. It means, in short, celebrating the underlying beauty of being a woman in terms of accomplishment.

Revlon will create a more successful company by applying the *Seventh Truth: Co-Parenting Is the Best Way to Raise a Brand*. Charles Revson innovated in this way without fully realizing what he was doing. When he picked up the executive telephone in his sky-high and palatial office, to talk to an ordinary woman living in an ordinary suburb, he was giving her the opportunity to help him define his next product.

Imagine how Revlon could reach out to women, creating a Co-Parenting product environment with today's instant and digital means of communication. The Web, of course, is the logical place to start. Right now, the only way the women can reach Revlon is through a half-hearted e-mail system that is handled through Customer Service.

Wouldn't it be thrilling if the real decision-makers at

Revlon had their own, personal e-mail addresses listed on the Web site? I'm talking about the people in charge of product form, texture, and color; in charge of packaging; in charge of pricing. Currently, these decision-makers—at best—are in touch with some of their consumers twice a year at focus groups. And they're sitting on one side of a glass window, observing, but not collaborating with.

There are other ways that Revlon can start the Co-Parenting process. Computer software companies have been among the first to interact with "user groups." They distribute test versions of their software to clusters of their most sophisticated users whose experiences, reactions, and product insights become part of a "feedback loop." This process helps sharpen and refine the products prior to launch.

Hint, hint. If software companies get the message, why doesn't Revlon? Women are genetically-programmed to share their opinions and to make things better. It's time for Revlon to invite more women into the boardroom (yes, we know they have a couple of female board members, including Martha Stewart. And she is doing her bit. On her pre-Christmas TV show, Martha made a glorious Christmas wreath, using little red glass balls pinned onto a Styrofoam form. To cover up the many metal pinheads, she painstakingly painted every one with a coat of nail polish. Martha smiled, showed the familiar bottle, and said, "Revlon Red. It's a good thing.").

And another idea for Revlon: What about welcoming some female consumers to come right into the laboratory? This could create a national network of user groups, turning *in*put into *win*-put.

But using women to shape and contour Revlon's products is just the beginning. If Revlon truly is to become a company that celebrates the underlying beauty of women, it needs to rely on women to help point it in new directions. Revlon daycare centers? Revlon state-of-the-art plastic surgery facilities? Revlon teen spas? Just how much width does the brand have? Revlon and its customers, not Revlon and its investment bankers, should make those decisions.

The last EVEolutionary Truth is what might be the most important one of all. By the *Eighth Truth: Everything Matters—You Can't Hide Behind Your Logo,* I mean that *everything* Revlon does defines the company to its women consumers. It used to be that just the product mattered. Today, the company is the product.

Where does Revlon source its raw materials from? The problems Kathie Lee Gifford has faced (true or false) are not limited to products that are made in Third World countries. Is the glycerin in ColorStay lipstick made by any companies that dump their industrial waste? It took The Body Shop to put the issue of animal testing in our consciousness. How exactly does Revlon test its products?

Does Revlon make sure that it buys enough product and services from female-owned and run businesses? Where does Revlon bank, who is its accounting firm, who does its legal work? Let's look through that corporate keyhole and see what's really going on (like, exactly how and why they agreed to hire Monica Lewinsky). In fact, I see a time when companies like Revlon will actually list the names of the female-led businesses they support on their products. What woman wouldn't feel great about a brand if they found that on the package?

I began this chapter by talking about Ron Perelman, and how he has let Revlon slip down. I want to end it by coming around full circle. Because there is a tremendous opportunity for Ron to lift Revlon up, to embody the Everything Matters Truth by becoming a dedicated and committed ambassador of the company and hero to women. Is it too late? I don't think so. Women are forgiving—but only if Ron genuinely changes his thinking, and it isn't—excuse me—just cosmetic.

To show personal commitment and involvement with

Revlon, Ron could ask his paramour, the believable, beautiful and not-25-year-old Ellen Barkin, to be a spokesperson for the brand. Instant credibility. A little lightness.

A good place to start is philanthrophy. Now I know that Ron has been relatively generous, but I am suggesting that he refocus Revlon and expand its giving to center on more women's issues. Credit where credit is due: We know they sponsor The Revlon Run Walk for UCLA Women's Cancer Research Program; the 1999 Lilith Fair Concerts; and East Hampton's Ellen's Run for Breast Cancer Research and Pain Control. But health and wellness are areas that clearly need more help, more personal involvement, as do shelters for battered women.

I also see an opportunity for Ron to get involved in the rapidly emerging field of "venture philanthropy." In this model, nonprofits are accountable for their contributions, and have to show results. This is a perfect way for Ron to blend his business skills and his philanthropic instincts.

I also see a chance for Ron and Revlon to start business incubators. These are happening in the high-tech world, where start-ups are given initial funding and services. So wouldn't it be fabulous if Ron Perelman announced that he was allocating $50 million to start an incubator for female-owned start-ups? Revlon could provide the seed capital, offices, and basic business services such as legal and accounting. In exchange, Revlon gets an equity position in each company. And what makeup do you think the women in these companies would wear?

Ron should also take a page from Oprah's book—literally. We all know the profoundly positive influence that Oprah has had on reading and literacy in America. Ron should become a spokesperson for art, aesthetics, and beauty. They are subjects related to Revlon's business and ones that are in serious need of support. As school budgets come under pressure, art appreciation and art education are usually the first to take the hit.

With this platform, Ron can identify and support up-and-coming female artists (much as Oprah identifies authors)—featuring them and their work on a special area of the Revlon Web site. Like the famous Absolut Vodka campaign, Revlon can also use these artists to design innovative packaging and pick out new color palettes for the product lines. Ron can fund programs that take inner-city kids or seniors to museums or one that brings the artwork to people who might not otherwise get to see it, on a new kind of touring Museum Bus.

The possibilities are endless—and so is the upside for Revlon. It won't happen overnight—just like Revlon's decline didn't happen overnight. But sooner than later, if Ron Perelman embarks on this bright EVEolutionary path, Revlon will be a changed company and a changed brand.

And Ron a doubly richer man.

Chapter 10

In Conclusion:

Making the World Safe

for EVEolution

I f there's one motto I'd like to see on every desk in every corporate office, it is: EVEolution, EVEryday. To serve as a reminder that EVEolution should be the benchmark that every business decision is judged in light of. Considered against. Viewed in the context of.

EVEolution is the successful road map to follow so that today (and EVEryday) when you look at a business plan, you will no longer be imprisoned by the myths that have defined marketing for so long. Remember that other bit of historical wisdom: Species that don't EVEolve, die.

You see, EVEolution isn't about doing things partially. About getting there halfway. True, it's a process—but it's a process that needs daily progress. Women can't be won over by promises, by good intentions.

At BrainReserve, we think about EVEolution EVEryday. Do we measure up, we ask ourselves? Are we the role model we must be? After all, EVEolution begins at home. So here's our own, personal progress report:

- Connecting our customers. We work hard at cross-pollinating all our consulting clients. As an example, we have TrendSalons once-a-month on Thursday evenings where clients (past, present, future) meet with our staff and some of our TalentBank members and BrainJam on topics that will affect our mutual future.
- Marketing to Multiple Lives. We have many, many female clients. And our relationships with them are different. They bring their kids or dogs to meetings here; we accommodate their odd hours; we meet them on weekends (and not on the obligatory golf course). The artificial boundaries of business and personal relationships are, in my view, old-think—obstacles to growth, deeper development, success.
- Anticipatory Marketing. This is the essence of what we do. We get to the future first. We identify the problems and laser in on the answers before the consumer arrives there. Think: How can you do this for your business?
- Peripheral Vision. Whenever you see me on CNN or *Oprah* or *The Today Show*, that's an example of the way we take this Truth to heart. Not every business has the opportunity to turn up on national television—but every one can find a way to appear and reappear in the warp-and-woof of the lives of its customers. Local TV, radio,

town meetings, school boards, charities—you get the point. Show up everywhere.

- Going to our customers. Increasingly, we're using our Web site to help service our clients and wider audience of interested-in-EVEolving businesspeople, homebodies, students, other professionals around the world. And I spend lots of time on the road (and in the air), holding seminars globally, to do my utmost to spread the EVEolutionary message to women and men.

  And there's more I'd like to do. And plan to do. I envision a BrainReserve University that trains women and men in the principles of EVEolutionary marketing, and sends them out into the marketplace to educate, advise, inspire. My first foray—I'm teaching EVEolution to two of Susan Fournier's classes at the Harvard School of Business.

- Brand-Me-Downs. Since BrainReserve has been up and running toward TomorrowLand for a quarter-century, I'm starting to work with the children of certain female clients. So I'm just one genetic jump away from the next generation. Aside from that: I have gotten assignments from identical twin sisters in two Fortune 500 companies, in a typical female pass-along-brand way.

- Co-Parenting. Absolutely. All our projects at BrainReserve involve our clients in the solution process. They're there at our TrendProbes, our BrainJams, our Creative-Thinks. Whether your business is selling products or services, never forget that making your consumer into your Co-Parent is the wisest thing you can do.

- Everything Matters. This could be the one I work hardest at. For one thing, since my business is located in the same building I live in, obviously I can't run, can't hide. So few walls, so little separation, makes for total transparency. Sometimes I can see our clients looking quizzical until they figure out what they're hearing: g.g. laughing (or on rare occasions, crying) upstairs.

That, in a microcosm, is what I mean by Everything Matters. When you have the courage to share your foibles along with your strengths, your customers respect you for it. Try that in *your* business and see that I'm right.

Having looked both outward and inward, the time has arrived for me to wrap this book up. But how can you write a conclusion about a subject that is just beginning? Every time I stop, there's another idea that comes into my head, another example I see in EVEryday life that makes me want to say "Come over here and take a look at this."

My Web site (faithpopcorn.com) will be EVEolution Central for years to come. Please drop by, visit, and add your opinions. In other words, Co-Parent the site with me.

The Evolution of EVEolution

Researchers are beginning to take seriously that women are the pioneers in the world of consumerism. They represent the future: Future purchasing habits, spending patterns, and product demands. The direction that women consumers take—like using computers to build relationships, or wanting to know more about a brand than its price and positioning—is the way all consumers are headed. Male consumers. Teen consumers. Aging boomers. Latinos. African-Americans. Asian-Americans. Or Native Americans who, by the way, are starting to object to this appellation. Reasoning: Isn't everyone born here "native"?

Understand that you don't have to be a woman to be EVEolved. You just have to be awake, attuned to details, relationship-oriented, and process-aware. Although women and men are hugely different, many of the Truths can be applied to both markets.

Younger men, in particular, are real candidates for EVEo-lutionary marketing. Take the Audi commercial. It shows a young father and his 10ish-year-old daughter driving along somewhere in the Heartland. The Dad talks about looking for all the detours on the map, saying something like, "If I take all the backroads, I may hold on to my daughter a little while longer." Instead of talking about a car in terms of steel and glass, sleekness, and speed, Audi is going after connections, life journeys.

Or take Gillette. Their marketing hasn't changed in generations. If I ran Gillette, I would start to target younger men—their customers of the future—by using EVEolution. How about showing multi-roles, connecting men up to each other—about such topics as the future of sexual attraction or taking care of their aging fathers. Gillette could link men through their Web site (going one better than ESPN Sports Zone).

EVEolution, combined with technology, is pure combustion. While you can't stop the progress of EVEolution, technology is flash-firing it to a remarkable degree. And not just the Internet, which we've explored a lot, but other leaps of possibility. Wireless technology, for example, will change the way brands connect to their female customers. For example, if a woman is remodeling her house, she can be given a wireless device by her contractor. Think of the connection. She could get instant updates on the status of the job—letting her know when the stove will be delivered, when she should come and check the tile in the bathroom. If one molding is out of stock, she'll be alerted and can instantly choose another. Think of the control.

In fact, it's time for more places than the MIT Media Lab to start studying technology as it relates to women in a serious way. What an opportunity for brands like Cisco Systems and Motorola to fund this research. And own its results.

- EVEolution and Minorities. Currently we're working on the different ways the different cultures are EVEolving. The growth of the Latino and Asian markets, and the power of women within these markets, presents a big opportunity. For example, in Asian cultures, where tradition is vastly important, the concept of Brand-Me-Downs has even more meaning. And in many Latino markets, where there is a tradition of direct selling, the Go to Her Truth needs special examination. Being EVEolutionarily Correct and Culturally Correct needs to be carefully balanced, and is worthy of its own book.

- EVEolution and Younger Women. EVEolutioners need to address the 8–12-year-old girls' market, currently 15 million strong. You don't need a fun-house mirror to exaggerate this group. These youngsters are now spending $5 billion per year in clothing alone. More than two-thirds of these girls are on computers, a slight edge over the less than 60% of boys. (Guess how you should reach them?) Girls use their computers to connect to each other—and for ways to stretch their imagination. Playing "dress-up" in a more grown-up way.

- EVEolution and Fifty, Sixty, Seventy, and Eighty-plus. Consider that these women will be on their fourth, fifth, and sixth career choices (not to mention husbands, boyfriends)—opening up Internet stores, craft centers, giving counseling to generations below, and consulting with their peers. The range of knowledge is wide: Everything from romance to recipes to refinancing. When looking to implement the Eight (Elder) Truths, marketers could spend decades on the many issues that these women face.

- EVEolution and Management. As these Eight Truths prove, a female-run and female-filled company would be different from anything the Fortune 500 (or *any* company) has experienced up to now. More discussions, more detail, more compassion.

● ● ●

Let me leave you with this. The last three letters in "believe" are EVE. It means:

> Believing in EVEolution can change your business for the better.
>
> Believing in EVEolution can change you—to forge new and deeper connections with your consumer.
>
> Believing in EVEolution will create more value in your business and your life.
>
> Believing in the Eight Truths of EVEolution brings you to your own best future.
>
> Because women can change your brand and your company, forever.
>
> But only if you have the courage to let them.
>
> Do you?
>
> Will you?
>
> You must.

EVEolutionary Reading

Books:

Awakening Intuition, Dr. Mona Lisa Schultz
Backlash, Susan Faludi
The Ballad of Sexual Dependency, Nan Goldin
Bastard Out of Carolina, Dorothy Allison
Beauty Fades, Dumb Is Forever, Judge Judy Scheindlin
The Beauty Myth, Naomi Wolf
The Bell Jar, Sylvia Plath
Beloved, Toni Morrison
*Bosom Buddies: Lessons and Laughter on Breast Health and
   Cancer*, Rosie O'Donnell, Tracy Chutorian Semler,
   Deborah Axelrod (Preface)
Bridget Jones's Diary, Helen Fielding
*Cherishing Our Daughters: How Parents Can Raise Girls
   to Become Confident Women*, Evelyn Silten Bassoff
Chic Simple Women's Wardrobe, Kim Johnson Gross and Jeff
   Stone. Rachel Urquhart (Text), James Wojcik (Photographer)
The Courage to Be Rich, Suze Orman
Deborah, Golda, and Me: Being Female and Jewish in America,
   Letty Cottin Pogrebin
Divine Secrets of the Ya-Ya Sisterhood, Rebecca Wells
DV., Diana Vreeland, George Plimpton (Editor)

The End of Fashion: The Mass Marketing of the Clothing Business,
  Teri Agins
Fear of Fifty: A Midlife Memoir, Erica Jong
The Female Advantage: Women's Ways of Leadership,
  Sally Helgesen
The Feminine Mystique, Betty Friedan
Fire And Ice: The Charles Revson Story, Andrew Tobias
*The First Sex: The Natural Talents of Women and How They Are
  Changing the World*, Helen E. Fisher
The Heidi Chronicles and Other Plays, Wendy Wasserstein
Hello, He Lied and Other Truths from the Hollywood Trenches,
  Lynda Obst
History Portraits, Cindy Sherman
Hope in a Jar: The Making of America's Beauty Culture, Kathy
  Preiss
How to Care for Aging Parents, Virginia Morris, Robert Butler
How to Make an American Quilt, Whitney Otto
I Know Why the Caged Bird Sings, Maya Angelou
The Improvised Woman: Single Women Reinventing Single Life,
  Marcelle Clements
In a Different Voice, Carol Gilligan
*Investment Basics for Women: The Essential Guide to Taking
  Charge of Your Money*, Kathy Buys, Jonathan Berohn
It's a Jungle Out There, Jane, Dr. Joy Browne
The Joy Luck Club, Amy Tan
Last Night in Paradise: Sex and Morals at the Century's End,
  Katie Roiphe
Life and Death in Shanghai, Nien Chang
Making Faces, Kevyn Aucoin
May I Kiss You on the Lips Miss Sandra?, Sandra Bernhard
Meditations for New Mothers, Beth Wilson Saavedra
*Men Are from Mars, Women Are from Venus: A Practical Guide
  for Improving Communication and Getting What You Want in
  Your Relationships*, John Gray

Midwives: A Novel, Chris A. Bohjalian
Mothers Who Think: Tales of Real-Life Parenthood, Camille Peri,
    Kate Moses (Editors)
The Names of Things, Susan Brind Morrow
A Natural History of the Senses, Diane Ackerman
The New Our Bodies, Ourselves, The Boston Women's Health
    Book Collective
No Time to Die: Living with Ovarian Cancer, Liz Tilberis,
    Aimee Lee Ball (Contributor)
Passages, Gail Sheehy
Personal History, Katharine Graham
The Portable Dorothy Parker, Dorothy Parker; Brendan Gill
    (Introduction)
Raising A Daughter, Jeanne Elium, Don Elium (Contributor)
Red Azalea, Anchee Min
Reviving Ophelia: Saving the Lives of Adolescent Girls,
    Mary Pipher, Ph.D.
Revolution from Within: A Book of Self-Esteem, Gloria Steinem
Rock She Wrote, Evelyn McDonnell, Ann Powers (Editors)
The Second Sex, Simone De Beauvoir, H.M. Parshley (Translator)
The Silent Passage: Menopause, Gail Sheehy
Simple Abundance: A Daybook of Comfort and Joy,
    Sarah Ban Breathnach
Strong Women Stay Young, Miriam E. Nelson, Ph.D.,
    Susan J. Douglas
*Talking From 9 to 5: How Women's and Men's Conversational
    Styles Affect Who Gets Heard, Who Gets Credit, and What Gets
    Done at Work*, Deborah Tannen, Ph.D.
The Vagina Monologues, Eve Ensler, Gloria Steinem (Foreword)
We Are Our Mother's Daughters, Cokie Roberts
What Do Women Want: Exploding the Myth of Dependency,
    Louise Echenbaum, Susie Orbach
What to Expect When You're Expecting (Revised Edition),
    Arlene Eisenberg, Sandee E. Hathaway, Heidi E. Murkoff

Where the Girls Are: Growing Up Female with the Mass Media,
    Susan J. Douglas
The Whole Woman, Germaine Greer
Why We Buy: The Science of Shopping, Paco Underhill
Woman: An Intimate Geography, Natalie Angier
The Woman's Encyclopedia of Myths and Secrets,
    Barbara G. Walker
Women, Annie Leibovitz, Susan Sontag (Foreword)
Women Can't Hear What Men Don't Say, Dr. William Farrell
Women of the Beat Generation, Brenda Knight
Women, Race and Class, Angela Y. Davis
*Women Who Run with the Wolves: Myths and Stories of the Wild
    Woman Archetype*, Clarissa Pinkola Estes, Ph.D.
Women's Bodies, Women's Wisdom, Dr. Christiane Northrup

Magazines:

Allegra (Germany)
Allure
American Health
Amica (Germany, Italy)
B. Smith
Bella (Italy)
Biba (France)
Bust
Cosmopolitan
CosmoGirl!
Curve
Depeche Mode (Germany)
Ebony
Elle
Elle Decor
Essence

Family Travel & Leisure
Fast Company
Femina (India)
Flaunt
Freudin (Germany)
Girlfriends
Good Housekeeping
Grazia (Italy)
Harper's BAZAAR
Harpers Queen (England)
Honey
In Style
Inc.
Jane
jump!
Junior (England)

Ladies' Home Journal

Latina

Lilith

Madame (France)

Marie Claire

Marketing To Women

Martha Stewart Living/Baby

Moxie

Ms.

Nylon

Parents

Passion Fruit

Petra (Germany)

Rebecca's Garden

Redbook

Self

Seventeen

Shape

Sports Illustrated for Women

Tatler

Teen People

Total Health For Longevity

Van (Spain)

Victoria

Visionaire

Vogue

W

Wallpaper

w.i.g. (women in general)

Women Outside

Women's Sport & Fitness

Working Mother

Working Woman

Yoga Journal

Faith's Bookmarks:

4women.org: National Women's Health Information Center lets you know the latest on health news and legislation.

4workingmothers.com: Puts you in touch with a big mix of professional organizations, publications. Advice on balancing life and work, childcare providers, plus a spa finder.

adoptioninstitute.org: Helps sort through the claims made by adoption agencies, not all of them reputable. It is also packed with adoption research and region-related data.

adventurewomen.com: A Fantasy Adventure site that sends you on sea kayaking adventures in Mexico, horseback riding in Ireland, or hiking in France. The trips are for women over-30, and rated by difficulty.

babycenter.com: Covers pregnancy and your baby's development. Use the site to shop weekly store specials from home, stay in touch with other parents and experts. They also have a childcare finder that is searchable by region.

beatboxbetty.com: Women's film Web site.

beingabroad.gol.com: Female perspective on being a foreign woman working in Japan.

coffeerooms.com: News, opinion, and message boards on topics such as TV, books, family, health, and friendship.

coolgirlsjapan.com/home.html: Web site on Japanese Youth Culture.

hersalon.com: Romp through a cyber-themepark for women— chat, learn, discuss, share, and be entertained. Site has feminist humor, information, sports, satire, and fun.

hipmama.com: A Web site for cool Moms.

igc.org: WomensNet is a global community of women, activists, and organizations using computer networks with the intent of increasing women's rights.

iVillage.com: The leading women's community on the Web. Informative, provocative, and welcoming.

journeywoman.com: A women's travel resource about tips, advice, and stories. Sign on for free travel-tip newsletter.

mountainwomen.com: Sells sleeping bags, climbing harnesses, and other equipment for women.

oxygen.com: Gerry Laybourne's latest female mentoring venture. Co-Parented.

she-net.com: An on-line community for intelligent women, with articles and discussion on everything from the arts to politics to health to sex.

sportsforwomen.com: Follows top female athletes such as Mia Hamm and Sheryl Swoopes, plus checks up on your favorite female teams. A Q&A section allows you to ask the experts your own sports and fitness questions.

wiredwoman.com: Canadian women devoted to technology join the World Wide Web.

womanowned.com: Helps future entrepreneurs through the launch process, from writing a business plan to raising capital. For those who have launched a business, there is advice on marketing, and scoring government contracts on the Web.

women.americanheart.org: From the American Heart Association, this site tells women how to spot female heart-attack symptoms, which are often different from men's, as well as other helpful information.

womenssportsfoundation.org: Advises you on the costs and basic fitness level required to participate in various sports. It also offers publications and videos describing sports careers for women.

wham.com: An informative and fun on-line magazine for mothers who work at home.

And more:

deja.com
disgruntledhousewife.com
hissyfit.com
mamamedia.com
medscape.com
priceline.com

thirdagemedia.com
wcn.org (women's cancer)
wellweb.com
womenconnect.com
women's.health.com

Index

A.1. Steak Sauce, 126–31
Abercrombie & Fitch, 231
Absolut Vodka, 237
Academy Awards, 230
Ackerman, Val, 165, 167
Advantix film system, 44, 46
Advertising, 157, 198
  Revlon, 221, 224, 230
  television, 105–6, 117, *164*, 230
Advocacy groups, 211
African-Americans, 242
Ahold, *86*
AIDS, 121–22, 126, *165*, 231
Airports, malling of, 144
Albright, Madeline, *113*
Ally McBeal, 34, 139
Alternative medicines, 2, 15
Alternative Work Arrangement Group, 54
Alumni Associations, 159
Amazon.com, 186
American Airlines, 168
American Association of University Women, 81
American Dialect Society (ADS), *192*
American Express, 27
American Menopause Foundation (AMF), 52

Amway (co.), 137
Angelou, Maya, 230
Angier, Natalie, 42, 43, 45–46
Annie's Homegrown Mac n' Cheese, *203*
Anti-bacterial soaps, 119
Anticipation Truth, 13, 79–103
  and BrainReserve, 240
  case study/Jiffy Lube, 98–102
  FutureCorner, 93–96
  Revlon, applied to, 229
Arm & Hammer, 201
Armani, 88–89, 127
Armani, Giorgio, 122
Army, U.S., 60, 97
Art of War, The (Tzu), 82
Aruba Sonesta Resorts, 33
As Good As It Gets, 50
Asian market, 242, 243–44
AT&T, 50, *159*, 207
Au Bon Pain, 144
Audi, 243
Autodesk (co.), *164*
Automatic Replenishment, 149, *149*
Automobiles *see* Cars
AutoNation USA, *172*
Auto-service industry, 98–102
Avon, 122, 133, 231
Awakening Intuition (Schultz), 107

Baby Jogger, 60–61

BabyGap, 142, 160

Backyard fence, 23

"Badge value," 198

Baechler, Phil, 60

Baker, Chet, 94

Balducci, 62

Banana Republic, 89, 112–13, 224

Bank of New York, *91–92*

Barbie and Ken, 154

Barkin, Ellen, 236

Barnes & Noble bookstores, 9, 126

Barzini, Benedetta, 224

Basketball, woman's, 165–67

Bass Weejun loafers, 154

Bassoff, Evelyn, Dr., 154

Bath and Body Works, 144

"Battle of the Burgers," 106

Baum, Herbert M., 73, 75

Beard, Lois, *60*

Beauty Fades, Dumb Is Forever
   (Sheindlin), 47

Beauty of being a woman, 225–27, 229,
   231, 233, 234–35

Beauty pageant(s) (proposed), 227

Beauty Parlor Night Kit, 144

Begley, Charlene, 139–40

Bell, Alexander Graham, 84

Ben & Jerry's, 112–13, 145, *203*

Ben Benson's, 130

Bernstein, Norris, 214

Big (film), 72

Big Brother (*BB*), *123*

bigbrother.nl, *123*

Bigelow, Mrs., 136

Bikers Against Breast Cancer, 25

Bitch (magazine), 230

BizRate.com, 93

Blamestorming, 34

Bloomingdale's, 63, 160

Board(s) of Directors, 178, 202–3, 234

Bobbie Brown (brand), 223

Body image, 25, 26, 34, 37

Body Shop, The, 235

Bookmobiles, 144

Books, children's, 157–58, *158*

Borg, Anita, *187*

Bowman, Hank, 59

Boyle, Lara Flynn, 34

Braille The Culture, 10

BrainJams, 34, 35, 172–73, 240

BrainReserve, 10–11
   brand look, 64, *110*, 111
   Eight EVEolutionary Truths,
      application, 240–42,
   EVEolutionary case studies
      A.1. Steak Sauce, 126–31
      Four Small Companies, 62–71
      Future: Revlon, 219–37
      GE Financial Assurance (GEFA),
         190–92
      Hasbro, 71–77
      Jiffy Lube, 98–102
      KitchenAid, 170–74
      Knox Gelatine, *118–19*
      Queen Mary, 214–17
      SnackWell's, 34–39
      Streamline.com, 146–52
   consulting, 62, 137–39
   involving clients in, 241
   Licensing, 54–59
   Multiple Lives needs of employees,
      55–56

BrainReserve Glossary, xxi–xxv

BrainReserve TrendBank, xix–xx

BrainReserve Trends, 3, 10, 128–29,
   139, 206

BrainReserve University (proposed), 241

Brainstorming, 34

"Brand-as-hero" philosophy, *200*

Brand building, 124, 129, 223
  with fashion, 64, 109–10, *110*, 111,
    122
  new framework for, 5
  Revlon, 231
Brand choice, intangibles in, 19
Brand connections
  childhood, 153–54, 160–62, *161*,
    164–65
Brand look, 109, 122
  BrainReserve, 64, *110*, 111
Brand-Me-Down Truth, 12, 74,
    153–174, 244
  and BrainReserve, 241
  case study/KitchenAid, 170–74
  FutureCorner, 168–70
  Revlon, applied to, 232–33
Brand skepticism, *157*
Brand success, *151*
Brands, 4, 83, 106, 135
  as a cause, 122
  on Internet, 120
  joining, 4–9, 49, 177, 199
  nostalgia evoked by, 153–55
  in unusual places, *127*
BrandWeek, 208
Brand-width, 37
Brandwise.com, 140
Bread & Circus store (Cambridge, MA),
  209
Breast cancer, 120, 122
Bridgehampton National Bank, *92*
Brightpoint, Inc., 210
Brill's Content (magazine), 230
Bristol Hum, *113*
Broderick Cup, *204*
Brooks Brothers, *131*
Browne, Joy, Dr., 107
Buddy system, 68
Bull, Johanna, 22

Burger King North America, 208
Busch, Johanna, 57
Business incubators, 236
Business travel, 30–32
  bringing children, 32
BusinessWeek, 48, 222–23
Business, women-owned and run, 7–8,
    62–71, 235, 236, 244
  financial services for, 190–92
Bust (magazine), 230
Buyer's stress, *157*

Calabro, Maria, 88–89
Calvin Klein, 80, 143, 224–25
Camel (brand), *165*
Campbell Soup Co., 85
Capellas, Michael D., 48
Car pools, 27
Cardioexpress, 144–45
Carnival (co.), 216
Carpenter, Candice, 28, 29–30
Cars
  Co-Parented, 182–83
  house/office calls for, 143
  shopping for, 141, *172*
  women buying, 7
Cartier, 221
Case studies
  Anticipation (Jiffy Lube), 98–102
  Brand-Me-Down (KitchenAid),
    170–74
  Connection (SnackWell's),
    34–39
  Co-Parenting (GE Financial
    Assurance), 190–92
  Everything Matters (*Queen Mary*),
    214–17
  Future (Revlon), 219–37
  Go to Her (Streamline.com),
    146–52

Case studies (*continued*)

Multiple Lives (Four Small Companies), 62–71

Multiple Lives (Hasbro), 71–77

Peripheral Vision (A.1. Steak Sauce), 126–31

Peripheral Vision (Knox Gelatine), 118–19

Cause-related marketing, 117–18, 120, 122

Cereals, 118–19, *138*, 159

Ceslow, Susan, 67

Chain restaurants, 188–89

Charitable giving, 199, 201, 208, 231–32

Charity Ribbons, 121–22

Charmin, *165*

Chastain, Brandi, 164–65

Cherishing Our Daughters (Bassoff), 154

Chex cereals, 159

Chicago Tribune, 207

Child labor, 202–3

Children

and brand name connections, 153–54, 160–62, *161, 164–65*

affected by experiences of parents, *157*

on business trips, 32

linking with products, 171–72

purchasing power of, *161*

summer camps, 142

transportation, 53

Children's clothing, 2, 14–15, 159–61

Cho, Margaret, 230

Chub Club, 26

Church and Dwight, 201

Cisco Systems, 243

Citigroup, 27

Claiborne, Liz, 160

Class to the mass, 13, 162, 224–25

Classroom Cameras, 59–60

Clayton, Paul, 208

Clicking (Popcorn and Marigold), 4, 87

Clinton, Hillary Rodham, *21*

Clockwork Orange (film), 136

Clothing, 63–65, 160

Anticipation Truth, 88–90

Brand-Me-Down, Truth 159–61

Brand look, 109, *110,* 111, 122

Clubs for kids, *166*

Clue, 158

CNN, 198, 240

Co-branding, 116–17, 229

Cocooning Trend, 3, 54, 129

Cocooning Chair, 57–59

Cocooning Collection Club Web site, 59

Cocooning Lamps, 59

Cocoons, 71

Co-couponing, 186

"Cola Wars," 106

Cold War, *165*

Collagen, *118*

Color Purple, The (film), 50

Columbia TriStar Motion Pictures, 50–51

Commercials, 105–6, 117, *164,* 198

Community, weakening of, 23

Community of women, 24

Companies

consolidated buying power, 205

ethical biographies, 201

relationship to female customers, 71–72, 74, 75, 139, 177–78, 180, 197–98, 225

relationship to female employees, 47–48, 50–54, 55

Web site monitoring (proposed), 202–4

Compaq, 48, *164,* 187

Computer software companies, 234

Computers, girls and, 168–69, 244

Condé Nast magazines, 230

Condominium builders, 97–98

Confetti, 63

Conley, Chip, 87

Connection Truth, 12, 13, 17–40, 170
  and BrainReserve, 240
  case study/Snackwell's, 34–39
  FutureCorner, 26–28
  Revlon, applied to, 226–27

Consumer purchasing
  children, *161*
  women, 7–8

Consumer Rating System (predicted),
  204

Consumer Reports, 185

Consumerism, 158, 242

Consumers
  companies' relationship with, 24–25,
    71–72, 74, 75, 139, 150, 177–78,
    180, 191–92, 197–98, 225, 240
  at epicenter of marketing universe,
    112
  interaction with brands, 135
  surrounding with messages, 109–10,
    112–14, 116
  see also Service

Construction industry, 96–98

Contradiction (brand), 80

Convenience, 134–35, 137, 145

Cookies, emotional connection, 34,
  35–36

Contemporary insanity, 135

Co-Parenting Truth, 15, 175–93, 242
  and BrainReserve, 241
  case study/GE Financial Assurance,
    190–92
  FutureCorner, 186–90
  marketing, 177–84
  Revlon, applied to, 233–35

Corporate Ethicist (proposed), 204

Corporate Soul, 120, 197, 212–13

Cosmetics,
  customized, 232
  for girls, 232–33
  marketing, 222, 224, 225
  testing of, 235

Cosmetics International, 223

"Cosmic Egg," 176

COSMO girl (magazine), 230

Crayolas, 158

CreativeThinks, 35, 241

Cunard Line, 214, 216

Customer parking, *91–92*, 118–19

Customers, *see* Consumers

Customization, 71, 147–49
  future, 93–96
  health and beauty, 144, 232
  technology, 186
  see also Service

Cutex, *118*

Cyberspace, *29*

Darwin, Charles, 107

Dayton Hudson (now Target), 206–7

dealtime.com, 140

Decorative accessories market, 68–69

Deja.com, 185, 186

Delivery Channels, 146–48, *149*

Delta Airlines, 130

DeMello, Tim, 147–48, 150–51, 152

Department stores, 89–90, 137–38,
    160–61, 221

Depends, 145

DeSanti, Rudi, *131*

"Design Your Dream Car," 183

Details, 196–97, *202*

Dial-10-10 long-distance services, 207

Dick Clark's American Music
    Experience, 216

Direct-delivery services, 146–47
Disney (co.), 156–57
Diving Divas scuba package, 33
Divorce insurance, 229
DKNY, 63–65, 144, 160
Dr. Seuss, 154
Dolce & Gabbana, 122
Door-to-door selling, 2, 14, 133, 231
Dopamine, 107
Dow, Elizabeth, 69–71
Dreesen's, *131*
Drink-O-Meter (proposed), 205
Duchess of York, 26
Duncan (yo-yos), 158
Dwyer, Kathy, 223

e.p.t., 145
E.R., 117
E & J Gallo, *115*
E-commerce, 28, 90, 93, 139, *148*
East Hampton High School, 168
Easy Bake Oven (toy), 76
eatZi's Market and Bakery, 86
eBay, 114
eBay (magazine), 230
Economic power of women, 7–10
Edu-tainment, 188
Eichenbaum, Louise, 81
Eight Truths of EVEolution, 2, 11–15,
        62, 120, 211, 245
  1. Connecting, 17–40
  2. Multiple Lives, 41–78
  3. Anticipation, 79–103
  4. Peripheral Vision, 105–132
  5. Go to Her, 133–152
  6. Brand-Me-Down, 153–174
  7. Co-Parenting, 175–93
  8. Everything Matters, 195–218
Eitel, Maria, 213
Electrolux, 133

Eli Lilly (co.), 52
Elium, Jeanne and Don, 175–176
Elizabeth Dow Ltd., 69–71
elizabethdow.com, 70
ELLE (magazine), 230
Ellen's Run for Breast Cancer Research
        and Pain Control, 236
EM (Everything Matters) index, 204
Emotional connection(s)
  with cookies, 34, 36
  with kitchen, 171
  with products, 222
  with Revlon, 225–226
Employee benefits, 48, 50, 51–52, 53,
        55–56
EnfaGrow, 85
Enfamil baby formula, 85
Ensler, Eve, 231
Enterprise (co.), 137
Environmental Protection Agency (EPA),
        203
ESPN Sports Zone, 243
Essence (magazine), 230
Esser, Judith, 180
Estée Lauder, 70, 90, 223, 224
"Ethical ingredients" list(s), 201, *202*
Ethics, 196, 199, 201, *202*–3, 204
eToys.com, 140
Evans, Gail, 198–99
Evans, Nancy, 28
EVEolution, 1–15
  believing in, 245
  Eight Truths of, 2, 11–15, 62, 120,
        211, 245
  EVEolving to, 10–11
  evolution of, 242–45
  importance of, 4
  making world safe for, 239–45
  and minority groups, 242–44
  technology of, 20–21

EVEolution EVEryday, 239
EVEolution Moment (the), 7–8
EVEolutionary Truths, 12–15
  and BrainReserve, 240–42
  Revlon, applied to, 226–37
Everything Matters Truth, 15, 63, 65,
    74, 77, 120, 195–218, 221
  and BrainReserve, 241–42
  case study/*Queen Mary*, 214–17
  Five "Ps" of marketing, 198
  FutureCorner, 201–6
  Revlon, applied to, 235–36
EVEsdropping, 29
Experience-centric, 129
ExxonMobil, 27, 143

"Faith Popcorn's Home Office Cocoon,"
  56–59
faithpopcorn.com, 242
Family Law, 117
Farberware, 156
Farrell, Warren, *43*
Fashion industry, 224
Fast Company (magazine), 179
Father-daughter relationship, 155
"Feelings exchange," 27
Fehrenbach, Mary, 90
Feller, Nora, 65
Female employees
  relationship of company to, 47–48,
    50–54, 55
Female market, 7–8, 10–11
Fergie, Duchess of York, 26
Fifth "P" of Marketing, 198
Financial services, 27–28, 169–70,
    190–92, 229
Fiorina, Carly, *115*
Fire and Ice (Tobias), 220–22
First Sex, The (Fisher), 42, 176
Fisher-Price, 121

Fisher, Helen, 42, 43–44, 176
Fisher, Lucy, 50–51
Fitzgerald, F. Scott, 5
Fitzgerald, Niall, *148*
Flaunt (magazine), 230
Flexible Flyers, 158
Flockhart, Calista, 34
Focus groups, 83, 97, 178, 179, 185,
    186
Food
  flash-frozen and delivered, 62
  relationship to, 36
Foodaceuticals, *119*
Foote, Cone and Belding, 38
Forbes (magazine), *115*
Ford Motor Co., 182–84, 228
Fortune (magazine), 219
Fortune 500, 8, 10, 14, 135, 195, 244
  female employees, 135
Four "Ps" of Marketing, 198
Four Small Companies, 62–71
Frango Mint, 207
Frederick's of Hollywood, 97
Free association, 22, 132
Frequency, 105–6, 117
Freud, Sigmund, 22, 80
Frito-Lay, *203*
Frogger, 77
Fugazy, 53
Fugitive, The (film), 50
Fuller Brush man, 133
Furby (toy line), 73, 76
Furlong, Mary, 23
Future (the), 2, 4, 10, 15, 242
FutureCorner, 12
  Anticipation Truth, 93–96
  Brand-Me-Down Truth, 168–70
  Connection Truth, 26–28
  Co-Parenting Truth, 186–90
  Everything Matters Truth, 201–6

FutureCorner (*continued*)
  Go to Her Truth, 141–44
  Multiple Lives Truth, 51–53
  Peripheral Vision Truth, 117–20
FutureScape, 10, 137–39

Gallo, Ernest, *115*
Gallo, Gina, *115*
Gap, Inc., 160
GapKids, 160
Garroway, Dave, 222
GE Capital Services, 152
GE Financial Assurance (GEFA),
    190–92
Gelatine, *118–19*
Gender differences, 2, 21–22, 106–9,
    113, 114, 116, 197
  neurological, 8–9
  in thinking, 42–45
Gender stereotyping, 9
Genealogy, 26–27
General Motors, 141, 210
Generation Gap, *164–65*
Generational marketing, *see* Brand-Me-
    Down
Generational Specialist, 155
Genetically transmitted diseases,
    26–27
Genie Joke, 80
Gifford, Kathie Lee, 235
Gift-giving, 87–88, 208
Gilda's Club, 22, 208
Gillette, 243
Gilligan, Carol, 21–22, 81
Girls
  computers, 168–69, 244
  cosmetics for, 232–33
  math/science, 168–69, 233
  sports, 164–67
Girls Inc., 37

Girls' market, 244
Gitlin, Josh, 171
Glamour (magazine), 230
"Go, Girl," 33
Go to Her Truth, 133–52, 244
  and BrainReserve, 241
  case study/Streamline.com, 146–52
  FutureCorner, 141–44
  Revlon, applied to, 231–32
Goldberg, Whoopi, 230
Goldstein, Ross, Dr., 107
Golfers, women, *31*
Good Housekeeping (magazine), 230
Good Humor man, 133
Goodnight Moon, 158
Grace Children's Foundation, 208
Graham, Karen, 224
Graham, Marc, 100
Gray, John, Dr., 6, 18
Great Gatsby, The (Fitzgerald), 5
Greenberg, Sandy, 38
Greenbriar Hotel (West Virginia), 216
Greer, Germaine, 89
Greeting cards, 27, 229–30
Groceries
  direct delivery, 148, 149, 150
  on-line purchase, *148*
Gross Rating Points (GRP), 112
Gucci, 160
Guess?, 160, 213
Gyms, 144–45

H. J. Heinz (co.), 25–26
H.O.G. (Harley Owners Group), 24–25
Haarlem, 86
Haenen, J. P., *123*
Hallmark, 27
Hand-Me-Down Brand, 170
  KitchenAid, 170–74
  see Brand-Me-Down Truth

Hanks, Tom, 72
Harel, Idit, Dr., 168
Harley-Davidson, 24–25
Harper's Bazaar (magazine), 120
Harsha, Mark, *166*
Harvard Business School, 9, 21
Hasbro (co.), 71–77
Hasbro Children's Foundation, 77
Hasbro National Resource Center for
    Boundless Playgrounds, 77
HasbroCollectors.com, 76
Hassenfeld, Alan, 72–73, 75
Hassenfeld Brothers, 72
Hayground School (Bridgehampton,
    NY), *158*
Health information (women), 228
Healthcare decisions, women
    influencing, 7
"Heirloom concept," 162–63
Heisman Trophy, *204*
Hellman's, 186
Herman, Stan, 217
Hermés, 160
Hewitt Associates, 51
Hewlett-Packard (HP), *115*, *187*
High Point, NC, 58
Hilton Jalousie Resort & Spa, 33
Hold Everything, 225
Hollywood Wings, 65–67
Home
    marketing that goes to, 14
    selling to women in, 136–41, 231
Home delivery, 133, *138*, 146–52
Home Depot, Inc., 163, 231
Home Office Cocoon, 56–59
Home Shopping Network, 144
Home spas, 1, 13
Home-workers, 19, 54, 56–59, 135–36,
Home-working environment, 54–59
Honda, *204*

Honey (magazine), 230
Hooker, John Clyde, Jr., 56
Hooker Furniture Company, 56
Hopfinger, Ellen, 89
Hostess Twinkies, 141
Hot Pockets, 186
Hotel, The (Miami), 123
Hotels, 30–32, 87, 122–24
Household cleaning, 143
Housewares stores, 189–90
How to Be Wrinkle-Free (Jacobson), 66
Huggies Pull-ups Training Pants, 85
Hynde, Chrissie, 42

IBM, 51
ideas@faithpopcorn.com, 59
IGA, *166*
Ikea, 225
Ilitch, Denise, 50
Image advertising, 106
ImagiNation, 74
In a Different Voice (Gilligan), 81
Income (women), 7
Industrial appliances and professional
    cookware, 2, 14
Information processing
    differences between the sexes, 8,
        106–7
Inspectah Deck, *123*
Institute for Women and Technology
    (IWT), *187*
Insurance industry, 190
Intel (co.), 94, 122
"Intel Inside," 122
Intel Science Talent Search, 168
Internet, 20–21, 28–30, *29*, 141, 148,
        173, 229, 243
    access to information through, 120,
        201
    brands on, 120

Internet (*continued*)
  children and, 168–69
  Co-Parenting on, 184–85
Intranets, 228
Intuition, 107
Intuition Group, 22
Irons, Jeremy, 121
It's a Jungle Out There, Jane (Browne),
  107
iVillage, 28–30, 183
  Ford's Women's Auto Center on,
    183–84
  Renova on, 30

J. Roaman (co.), 63–65
Jackson, Deanna and Felicia, 166
Jacobson, Carlotta Karlson, 66
Jacqua Girls, Inc., 144
Jager, Durk, *200*
Jane (magazine), 230
Jane Fonda's Workout, 63
Jerome Hotel, 65
Jerry McGuire (film), 50
Jiffy Lube International, Inc., 98–102
Johnson, Rick, 156
Johnson & Johnson, 27
Jokes
  Genie, 80
  self-deprecating, *108*
Jones Sodas, *127*
journeywoman.com, 33
Judging Amy, 117
Jung, Carl, 154
Jupiter Communications, *93*
"Just Ask a Woman," 179

Karan, Donna, 224
Kellogg School of Management, 9
Kennedy, Rose, 66
Kimberly Clark (co.), 85

Kinko's, 127, 228
Kiosks, 145
Kitchen(s), 2, 14, 190
  emotional connection with, 171
  hand tools, 61–62
KitchenAid, 170–74
  Web site, 173
Kmart, 163
Knight, Phil, 213
Knox, James, *118*
Knox Gelatine, *118–19*
Knox for Nails, *118*
Knox Nutrajoint, *119*
Koosh (toy), 76
Kraft Foods, 87
Krispy Kreme (co.), 112–13, 114
Kroger (co.), 144–45
Krugman, Scott, 160

Labels, peripheral marketing through,
  121
Ladies' Home Journal (magazine), 230
"Ladies of Harley Group," 25
Ladies rooms, 27
Lake, Celinda, *196*
Lake, Snell and Perry, *196*
Lands' End, 208
lang, k. d., 223
Latino market, 242, 243–44
Lauder, Estée, 136
Laybourne, Geraldine, 184, 185
Lenny, Rick, 37
Leonard, Stew, 180–82
Lepler, Lori Moskowitz, 22
Levine, Carl, 56, 59
Levine, Jen, 179
Levi's, 213
Lewinsky, Monica, 235
Licari, Louis, 109–10, 144
Licensing, 56–59, 116–117, 231

"Life-extended," 225
Lifetime TV, 38, 230
Lilith Fair Concerts, 236
Line extensions, 124, 225
Link, 17–19, 28, 32, 40
Liquor business, 186–88, 204–5
Little Ceasar Enterprises, 50
Liz Kids, 160
Logo, 195, 208
Long, Hank, 56
Long Beach, CA, 214, 216
Long-range planning, 84–85
Lorin Marsh (co.), 67–69
Loyalty, 24, 51, 62, 67, 131, 133–52,
    149, 159, 160, 171, 190
  to customers, 221
Lucky Dog (co.), 207
Lugano, Marie, 52

M&M's, 180
M. A. C. Cosmetics, 126, 223
McCann, Jim, 88
Mackey, John P., 209–10
McNeal, James U., *161*
Made in Japan (Morita), 85
Mademoiselle (magazine), 230
Maidstone Arms (East Hampton, NY),
    124
Majolica, 163
Make the Connection (Winfrey), 24
Malcolm X, 50
Malls
  in airports, 144
  Peripheral marketing in, 120–21
MamaMedia, 168–69
Management, EVEolution and, 244
Mandell, Sherri, 68–69
MapEasy, 93
Marigold, Lys, 10, *45–46*, 61, 67, 181
Marigold, Skye Qi, 61, *158*, *164*, 169

Marital therapists, 142
Market research, 83–84, 91–92, 97,
    178–80
  future, 186
Marketing, 2–3, 8, 46–47, 78, 84–85,
    157, 162, 177–80, 242–43
  EVEolved, 23
  Fifth "P" of, 198–201
  Four "Ps" of, 198
Marketing links, 86–87
Marketing tactics, 116–17
Marketing to women, 2–4, 9, 12, 79–80,
    90–93, 106, 195–96, 244
  Anticipation Truth, 82, 83
  Connection Truth, 18–19, 22–23
  Everything Matters Truth, 198
  Go to Her Truth, 136–39
  Multiple Lives Truth, 42, 48
  Revlon, 223
Marketing with women, 29–30
Marshall Field's, 207
Martha Stewart Living (magazine),
    230
Math/science
  girls and, 168–69, 233
Mattel (co.), 122
Max Racks, *127*
McDonald's, 13, *165*, 186
MCI, 28
Mead Johnson (co.), 85
"Media record," 143
Meditations for New Mothers (Saavedra),
    75
Men
  differences from women, 2, 8–9,
    21–22, 106–9, *113*, 114, 116,
    197
  single-focus, 42, 45
  and EVEolutionary marketing,
    242–43

Men (*continued*)
  and women's wants/needs, 80, *80*,
    81–82
*Men Are From Mars, Women Are From
  Venus* (Gray), 6, 18
Menopause management programs, 52,
  231
Men's Health, 43
Mentorship, 191
Mercedes Benz Manhattan, 163
Mercury Award, 130
Merrill Lynch, 53–54
Meyer, Terri, 38
Microsoft, 145
Mikasa, 143
Miller, Coco and Kelly, 166
Miller Brewery, 208
Minority markets, and EVEolution,
  242–44
Mr. & Mrs. Potato Head (toy), 72, 158
MIT Media Lab, 243
Miyake, Issey, 32, 160
Moment, Mary Kay Adams, *110*
Monopoly, 158
Morita, Akio, 84–85
Morrissey, Steve, 212
Morrison, Toni, 230
"Mosaic brain," 43
Moss, Kate, 34
Mother-child bonds, 36–38, 154–57,
  167
  Revlon and, 232–33
Mother/Daughter Journal, 37–38
Mother/Daughter Workshops, 37–39
Mothers, 175–76
  influence on buying habits, 154–57
  single, 169–70
"Mothers and Daughters: A Lifetime
  Bond" (documentary), 38
Motorola, 243

MovieFone, 206
MTV, 230
Multi-dimensionality of women's lives,
  45–47
Multiple Lives Truth, 12, 13, 41–78
  and BrainReserve, 240
  case study/Four Small Companies,
    62–71
  case study/Hasbro, 71–77
  FutureCorner, 51–53
  Perfessional, 49
  Revlon, applied to, 227–28
  Multi-tasking, 145, 184
My Best Friend's Wedding (film), 51

N.W. Ayer, 179
Nabisco, 34, 37, *118–19*
National Retail Federation, 160
Native Americans, 242
Net Perceptions, 87
Netherlands, 61, 86, 160, 186
Netpulse, 145
Netsmart-Research, 139
Networking, 68
Neurotransmitters, 107
New Coke, 180
New York Times, The, 57, 60, 119
New York Times Magazine, 107–8
Newlin, Kate, 65, 130
Next Step, 85
Nickelodeon, 184
Nike, 143, 213, 226
99 Lives Trend, 206
Nivea, 154
Noonan, Jerry, 87–88
Nordstrom (co.), 152, 160–61
Nordstrom, Bill, 160–61
Nordstrom, Dan, 152
Northrup, Christiane, 176
Nostalgia, 153–54

Nu Skin (co.), 137
Nuances, 120

o.b. tampons, 180
Ocean Copies (Bridgehampton, NY), 90
O'Donnell, Rosie, 26
Oldham, Todd, 123–24
Omaha Steak, 130
Omnibus, 83
On-line shopping, 139–41
    groceries, 148
Onboard Services Award, 130
"100 Best Companies for Working
        Mothers," 48
1–800–flowers.com, 87–88, 231
Oprah, 240
Oprah's Book Club, 125
Orbach, Susie, 81
Ore-Ida, 186
Organic foods, 2, 15, 202
Organization Man, The (Whyte), 107–8
OshKosh, 121
Overweightness, 25–26, 26, 34, 49–50
Oxford Health Plans, Inc., 142
Oxo® company, 61–2
Oxygen.com, 184–85, 186
Ozzie and Harriet, 7

Palm Pilots, 85–86
Palm Restaurants, 130
Paltrow, Gwyneth, 70
Pampering products, 1, 13
Parking Lots, 91–92, 118–9
Pass-along dynamic, 22, 154–55
Patterson, Terry, 97
Pennzoil-Quaker State, 98, 101
People of the Labyrinths, The, 160
Pepsi-Cola, 186
Perelman, Ron, 219, 220, 222–23, 225,
        235–37

Peretti, Elsa, 162
Perfessional, 49–50, 69, 70
Peripheral Vision Truth 12, 14, 105–32
    and BrainReserve, 240–41
    case study/A.1., 126–31
    case study/Knox Gelatine, 118–19
    FutureCorner, 117–20
    Revlon, applied to, 221–22, 229–31
Perlman, Willa, 76
Pez, 154
Philanthropy, 64–65, 236–37
Phoenix (hotel), 87
Picasso, Paloma, 162
Pinkdot, 147
Pipher, Mary, 196
Pittman, Stuart, 10
Pizza Hut, 127
Play, 71–77
Play Everyday, 75–76
Pleasure Revenge Trend, 3, 128–29
Point-of-purchase materials, 198
Pokémon, 76, 157, 208
Policy, 198
Politics, 196
Pop(corn) Quiz, 1–2, 13–15
Popcorn Report, The (Popcorn), 4, 87,
        119, 146, 147–48
Portantina, 206
Portraits of Hope: Conquering Breast
        Cancer (Feller), 65
Post Office, U.S., 117, 137
Post Ranch Inn (Big Sur, CA), 124
Postl, Jim, 101
Practice, The, 34
Prada, 160
Pre-need marketing, 84
Pretenders, 42
Prevratil, Joseph F., 214
Priceline.com, 185–86
PrimeAmerica, 229

Privacy, 145–46

Procter & Gamble, 117, 143, *200,* 232

Product placement, 117

PTA, 180

Public relations, 196, 201, 202–3

Publicis & Hal Riney, 212

Purchasing power

  of children, *161*

  of women, 7–8

Purdue University, 97

Queen Amidala, 77

Queen Mary, 213, 214–17

  "Image Bible," 217

Queen Mary Compass, The, 217

Quindlen, Anna, *21*

Quinlen, Mary Lou, 179

Quinn, Jane Bryant, 28

Raggedy Ann, 77

Raising a Daughter (Elium and Elium), 176

Ralph Lauren, 160

Rather, Dan, 109

Reach, 105–6, 112, 117

Recency, 106

Red Dog, 208

reflect.com, 232

Relationship(s), 4–5, 24–25, 75, 89, 90, 177–78, 179, 180, 191, 192, 197–98, 225, 240

  of company to female employees, 47–56

Relationship Managers, 191

Reliance Insurance Co., 152

Religious/spiritual life, 52–53

Renova, 30

Repositioning, 10, 139, 174

Reputation, 196

Research Tools, 178

Responding (marketing), 83–84

Restaurants, 122–23, 130

Retail industry, change in, 137–39

  garage sales, 143–44

Reviving Ophelia (Pipher), 196

Revlon, 219–37

  ColorStay lipstick, 225, 235

  emotional connection with, 225–26

  Fire and Ice promotion, 222

  reborn, 226–37

Revlon Expressions (proposed), 230

Revlon Run Walk, 236

Revson, Charles, 220–22, 232, 233

Roaman, Judi, 63–65

Rocker, John, 211

Roebling, Mary, 66

Romanzi, Ken, 62

Rothe, Sigrid, 224

RuPaul, 223

Saavedra, Beth Wilson, 75

Safeway (U.K.), 85

Sampling Store (proposed), 120–21

Saratoga Institute, The, 51

Saturday Evening Post, The, 20

Saturn cars, *20*, 163, 210–13

Sawyer, Diane, 109

Schacht, Caryn, 68

Schacht, Lorraine, 68

Schneider-O'Sullivan, Enid, 109

Schools, 81, 158–59, 180

Schultz, Howard, 124, 201

Schultz, Mona Lisa, Dr., 107

Scott, Willard, 136

Scrabble, 77

Sculley, Mary E., 169

Seagram, 205, 232

Sears, 143, 208

Seinfeld, Jerry, 161

Self-esteem, women's, 26, 37

Sellers, Paul, *204*
Sensory Integration Dysfunction,
     41–42
Sephora, 187, 224
Serotonin, 107
Services, 64, 87, 88–89, 90, *91–92*,
     137, 139, 146–52, 206
  e-commerce, *93*
Seurat, Georges, 112
777-Film, *91*
Shakespeare, William, 195
Shakespeare & Company, *158*
"Sharing-a secret" scenarios, *108*
SHE millennium, *192*
Sheindlin, Judy, 47
Shell, 27
Shop-ological, 2
Shopping, 134–35
  Anticipatory marketing, 85–87
  for car(s), *172*
  department stores, 89–90, 137–38
  kiosks, 145
  on-line, 139–41, 147, *148*
  proposed services in, 89–90
  as social experience, *138*
  virtual, 138
Single mothers, 169–70
Skelley, Georgeanne, *31*
Sleepy Bear's Den, *32*
Slim•Fast®, 228
Slinky, 158
Small companies
  marketing to Multiple Lives, 62–71
Smith/Greenland, 156
Smith, Lynda, 83
SnackWell's, 34–39, 170
Soccer, women's, 164
SocioQuake, 10
Soho Grand Hotel, 70
Sontag, Susan, 230

Sony (co.), 61, 84–85, 94, 143
Soviet Union, *164*
Specialty Equipment Marketers
     Association, 184
Spielberg, Steven, 51
Spin (magazine), 230
Sports, women's, 164–67
Stamps, selling, 137
"Stampvertising," 117
Stanford Business School, 9
Star Wars (film), 77
Starbucks, 124–26, 142, 225
Steakhouses, 130
Steinberg, Saul, 152
"Step Thinking," 42
Stew Leonard's (co.), 180–82, 184
Stewart, Martha, 70, 162–63, 234
Stiffel, 59
Stock market, women in, 7
Stocks, Everything Matters Truth, 204
Stoller, Phyllis, 33
Stonyfield Farm Yogurts, *203*
Streamline.com, 146–52
Stress, Trickle-down, *157*
Sun Microsystems, 94, *187*
"Sunday in the Park with George," 112
Sunset Boulevard (film), 65
Super Bowl XXXIV, 186
Supermarkets, 85, *86*, 118–19, *138*,
     147–48, 166, 181–82
  gyms in, 144–45
Susan G. Komen race, 65
Swanson, Gloria, 65
Swoopes, Sheryl, 166
Sylvan Learning Centers, 233

Take-out-foods industry, 1, 13
Talbots, 160
TalentBank, 10, 35, 35–36, 72, 128,
     214, 240

Talmage, Stephanie, 168
Tannen, Deborah, 18
Target, 206, 208
Techno-Isolationism, 20
Technology, 139, *187*
  Anticipatory, 85–87
  Connecting, 20–21, 186
  customization, and, 186
  EVEolution, and, 243
  Multiple Lives, 50
  toys, and, 76–77
  wireless, 243
Teen People (magazine), 230
Telecommuting, 54, 136
Telephone, 84
Telephone communications, 28, 50,
    159, 205
Television, 38, 105–6, 109, 117, 139,
    230, 240–41
Third Age Media, 23
Tiffany & Co., 82, 161–62
Time, *147*, 205–6
Timex, 49
Titanic, *165*
Tobacco industry, 204
Tobias, Andrew, 220–22
Today Show, The, 136, 222, 240
Tommy Hilfiger, 213
TommorowLand, 241
Tony Awards, 121
Toskan, Frank, 126
Toy Story 2 (film), 158
Toys, 157–58
  Hasbro, 71–77
  replicas of kitchen appliances, 172–
    73
  technologically based, 76–77
Tracy, Bernadette, 139
Transparent brand, 198–200, *200*,
    202–3, 218

BrainReserve as, 241–42
  Saturn as, 212–13
Transportation of children, 53
Travel
  Business travel, 30–32
  with children, 32
  women only, 33
Travel agents, 142–43
Travelodge, 32
TrendProbes, 10–11, 74, *119*, 193
  and BrainReserve, 241
TrendSalons, 240
TrendTreks, 128, 214
Trucking industry, 117–18
Trudell, Cynthia, 211
Trust, 150, 196
2wice (magazine), 230
TwinLab, 94
Tyson (co.), 186
Tzu, Sun, 82

Uber-Truth, 225
UCLA Women's Cancer Research
    Program, 236
U-God, *123*
Ullman, Tracy, 230
Unilever, *118*, *148*
United Airlines, 94, 208
Ur-club, 36
Urbanfetch.com, 141
USA Today, 183
U.S. News & World Report (magazine),
    211
User groups, 234

Vagina Monologues, The (Ensler), 231
Values, 198–99, 201
Vanderbilt, Nicole, 93
Vasilchik, Tiffany, 217
Venture philanthropy, 236

VH1, 230
Victoria (magazine), 230
Virtual Shopping, 138–39
Virtual survey, 186
Visibility, 106
Viva Glam lipstick, 126
Vogue (magazine), 224, 230

W Hotels, 124
Wallpaper, 69–71
Warner Lambert, *127*
Weatherspoon, Teresa, 166
Web (the), 20, 139, 232
    Co-Parenting and, 186
    privacy on, 145–46
    Revlon and, 233–34
Web sites, 71, 82, 186
    BrainReserve, 241
    health-related, 29
    meditation, 140–41
    monitoring companies (proposed),
        202, 203–4
    Popcorn, 242
    Revlon, 227, 237
    travel related, 31–32, 33
    "Women Only," 1, 13
    Women-specific, 29
"Web Thinking," 42
WebVan, 147
Weight Watchers International, 25–26,
    49–50
Westinghouse competition, 168
What Do Women Want (Eichenbaum
    and Orbach), 81
Whole Foods Markets, Inc., 208–10
Whole Woman, The (Greer), 89
Whyte, William H., 108
Wick, Doug, 51
Widows, 27–28
Wild Women Adventures, 33

Williams, Serena and Venus, 166
Windstar Minivan, 182–83
Winfrey, Oprah, 24, 236
Wings, *see* Hollywood Wings
Wireless technololgy, 243
WNBA (Women's National Basketball
    Association), 165–67
Woman: An Intimate Geography
    (Angier), 42
Women
    consistent behavior in, 114
    different from men, 2, 8–9, 21–22,
        42–45, 106–9, *113*, 114, 116,
        197
    economic power of, 7–9, 10, 27
    and errands, *147*
    how to please, 6
    joining brands, 4–5
    nurturing, 175–76
    older, 244
    pioneers in consumerism, 242
    roles of, 44–45, 46, 47, 134
    in workforce, 14, 27, 54, 74–75,
        133–34
    younger, 244
Women Can't Hear What Men Don't Say
    (Farrell), 43
"Women on Their Way" Web site,
    30–31
Women-only travel, 33
Women's Bodies, Women's Wisdom
    (Northrup), 176
Women's Movement, 9
Women's support groups (proposed),
    227
Women's Travel Club, 33
Women's Wear Daily, 223
Workforce, women in, 14, 27, 133–34
Working Mother (magazine), 48
Workout Strollers, 60–61

Workplace
  EVEolution in, 47–57, *110*
  opportunities for Revlon in, 227–28
Wu-Tang Clan, *123*
Wyndham Hotels & Resorts, 30–32

Xerox, *164*, *187*

Yankelovich (marketing research firm),
  22, *157*
YM (magazine), 230
Yoma (co.), 70

You Just Don't Understand (Tannen),
  18
Youth Monitor, *157*

Zagat, Nina, 182
Zagat, Tim, 182
Zagat Survey Restaurant Guides, 62, 182,
  184, 185
Zaki, Sonia Trulli, 61
Zobel, Gretchen, 183
Zona Research, 93
Zoomerang.com, 185